WHERE TO GO WHEN THE BANK SAYS NO

Financing your small business in Canada

GARY FITCHETT
WITH JOHN ALTON
KATHLEEN ALDRIDGE

 McGraw-Hill
Ryerson

Toronto Montréal New York Auckland Bogotá Caracas
Lisbon London Madrid Mexico Milan New Delhi San Juan
Singapore Sydney Tokyo

McGraw-Hill
Ryerson Limited

A Subsidiary of The **McGraw·Hill** *Companies*

ISBN: 0-07-560225-3
1234567890 GTC 7654321098

Canadian Cataloguing in Publication Data

Fitchett, GaryA.
        Where to go when your bank says no: financing a business in Canada

(SOHO solutions for Canadians)
Includes index.
ISBN 0-07-560225-3

1. Small business – Canada – Finance. I. Alton, John D.II. Aldridge, Kathleen. III. Title. IV. Series.

HG4027.7.F572 1998   658.15'2'0971   C98-931078-7

Publisher: **Joan Homewood**
Production Coordinator: **Jennifer Burnell**
Editor: **Rachel Mansfield**
Electronic Page Composition: **Pages Design**
Interior Design: **Dianna Little**
Cover Design: **Sharon Matthews**

Printed and bound in Canada.

This book is dedicated to the many clients, business associates, bankers, lenders and investors who have shared their experiences and encouraged us to write this book.

ACKNOWLEDGEMENTS

We would like to thank the following Contributing Authors to *The Canadian Business Financing Handbook* who loaned their specialized knowledge and expertise to certain indicated topics, where these sections or parts thereof, have been adapted for this book:

Jake Thun, B. Comm.
Brian K. McArthur, HBA, FICB
Royal Bank Leasing Inc.
- *Leasing*

Larry Levine, M.Sc. (Eng), P.Eng.
Henriques Canada
division of North American Trust Company
- *Trade Finance*

David Morrison, B.A., LL.B.
Morrison Financial Services Limited
- *Factoring*

Paul H. Harricks, LL.B.
Smith Lyons
- *Going Public*

RoyNat Inc.
Vengrowth Capital
- *Financing Commitment Letters and Loan Agreements*

Table of Contents

No! ... A word that echos finality. Sometimes the "no" is blunt and uttered without conditions, explanations or even a glimmer of encouragement. What's your next step?

You're facing a devastating situation - and whatever the cause, the bank's on your back! This chapter will help you understand your bank's communications, whether direct or subtle, and will give you strategies for generating cash and developing a co-operative action plan for recovery.

From indiscretions of youth through to medical catastrophes, sometimes past situations haunt the borrower's financial future. Often these matters have nothing to do with the borrower's past business performance, moral obligation to repay debts, or prospects for operational success in the future. How do you deal with special circumstances which affect either your personal finances or the business itself?

Once only the domain of large business, term loans are now available to small businesses through many and varied members of the financial services industry. Interest rates today are better than ever as more players try to attract the small business market. The cornerstone of long term funding, a term loan is particularly attractive for the acquisition of fixed assets.

When you've exhausted your avenues for fully secured financing, mezzanine debt financing is often the next logical source for term financing. As a newer financing structure, this type of term loan is an excellent way to get more debt financing with reasonable operating flexibility than would be otherwise possible.

Equity is the foundation of all business financing. While it's a major concern for start-ups, most businesses will suffer from a lack of equity capital at some point during their life cycle. This chapter explains the different sources of equity financing in relation to the growth stage of a business and shows how to structure a deal that will work.

In today's fast-moving environment, you can't afford to overlook the potential for financing through government programs. It could be the means for you to find those additional funds you need to gain competitive advantage or get moving on a new market opportunity. And generally, the price is right.

Chapter 8: Leasing – A Workable Financing Option / 135

With more than 10% of all business equipment now being lease-financed, leasing is a rapidly growing, multi-billion dollar industry across North America. When compared to traditional sources of financing, the bottom line benefits of leasing can be very attractive.

Chapter 9: Factoring – Another Source of Financing / 149

Factoring is a widely misinterpreted source of funding for the day-to-day operations of a business. Essentially, a factoring transaction involves the purchase and sale of an account receivable. Factoring can carry a start-up or small company through extraordinarily rapid growth for which the business might otherwise be undercapitalized.

Chapter 10: Trade Finance – Funding International Imports and Exports / 169

Still not well known by Canadian businesses, trade finance companies fill a specialized niche in the finance industry, particularly for importers, by providing a means for a business to expand and improve its profitability, without compromising its working capital, financial strength or ownership.

Chapter 11: Franchising – A Jump Start to Expansion / 177

If you want to expand your business quickly, franchising is an imaginative and often very viable strategy for broader distribution and vigorous financing. It's also very attractive to new entrepreneurs who are looking for a lower-risk means of becoming an owner/operator of a business.

Chapter 12: Going Public – Ready, Set, Wait! / 193

A company's initial public offering is a major undertaking which will have lasting effects on the company, its shareholders, its officers and directors, and its methods of conducting business. It's one of the most important strategic steps for a company at the top of the heap… but it's not for the faint of heart.

Chapter 13: R&D – Financing the Better Mouse Trap / 209

Got an innovative idea that's bound to make millions but just needs a little financing to get it off the ground? Because of the costs, risks, and long-term payback associated with innovation and research, many businesses find financing their sure-fire idea difficult, if not impossible. But with commitment and the right strategies and contacts, R&D financing can be found.

Chapter 14: And Now … Back to the Bank / 217

Back to the bank! You may want to keep your bank as just one of many financing sources. Or you may have outgrown the need for alternative sources of financing altogether and the bank can now meet all of your financing needs. This chapter will help you understand bank operations and the various financing services they offer and give you some practical guidance for assessing and improving your relationship with your bank.

Epilogue: Looking to the Future: Tomorrow's Bank / 247

Glossary / 249

Index / 265

Preface

THE BANK SAYS NO! WHAT'S YOUR NEXT STEP?

Entrepreneurs across the country are constantly concerned with financing. But what do they do when the bank refuses to help them finance that sure-to-succeed widget, start-up or expansion? Many business people think of the bank as the first place to go for financing. And too often, when they are turned down, they do not know where to go for alternative sources of financing. Sometimes they even fold.

This book is about overcoming that resounding NO, discovering the many and varied sources of financing that can help your business succeed and learning how your bank can be an effective player on your financing team, but not necessarily the only one. As you read this book, you'll discover viable, available financing alternatives - discussed in a practical and straightforward manner and with gems of *real-world* wisdom and strategies for succeeding both with your bank and with other lenders.

Strategies for Winners

This is the book that will help you understand financing, gain focus and take the next step with greater confidence. You will also learn from the anecdotal, actual stories throughout that you are not alone in your financing needs and frustrations. Best of all, you'll see that others who have gone before you have been successful, sometimes immensely successful. Their roads have also been bumpy but they've found the new directions and new sources of financing they've needed and they've succeeded.

THE SCOPE OF THIS BOOK

This book is a road map. It offers general information and directions. It is not intended to be a specialist book with all the technical guidance and materials to solve every financing problem — an impossible task for any one publication.

While every effort has been made to ensure the information is complete, thorough, and up-to-date, the reader is cautioned that the topic of business finance is very broad, subject to many interpretations, and constantly changing.

For more detailed guidance and lists of specific sources, refer to *The Canadian Business Financing Handbook,* a technical reference service published by the Canadian Institute of Chartered Accountants (you'll find the three volumes in a business library or professional accountant's office). Better still, get a professional advisor on your team.

Keeping Up-to-date

As statutes and practices change rapidly, this book may be updated periodically. But keep in mind, data could change the day after it goes to press. In using statutory information from this book, you should always cross-reference to the current status of the laws and regulations as well as talk to your professional advisors.

Opinions and Data

The information and opinions expressed herein are those of the authors and the contributing authors where indicated, and do not represent the position on any matters of the publisher, McGraw-Hill Ryerson. In many instances, the opinion of a contributing author may represent the policy or practice of his organization, which may not wholly reflect the policy and practice of other members of the particular financing sector.

This Book is Not About Bank Bashing!

"Can anybody remember when times were not hard and money not scarce?"

Ralph Waldo Emerson (1803 - 1882)

"At the pleasure of the Bank..."

The opening words of the typical bank commitment letter
(35 years ago)

Give me $$$... that's what I want! We've all heard, and unfortunately some of us have experienced, the big bad bank stories. The walking wounded frequently describe their relationships with banks and bankers in less than positive terms....

The bank gave us a line of credit of $250,000 and we were rolling... but over the next three years, we had to "train" six different account managers at the branch!

The bank liquidated us! They called their $4,500,000 loan to our company. For 25 years, we'd operated profitably, but had just one year of losses — we built a new facility for expansion immediately before the last recession — and poof, we were gone. The bank approved the new increased credit for expansion, yet when the recession hit, blamed us for "poor management" for our error in judgement. Like if we knew it was coming we would have borrowed 4$\frac{1}{2}$ mill? We were forced to liquidate and the bank took a $1,000,000 loss on liquidation of the assets. But we're back! We bought back the assets in the liquidation sale (at 50 cents on the dollar) and we're once again pulling in very nice profits!

The bank issued a sudden demand for repayment of a loan we had taken to finance our real estate development project, even though there was no default or arrears. In fact, we later discovered that the bank's senior management had mismanaged its own business. The bank's own credit rating was impaired because of the number of real estate-backed loans on its books. We couldn't repay without catastrophic financial consequences. For six years, we worked hand in hand with the bank's Special Loans Department making small monthly payments of principal plus interest... and we survived.

I needed to meet my new account manager to negotiate a small variation on the monthly loan repayment schedule so I called and suggested a lunch meeting the next day. Arrived at bank at appointed time, waited for 30 minutes, and account manager didn't show up. Left business card with receptionist, with request that account manager call in afternoon to rearrange meeting. Received a letter 45 days later demanding payment, with apology for missing lunch!

As a sequel to the missed lunch, the account was moved to a central administrative office and we soon worked out a payment schedule and provided post dated cheques. A week after the deposit of the first cheque, I received a telephone call... "Bad way to start off the new repayment schedule. Bad for credibility." Of course I pointed out that I had not had an NSF cheque in 20 years. I asked them to fax a copy of the returned cheque. The next day, I got a telephone call again, but this time advising that everyone has a time in their career when they must be humble. It turned out that "accounting" made a bookkeeping error, which someone interpreted as an NSF cheque.

One day the senior account manager and branch manager were suddenly "gone" from the bank — no explanation and no replacements. Our cheques were returned NSF on accounts where approved facilities were not recorded into the computer. Replacement bank drafts were only provided after new bank staff re-negotiated existing credits (all of which were current and in good standing). Our existing loans had been "earned" through 29 years of solid relationship banking and credit performance.

The stories are endless and nerve-wracking. Across the country, entrepreneurs bond in their sharing of their war stories about "The Bank." Some rank banks right up there with politicians and lawyers. Others suggest that "BANK" is the new four-letter word!

BUT THIS BOOK IS NOT ABOUT BANK BASHING

Most banks have excellent personnel, are positive in their approach, and frequently and skillfully help individual borrowers and investors with their financing requirements.

So What's the Problem?

So why do we continue to bank bash? Many times a bank will be criticized for refusing financing assistance where it is truly not the proper role of a bank to participate in such a situation. The root of the problem is a lack of knowledge and understanding of banking and of the many alternative sources of financing for small- and medium-sized businesses. Simply put: sometimes we expect the bank to play in a game it's just not equipped to do. So maybe it's time to look at some other playing fields.

Throughout this book, you'll learn about:

- the attitudes of banks and the criteria they must apply when approached for business financing
- the type of financing required in a given business situation
- the proper source for each alternative type of financing.

And you'll learn some valuable tips for understanding your bank and making the relationship work. The bank will likely always be a part of your financing team, but it doesn't have to be the whole team.

WHAT DO BANKS REALLY DO?

Banks lend money and they provide various financial services.

When they need money to lend, where do they get it? Their principal source of funds to be loaned is from depositors. Simply stated: the bank rents the depositors' funds.

When making a loan, the bank must charge interest and sometimes other fees for the use of the funds to cover:

- the cost of funds from depositors
- the overhead of the bank
- the profit of the bank (don't forget the bank has shareholders!).

As the safety of the depositors' funds is paramount, when the bank makes a loan, it is very preoccupied with safety and low risk.

The 1990s Changed the Playing Field

For almost as long as can be remembered, the financial community in Canada was comprised of four pillars:

- banks
- trust companies
- insurance companies
- investment dealers

Each played a distinct and unique role in the financing hierarchy for business.

The Walls Come Tumbling Down

Since the late 1980s, federal legislative changes have fractured this structure — and several of the pillars have tumbled down. Banks have become ever powerful, gaining the rights to own trust companies, sell certain insurance and take over established investment dealers.

Bigger... but Better?

Consolidation has allowed the banks to become bigger, more powerful, and obviously, v-e-r-y profitable (read "happy shareholders"). The banks argue that BIG is a key requirement for maintaining financial stability and competing in the international arena. In reality, despite this substantial growth, large Canadian banks, in terms of size, are falling further down the list of major international banking institutions.

This changing profile of the financial community is having a profound impact on the sources and availability of capital, and also on the way business is conducted. Here are just a few examples of typical changes:

- Large businesses now place major fundings in the form of commercial paper (promissory notes) through the investment dealer arms of their bankers.
- RoyNat, a term-lending specialty firm formed in the 1960s to fill a void in banking in the long-term availability of funds, is now owned by the Bank of Nova Scotia.
- Life insurance is placed by a bank (usually with its insurance subsidiary) to insure the outstanding indebtedness from loans.
- Not only will the bank provide savings accounts and certificates of deposit, but various money market and securities investments are available through the investment dealer divisions.

The Score: Business loans 35 — Personal loans 65

When you analyse the Canadian loan portfolios of the Canadian chartered banks, you can clearly see their game plan:

Business and government loans   35%
Personal and credit card loans   15%
}Total personal lending
Residential mortgages   50%
Total Canadian loan portfolios   100%

The trend of the past few years continues — mortgages up, business loans down!

Mortgages Up, Business Loans Down

What else is contributing to this trend? Here are just some of the other factors:

• As banks acquire trust companies, they're also acquiring more residential mortgages.
• Banks have made retail lending to individuals a strong policy initiative.
• The banks are driven in this direction to gain from the synergy resulting from cross-selling of mortgages, car loans, insurance, RRSPs, mutual funds, and GICs.
• From the bank's perspective, it is easy to see the advantage of a five-year solidly secured realty mortgage, payable with an automatic debit, compared to a fluctuating business loan secured by volatile accounts receivable and inventories of a small business.

Getting Their Financial Houses in Order

In 1988, another significant impact on Canadian banking emanated from Basel, Switzerland when the members of the Bank for International Settlements (known as "BIS") legislated that all member banks increase their capital base (and thereby decrease their leverage — the amount of assets in relation to capital).

As a result, banks could put their financial house in order by increasing capital (raising new equity) or decreasing assets (e.g., decreasing new lending or calling in unproductive loans). The ensuing recession didn't allow the banks to raise capital at good values. The cutback in credit probably helped to strengthen the recession.

The Mating Game

The January 1998 headlines blared the prospective merger of the Royal Bank of Canada and the Bank of Montreal. It caught everyone off guard — politicians, business people, regulators, and even the employees and shareholders of the respective banks! In April the Canadian Imperial Bank of Commerce and Toronto-Dominion Bank also jumped in.

The banks put forward their arguments for their action: they have to be MUCH BIGGER to compete internationally. But really, does international competitiveness do much for "Main Street, Canada?"

There are currently nine domestic banks registered in Canada, but in reality there are only five major national banks — representing limited local competition. The approximate 45 foreign (Schedule 2) banks do not operate on "Main Street, Canada."

"Small Town, Canada" currently has only two or three banks represented. If two of those are Royal Bank and Bank of Montreal, the competition is substantially reduced. Certainly, the residents and business people of that town will not benefit from the international competitiveness of the new "BIG Bank"; however, they will notice the impact of the reduced competition.

Another factor is that all the major banks are closing branches in smaller communities, already reducing competition. On the other hand, it is said that fewer banks can be an advantage to the business person — one can solicit all the "No"s much faster.

BUT THE BANKS REALLY DO WANT YOUR BUSINESS!

Over the years, there have been many surveys and studies undertaken to identify and quantify the attitude and problems of small- and medium-sized business in dealing with their banks. The studies are not lip service. The banks really are trying to respond with many initiatives in providing services to small- and medium-sized businesses.

"Banks and Small Business Borrowers"

This study, commissioned by the Canadian Bankers' Association, was completed in January 1991 by Larry Wynant and James Hatch of the University of Western Ontario. It examines the complex relationship between small business and its bankers, and draws conclusions about the difficulties and conflicts which beset this relationship.

The issue of *dissatisfaction with their banking relationship* was reviewed in detail. In summary, the dissatisfaction was prevalent among approximately one-third of borrowers, the businesses were mostly high-risk, and the clients were dissatisfied with most aspects of the relationship. Dissatisfied clients were more often located in a major urban area where they deal with a commercial banking centre.

Clients' complaints centred on the following aspects of bank practice or service:

- The banks demand excessive amounts of collateral support and pay inadequate attention to the firm's earnings prospects.
- Borrowing costs (primarily fees) are excessive and poorly explained or justified.
- The banks are too conservative in the amount of financing they provide.
- Bankers are unprepared or incapable of providing general business advice, a service which most small businesses expect.
- Rapid turnover of account managers destroys the quality of the firm's relationship with the bank, causes extra effort for the entrepreneur to "train" a new banker and increases the likelihood that new rules of the game will emerge in gaining bank support.
- Bankers can be arrogant and uncaring when turning down a loan request.

All of the areas of dissatisfaction are indicators of disagreement and/or conflict between the client and banker. A deeper analysis of these matters led to an understanding of *six key factors which generated the levels of dissatisfaction:*

1. The Client's Understanding of a Bank's Role and Lending Criteria

Most business people do not appreciate the minimal level of risk which banks are prepared to accept. This often results from:

- the inability of account managers to articulate clearly the banker's role and lending policy
- the banker's use of confusing terminology
- the client's lack of financial skills needed to relate to the banker's analytical process.

2. The Client's Understanding of the Risks and Opportunities Facing the Business, and the Lack of Skills at Communicating a Financing Proposal

Poorly understood and documented business plans result in incomplete and inadequate communication of information about the business to the banker. Furthermore, the business person is typically overly optimistic about the prospects facing their firms.

3. The Banker's Lack of Skill at Communicating a Credit Decision

Ambivalence and abruptness by the banker leave the client confused and without an understanding of the bank's position and the available alternatives.

4. The Banker's Knowledge of the Business and its Risks

Rapid turnover of account managers generates uneasiness for the client, and probably inhibits the account manager from gaining a complete understanding of the client's business, with the inherent capability of properly assessing the risks.

5. The Differences in Judgement and Perspective Between a Banker and an Entrepreneur

By their very nature, these two parties approach the questions of success of the business from opposite perspectives. Typically, the entrepreneur believes in the ability to succeed, and sees only the highest value in assets — failure and auction sale liquidation prices are inconceivable.

6. The Client's Perception of Alternative Financing Options

Most entrepreneurs have a limited awareness of other financing sources, and often get limited guidance from the banker, leading to a feeling of acute frustration if total financing is not approved by the bank.

In responding to these areas of conflict, the study made specific recommendations:

1. There is a need for better communication of the bank's commitment to small business.
2. There should be clarification of the types and levels of business counselling which bankers are prepared to provide, with appropriate training of account managers.

3. The banks must do a better job of managing and controlling turnover.

4. There should be training for account managers in the skills to communicate more effectively bank terminology and contractual obligations (the "difficult fine print") for clients' complete understanding.

5. There should be a clear description of the levels of risk which the bank is prepared to assume.

6. Account managers need to improve interpersonal skills in order to impart empathy and a supportive attitude to a client when full requests cannot be approved. Will the client come back to the same account manager if he/she becomes a success story? Will the client choose the same account manager if the business is in trouble?

"Small- and Medium-sized Businesses in Canada: Their Perspective of Financial Institutions and Access to Financing"

This survey was completed in 1996 by Thompson Lightstone & Company Limited and presented to a House of Commons Committee on Industry. In response to certain key conclusions, the banks responded that "the results reveal a communications gap between account managers and small-business people."

Some of the interesting conclusions include:

• Banks receive a positive satisfaction rating from their clients. Even in tough economic times, seven-in-ten small business bank clients are satisfied with the service they receive from their bank.

   (Indeed, but what about the other three-in-ten? No other business can survive while pleasing only 70% of its customers!)

• Small businesses are very satisfied with the performance of their main contact at their bank. 77% of bank clients report satisfaction with their main contact.

   (Indeed, but what about the other 23%?)

• Small businesses are generally satisfied with service delivery, but are less likely to be satisfied with availability and flexibility of credit.

   (Indeed, but credit is what it's about!)

Entrepreneurs Call It As They See It

In 1993, a survey by Arthur Andersen of 8,500 small businesses across Canada found that securing financing was one of the most important issues currently faced by entrepreneurs. One-third of the respondents found it more difficult to obtain financing than a year earlier (up 17% from a similar 1988 survey).

Task Force on Access to Capital by Small Business

In August 1994, the Federal/Ontario Liberal Caucus reported on their hearings from 16 Ontario communities. Many small business operators appeared and expressed the following concerns with Canada's major lending institutions:

- There is a lack of competition in the financial industry.
- Many account managers do not have sufficient skills to understand competently the specifics of a small business.
- There is a frequent turnover of account managers.
- Local managers lack the authority to make credit decisions.
- Credit decisions are not communicated in sufficient detail.
- Banks are no longer willing to lend on character.
- Banks do not tell individuals who have been turned down for a bank loan about other sources of capital.
- Excessive fees are applied by banks.
- Banks demand excessive amounts of personal guarantees and collateral.

Let's Look at Some of the NICE Things Banks Do

Many banks have taken very positive approaches, and indeed shown excellent judgement. The most successful ones have largely built on their relationships with their clients by following the axiom: "know your client." These are the stories we don't hear all the time; they're nice stories:

- A $50,000 short-term line of credit was granted to bridge the receipt of certain anticipated investments. It took a lunch to explain the circumstances; no paperwork, no fees.
- A $45,000 line of credit put in place, taking about 30 minutes to prepare the offer of credit letter.
- A U.S. $85,000 line of credit, unsecured, offered after banker read newspaper article about an exciting corporate project.
- At a head office meeting to discuss financing for the purchase of an established and successful business from the former owner's estate, there was a $150,000 shortfall in security. The quick and timely response from the senior banker was that the balance of the security could be the "cash flow of the new business."

Financing: Knock on the Right Door!

If you are having difficulty in your dealings with the bank, the first step is to assess the seriousness of your problem. The first three chapters should help you formulate your strategies. You may discover that for your particular business, you've simply been knocking on the wrong door.

If alternative sources of financing are the right solution for your business, the remainder of the book will guide you in approaching/completing such alternative financing.

And finally, when your business is again in a position to utilize bank financing properly, Chapter 14 will explain the major financing products as well as help you assess and improve your relationship with your bank.

People Are Critical Factors

Underlying both the good experiences and the bad experiences are people. You are only as good as the people you work with. The banks are only as good as the people dealing directly with your particular problem. If you have been fortunate in being served by experienced, competent people you will likely have a positive result. If, on the other hand, your contacts are less experienced or less competent, you may have an unpleasant experience. The past experiences of the lender will also have a bearing. Sometimes an entrepreneur is turned down by a lender who had a bad experience in a particular industry only to find another lender more accommodating, with the business ultimately being very successful.

Know Your Sources of Alternative Financing

The focus of this book is on the sources of alternative financing. However, it is not just enough to find the source and show up at the doorstep.

Credibility is what it's all about. Lenders scrutinize the credibility of the management, of the business, of the prospects. Communication, both oral and written, must be credible and instil confidence.

Plan and Prepare

Proper planning and preparation are the keys to successful completion of financing. There are four essentials to keep in mind:

1. Make sure you fully understand the five Cs of credit: Character, Conditions, Capacity, Collateral and Capital (particularly, the priority of character and capacity).
2. Develop a thorough and comprehensive professional business plan.
3. Clearly define and analyse your market.
4. Clearly establish the capacity of the business. Prepare reliable forecasts outlining the required financing and the prospective cash flow available for debt servicing.

So, turn the page. You're on your way to successful financing!

Rejection!

No...! A simple, but profound two-letter word. A word that echos finality.

Sometimes the "no" is blunt and uttered without conditions, explanations or even a glimmer of encouragement. Regardless of how positive the discussions have been, how upbeat the loan officer has been about your prospects, and how much the loan officer really would like to say "yes," the answer is "no." What's your next step?

Why "no" you ask? Maybe the loan officer pleads distance from the decision-making process, it was the approval committee's decision or gee whiz I'm not really experienced... And now that same loan officer who encouraged you initially even points out several weaknesses in your proposal!

Listen, Don't React!

Listen carefully to the "no," and particularly what follows.

A bank's loan officer must make a business decision based on the facts and circumstances of the company, not on your personal attributes. It is a decision based on the qualifying of the loan request within the bank's defined parameters.

WHEN THE ANSWER'S "NO"

Do not get mad.
Do not become defensive.
Do not look hurt.
Do not feel betrayed.
Do not say anything that may irreparably damage your future opportunities to obtain financing from this lender.

Do get going!

When the Going Gets Tough, the Tough Get Going!

No matter how well or how badly the lender delivers the "No," keep your composure: focus on being positive and very cordial. *The game's not over* — this is your opportunity to learn and succeed. Remember, the loan officer may be able to help you understand the reasoning behind the rejection. With this information, you can refine your proposal and take it back to the bank... or submit it to another lender. Maybe you were knocking at the wrong door to begin with.

HOW DID THE LENDER SAY "NO"?

"No" can be said many different ways. Listen. This is a time when you must calmly and confidently plan for your next step. What the loan officer says is important: the explanation, the details, the analysis of your company's position.

Variations on a "No!"

"No, but ..."

Ask if there are specific ways you can change your proposal. If you only hear the no, you'll miss the rest and it could be important.

"No, unless ..."

This "no" is conditional and can be changed to "yes" if you meet specified conditions or agree to more restrictive terms.

"I cannot say yes because ..."

The lender is waffling. Listen. There may be a way you can overcome any reservations and get a "yes."

"Not yet ..."

Maybe your application was submitted too early. Is the bank telling you that it's not yet comfortable with the business' level of success? Is it too early to substantiate trends that justify your expansion? This "no" might simply mean "wait."

"No, because the bank ..."

Sometimes the bank will have specific restrictions — your request is outside the lender's market area, is beyond its industry focus, or is greater than its lending limit. If the answer is "no" because that particular bank can't do it, take this as encouragement! Your request is valid; the source is just wrong. Find a lender that deals with your market or industry.

"Hell No..."

The blunt "no!" Maybe you need to revisit your proposal. Is it realistic that any lender will be able to extend the financing? A "no" without an explanation could indicate fundamental weaknesses in your presentation. This is a "no" you can use constructively. Ask questions and take notes. If you can identify weaknesses in your proposal, you can revise your business plan or the financing structure and succeed next time. Maybe you need expert help.

There are as many ways to say "no" as there are people and situations. While it's certainly not the answer you want, it really is just the beginning.

TIP

SNAP

When the answer's "no," listen very carefully — this is your chance to improve your business plan or finance structuring and get the bank to approve the loan at a later date or take it to another lender.

OKAY, SO WHAT DO I DO NOW?

There are many ways to respond to a loan denial. Scream, kick, punch... Remember your decorum. If you can prepare yourself and handle your response well, the information you can gather could mean financing approval the next time you present your proposal — there or elsewhere.

Set Up a Meeting

Several days later, call the lender to request an appointment for additional information about why the loan was rejected. Your purpose for this meeting is to learn by seeking answers from someone with a degree of expertise. These discussions are not intended to change the lender's mind about the proposed transaction, but rather to prepare you for the next round or the next lender.

In preparing for this interview, focus on business issues rather than personal reactions. By encouraging the lender to respond with directness, you may hear instructive commentary. Often, loan officers do not think in terms of what can be done, but rather in terms of what cannot be done. It's up to you to ask the right questions and determine on what basis the loan officer will respond affirmatively.

Prepare Your Questions

- From the lender's perspective, what factors about the business were not acceptable: the industry, location, products, employees, capitalization, track record, deal, or even management? What weaknesses need to be addressed and underpinned for the next loan proposal?
- Was the negative reply due to the lender? Often lenders steer away from particular loans because of a previous bad experience in the industry or because of the type of loan. Maybe the lender's loan policies, market focus or lending limits restrict participating in your request.
- Was the lender's rejection intended to be permanent, or can conditions or specific benchmarks change the response? Will the lender ever consider this financing? If so, exactly what changes or conditions are required? Where is the lender's level of comfort, and can the borrower attain it? This information will give you parameters in which to respond and make future choices.
- Is the lender telling you to move on to the another lender? Can the lender make recommendations about where else to apply? Ask if and why the proposal may be acceptable somewhere else. The answer might direct you to a more suitable source of financing and help you fine-tune your approach.

Listen, Listen, Listen

Make sure you fully understand how and why the lender turned the application down.

Without putting the lender on the defensive, you need to be prepared to ask questions. Make respectful inquiries and elicit specific answers that will help you succeed at a later date.

RESPOND TO THE LENDER'S OBJECTIONS

Identifying the qualifications, exceptions, and finality of the lender's rejection will help you determine and understand why the lender said "no." Here are some of the most common reasons a lender will reject a loan request and some logical responses for the borrower:

"The business is under-capitalized."

Lenders want the borrower to have either contributed or earned and retained a substantive portion of the net worth of the business.

In comparing the total debt to the total equity (the debt to equity ratio), there should be some measurable part of the company's financing provided from a source other than the lender.

YOUR RESPONSE

You can increase equity in the business a number of ways:

- You can inject more money into the company from such sources as savings, a second mortgage on an owner's home, liquidated investments, and the cash surrender value of life insurance policies.
- You can convert any subordinated debt or notes payable from the company to equity. Although this act may have consequences if and when the holders want to withdraw the money, it will show the lender your commitment to the success of the business.
- You can reduce any other liabilities of the company to a reasonable extent, at a discount if possible. Lowering the debt leverage will put the lender in a stronger position, without other liabilities distracting from its ability to be repaid.
- If you do not have additional capital to contribute, maybe relatives, friends, employees or suppliers are willing to invest in the business. This additional capital could be structured to ensure its priority in redemption as soon as the business accumulates additional capital to satisfy the requirements of the lender.

"The business has not earned a profit yet."

Lenders expect that the borrower can support the business strategy with a track record of business success. If the company has perpetually lost money, most lenders may reason that additional financing will compound those losses and the borrower will be unable to repay the borrowed funds.

YOUR RESPONSE

Your explanation of the financial history of the business was not sufficient or was not reasonable. If the business has failed to profit, it is important to demonstrate why and to explain how you plan to correct the problem.

Your strategy might be as simple as a plan to increase profits by acquiring more efficient assets and enhancing productivity. Lenders can usually accept this strategy if the borrower can prove that increases in productivity will indeed provide profits.

Don't make vague promises, such as you plan to make additional expenditures on advertising and marketing. Lenders are less comfortable about financing this strategy since there are so many undefined and poorly understood variables which can cause failure.

Instead, you will need to provide candid and detailed documentation which explains the periods in which a profit was not earned. In comparing those loss periods to periods in which the business did earn profits, you can explain how the operations may have been different. Then explain how the loan proceeds will be used to return your company to a profitable position.

"The proposed loan is too much money."

Lenders try to minimize loan requests by either reducing the marginal funds or trying to force the borrower to spend less in a particular part of the proposal. They want to control their exposure and perhaps get the loan balance down as a percentage of the collateral and in relation to the equity base of the business.

YOUR RESPONSE

Only you can decide if the business strategy can be achieved with a lower amount of funding. Only you will know how much extra financial padding you have incorporated into the request that can be reduced without affecting the business. If you do tighten some areas in your proposal, be sure there are sufficient funds under the heading "contingencies" to cover Murphy's Law: What can go wrong, will go wrong.

Your response has to be based on how much money is actually needed and how an expenditure can be reduced without having a negative impact on the business plans. Alternatively, if you can offer to provide additional collateral, the lender may reconsider its restriction since you will have reduced the perceived risk in the transaction.

"The business is too risky."

Lenders exclude some industries from their market because of real or perceived risks. Certain risks are inherent in some businesses and may be beyond the acceptable parameters of the lender or a specific financing program. These exclusions may apply only to the local lender, or they may be fairly common among most lenders, depending on the industry within which your company operates.

YOUR RESPONSE

Perhaps you have not effectively communicated how some of the risks can be underpinned.

Depending on the locale and nature of the industry, the lender that doesn't want to finance your business may be the only lender that can. In this case, you will have to convince the lender that the risks can be eliminated or limited. For example, by accepting tighter terms or providing sufficient collateral, you can structure the transaction to protect the lender from exposure to costly servicing or potential loan losses.

"Your business strategy is not sound."

In evaluating whether the business has a reasonable chance of succeeding, loan officers sometimes test your ideas against their experience (or inexperience). If the loan officer has strong reservations about your prospects, it's unlikely you will get the financing there.

YOUR RESPONSE

The bank is not always right — and almost always conservative. Maybe you did not explain the business concept sufficiently to the loan officer, or maybe the loan officer has an incorrect or incomplete understanding of exactly what you plan to accomplish.

Review your business plan and strategies carefully. Make sure that your plan fully describes each detail of the concept. Support your ideas with articles, surveys, market studies, and demographics that influenced, inspired, or convinced you.

"Not enough collateral."

This objection is probably the one the rejected borrower will hear most often when a lender turns down a loan application. The lender has a minimum standard of collateral coverage, based on a discounted valuation of that collateral. Usually, lenders will use their leverage to encumber virtually every asset the borrower has, even if those additional assets contribute little or no value as collateral to secure the loan.

The quantity and sufficiency of the collateral you can offer will overcome many objections.

YOUR RESPONSE

Your response should be based on an honest recognition of the true value of the collateral. How much would it be worth in liquidation, in a distress sale? Lenders are inclined to sell off repossessed assets quickly and drastically under market value, seeking merely to recover their loan balance rather than getting the full value of the assets.

Make sure the lender does not undervalue your collateral.

You need to be knowledgeable about the market for selling assets similar to those you are offering as collateral. For example, a 10-year-old lathe that cost $5,000 has a discounted value for the lender. Consider having a used-equipment dealer or auctioneer appraise the equipment. The appraiser can quickly assess what it would bring in a timely sale or in an auction. While you will have to pay for this appraisal, this is information that will directly determine the leverage the lender will give you on those assets.

Real estate assets also have to be valued, based on appraisals. The lender will typically advance a standard proportion of the market value to provide a margin to cover its time and associated costs if it is necessary to repossess, secure, hold and sell the property.

If the lender has under-valued the collateral, you can provide additional information to prove the value is higher. But you will need documentation to prove a different value than the one assessed. When asked to review the reasoning for the valuation, the lender can at least recognize a compromise value based on the evidence you provide.

If the assets are insufficient, offer to provide more collateral. Sometimes there are creative solutions to obtaining collateral value from assets which cannot be pledged. Review your personal and business financial statements carefully. You may find a way to assign values to the lender.

If you don't have any additional collateral, seek assistance from relatives, friends, associates, or investors who might be willing to hypothecate personal assets to the lender in order to additionally secure the loan. In effect, these third parties would be providing a limited guarantee for the loan, only to the extent of their ownership in the assets they would agree to use as collateral for the loan.

"The financial projections are unreliable."

Lenders will pay particular attention to the financial forecasts of the proposal to determine exactly how the borrower intends to repay the loan. Based on contributing factors, the loan officer does not always agree with the conclusions about revenue production or the cost of operations.

The loan officer will know from experience with other business deals that it invariably takes longer for sales to be generated and the business to grow to projected levels. If the loan officer does not accept the forecasts, your ability to service the debt becomes questionable.

YOUR RESPONSE

Examine the forecasts carefully to ensure that the expectations have been adequately assessed and communicated. Review the data or historical figures on which these projections have been based and ensure that this evidence is documented in the footnotes of the forecasts.

If the lender has discovered an error, you will need to modify your forecasts and the calculations. When you compare the new numbers against the debt service to pay back the loan, you should readily see if the deal is still feasible.

Once you're confident with the numbers, present them again with a line-by-line discussion (as necessary) to convince the loan officer of the soundness of these expectations. If you know the basis of the loan officer's questions or doubts, you can attempt to validate those specific entries thoroughly.

A STEP IN THE RIGHT DIRECTION

Your response to any of these objections does not guarantee that the lender will change the "no" to a "yes," but it is the logical next step after the loan has initially been rejected. You've invested considerable effort in educating this lender about your business before the loan was turned down. At this point, it's wiser to address the lender's concerns before starting over with a new proposal to a new lender.

Improve the Proposal

It is up to you to convince a lender to change a decision. The lender is only responsible for evaluating the information you present.

In fact, after a decision has been made, it can be more difficult to persuade someone to change it. But if the loan officer is candid about what influenced the decision, you may be able to challenge and overcome these objections. The loan could be approved quicker on reconsideration than if you started over with a new lender.

While you are pursuing financing, continue to update your proposal with fresh information as it is available or acquired. As your company is completing a financial period every 30 days, you need to keep the lender current on the company's financial position.

If you discover new information about the business, industry or strategy, revise your application to add this information. Even if the proposal has already been submitted to the lender, you should still send the additional information for review.

Every 60 to 90 days (if your search for financing lasts this long), you should review your entire plan from beginning to end and add updated information and make corrections. While your application is being reviewed, you can take advantage of any information or ideas obtained from a lender that turned down the request. The more you polish your proposal, the greater your chances for success.

Three Strikes, You Need Help

It may be that your business proposal does not qualify for the loan you're seeking — not only with the lender who rejected the loan, but with any lender. If your loan application is turned down more than three times, there may be an inherent weakness in your proposal that prevents approval from any source.

Find someone who can objectively evaluate the situation and the financing. Whether you talk to a business consultant, accountant, or experienced lender, a professional advisor's direct experience and practical advice could make the difference — a "yes."

A LOAN IS NOT THE ONLY WAY TO FINANCE A BUSINESS

There are other ways to accomplish your objectives. Beyond borrowing money, financing includes such diverse options as selling part or certain rights of the business, franchising, or bartering — all other ways to exchange value owned for value needed.

Or, you could reduce the loan by financing part of the transaction in another way. There are many possibilities. Although many of these strategies can be more difficult, more expensive, and more time-consuming, when you need financing, you have to take it the way it is available.

Maybe it was too early in the game to obtain financing. The best investment you can make in your business is time. Another six, twelve, or eighteen months might give you the time you need to improve the chances of approval by demonstrating the validity of the business strategy or other measurements of financial success.

To get the financing you need, you need to be in a position of strength. When you can present an established and stable operating record and profits of a business, you decrease the lender's exposure as well as your own inherent risk.

THERE ARE OTHER SOURCES!

There are literally hundreds of potential lenders. Within these hundreds of lenders, there are even more loan officers. Your initial rejection may have come from a person with less experience in business than you and the decision was based on a limited career.

You need to feel extremely confident about the merits of your loan proposal. Don't let one lender's "no" prevent you from enthusiastically presenting your plan to another lender.

Know Your Options!

Different lenders have different loan appetites (particularly at a given point of time), different expertise, even different levels of acceptable risks. Keep searching until you find the right lender — one who understands your business and feels comfortable with your management of it. They are out there! They're just harder to find. And there are other financing strategies you may not have considered. This book is your road map!

RECAP

We have looked at:

- the many ways a loan officer can say "No"
- the right way to react at the time
- how to gain from rejection, getting helpful hints for improving your proposal
- how to respond constructively to the various objections that have been made
- how you should always remember that there are other lenders
- but how sometimes you may just have to revise your ideas.

CHAPTER 2

The Bank's on My Back!

THE ONSET OF FINANCIAL DIFFICULTY

It may have been the loss of a major customer or a catastrophic fraud, fire or natural disaster. Maybe you've watched a pervasive deterioration of the business over a period of time. Whatever it is, you're facing a devastating situation — and whatever the cause, the bank's on your back!

For both owners and management, financial tough times in a business can be times of anguish, despair and unrelenting stress. It's happened; you're there. If you lose your objectivity or give in to panic, this can be an exceedingly dangerous time.

This chapter will help you understand your bank's communications, whether direct or subtle, and will give you strategies for generating cash and developing a co-operative action plan for recovery ... and in the worst case scenario, plan for a successful wind-down.

Take a Deep Breath

This is the time you must be pro-active in dealing with secured and unsecured lenders and creditors. You cannot afford to bury your head in the sand, hoping that the problem will go away. It won't go away; but it can be resolved!

Stand back, assess the conditions, analyse the causes, develop an action plan and carefully carry out a strategy for turning the business around.

Seek the right support. Turn to your professional advisors for guidance and assistance. As they will have seen these types of problems before, they can offer an objective viewpoint and proven strategies for effective resolution.

Know the Early Warning Signs

Management often does not recognize the longer-term symptoms or early warning signs. As lenders must be attuned to recognizing potential problems at early stages, they will often be the first to wave the flag signalling potential disaster.

View Matters in the Same Light as Lenders Do

When you sense financial difficulty, your first step should be to review and interpret the early warning signals that lenders look for. Lenders know a business is in trouble when they see one or more of the following situations:

- under capitalization (often evidenced by inadequate equity capital)
- lack of management depth (including a lack of specific skills for the particular business or second tier backup management)
- conflicts within the management team
- lack of up-to-date financial information
- historical operating losses
- deteriorating trends of financial ratios
- new and significant competition in the marketplace (this can be a result of product obsolescence, poor services or competitors' aggressive pricing)
- concentration of sales in a few customers or loss of a major customer
- continued failure to meet sales or margin objectives
- frequent bank overdrafts
- inability to meet monthly carrying costs of term debt
- high fixed costs in an industry vulnerable to economic fluctuations
- difficulty in raising new capital
- rapid expansion, with failure to keep pace with personnel, systems and controls, and required financing
- high break-even point, particularly on a cash flow basis and
- exposure of the business to external conditions beyond its control, such as a construction project delayed by continuous bad weather or protracted labour strife.

Take Action

Astute owner/managers will recognize the signs above *before* they hear from their banks. If you identify any of the above (deteriorating trends of financial ratios being the most significant), evaluate the factor fully and move immediately to the section on generating cash.

If you've missed the warning signs, it's likely the bank has already given you a wake up call. You may wish to skip the next section for now and turn to the section that follows to enhance your understanding of banks' specific communications and the degrees of seriousness of each.

FOCUS ON GENERATING CASH

Your first line of defense is to focus on generating liquidity — cash establishes flexibility. You need to be objective and hard-nosed in examining the many strategies that follow here. All too often, management will rationalize why particular actions can't be taken. And time and time again, when receivers must enter the picture, they confirm the validity of a particular action. But so often it is too late for the business to benefit.

How can you generate cash? Quick Check 2.1 provides some typical steps to consider, perhaps with the assistance of your accountant.

TIP

SNAP

Rejuvenate your business and enhance liquidity by developing fresh sources of cash, either from within or outside the business, to sustain operations.

Quick Check 2.1 Cash Generating Strategies

Asset Related Cash Generating Strategies

❑ Inventory
- ✓ Reduce and liquidate excesses
- ✓ Speed up production cycle
- ✓ Establish consignment stocks from suppliers
- ✓ Introduce "just-in-time" supply of inventory requirements
- ✓ Sub-contract production of certain components
- ✓ Investigate the possibilities of manufacturing offshore
- ✓ Obtain deposits/prepayments from customers.

❑ Accounts Receivable
- ✓ Aggressively follow up collection of delinquent accounts
- ✓ Offer customers a significant prompt payment discount
- ✓ Factor the outstanding accounts to realize a higher ratio of cash from the receivables, and retire the existing operating line.

❑ Fixed Assets
- ✓ Dispose of non-performing divisions, departments, or assets
- ✓ Sell and leaseback certain assets.

❑ Other Assets
- ✓ Dispose of various assets or divisions
- ✓ Sell or license various "rights" that the business may possess.

Liability-Related Cash Generating Strategies

❑ Accounts Payable
- ✓ Persuade trade creditors to accept payment on extended terms: for example, extend a portion of account to a term basis of 6-12 months with interest; offer a Purchase Money Security Interest, a form of applicable trade creditor security under applicable provincial personal property security legislation, in return for extended terms
- ✓ Consider a Proposal to creditors, either formal or informal, to freeze existing unsecured creditors
- ✓ Informally extend payment schedule.

❑ Operating Costs
- ✓ Assess all operating costs, overhead and personnel and make significant critical cutbacks.

Capital/Equity Related Cash Generating Strategies

❑ Share Capital
- ✓ Raise fresh capital from employees, suppliers, customers, venture capitalists or existing shareholders.

❑ Hidden Values in Assets
- ✓ Realize hidden values in assets through sale/leaseback or remortgage.

❑ Restructuring
- ✓ Through arrangements with secured creditors, postpone and/or capitalize certain debt or fixed payments.

UNDERSTAND YOUR BANK'S SIGNALS

Apart from the obvious Delinquency Notice for missed payment(s), there are many other signals which a bank dispatches. If your bank is waving any of the flags discussed here, move quickly and appropriately to avoid more serious consequences.

Since banks are often the centre of the business' financing, we'll examine the signals from their vantage point. All of these apply equally to other financial relationships and lenders.

In isolation, these signals do not necessarily mean difficulties with your bank. However, when a number occur collectively, you must assess them in the context of your business' present financial circumstances. Your bank may well be sending a strong and very serious message.

To focus on the relative significance of each, the signals are discussed under these categories:

- subtle signals
- moderate signals
- strong and direct signals.

Subtle Signals

On an individual basis, these subtle signals may not indicate a negative situation. But when coupled with other factors, they may give clues as to matters which you need to address.

More Frequent Contacts from Bank

When a bank perceives a possible deterioration in an account, there may be a closer monitoring of the business through more frequent telephone calls and visits. You might even have visitors from the bank's head office who want to see the business and meet management face to face.

A Change in Account Supervision

If your account supervision has been changed, you may now be dealing with staff, perhaps from a regional office, who are in fact specialists used to dealing with troubled accounts (these departments are often called "work out" or "special loans").

You may also notice the pace of decision making has quickened in respect of your account. These departments usually have a shortened chain of command.

Delays in Responding to Requests

If your bank delays responding to your requests, the bank may be assessing the deterioration of your account and trying to reach a consensus within the bank on an appropriate reply and course of action.

Request for More Information

While assessing a credit application, a bank may request additional information to gain time while a request is being debated internally. On the other hand, the information may be requested because the omissions were nothing more than oversights at the branch level.

Reluctance to Increase Line of Credit

Reluctance to increase your operating line of credit may be a forewarning of a level of concern about your account.

Requests for Asset Appraisals

A new request for updated appraisals on assets or new appraisals on assets not now encumbered is probably an indicator that the bank is re-examining its security position.

Moderate Signals

While these signs indicate the bank's considerable displeasure and uneasiness, there may still be time for a careful analysis of circumstances and development of a new financing strategy.

Imposition of New Loan Terms and Covenants

Loan agreement covenants are often minimal and seldom exercised. However, the strengthening and enforcement of these covenants may be an indication that the bank is setting the stage, through appropriate documentation, to call the loan.

Request for a Management Action Plan

Certain negative trends and performance may cause a level of discomfort that will cause the bank to request an outline of planned management action and response. The bank will then assess this plan and establish whether it finds it a satisfactory first step. Obviously, achievement of the plan will be the second step they expect you to carry out.

Additional Security

A request for further security is certainly an indication of a bank's concern. Additional security may consist of pledge of assets which were previously unencumbered or it may consist of new forms of security covering the same assets.

In many instances, this requirement will extend to asking the owner/manager to pledge personal assets, often on the basis that this gesture "demonstrates a commitment to the business."

More Equity

A request for more equity may reflect the bank's desire to see that the customer's business has a solid foundation upon which to build for future expansion and success. On the other hand, it may be a direct means of reducing the bank's loans and inherent exposure.

Requirement for a Consultant's Review

In situations where a loan condition is deteriorating, the bank will require an independent review and assessment of the customer's business operations and financial condition.

The latter usually includes an evaluation of the bank's security documentation and coverage. A positive assessment will benefit your relationship with the bank, perhaps even leading to increased credits. However, a negative assessment greatly enhances the bank's justification for more severe action.

New Support Professionals

If unfamiliar lawyers, accountants or insolvency specialists call or visit your business, it is likely your bank is seeking additional technical support in dealing with a troublesome situation. It may take very direct questioning to determine the background and purpose of these individuals.

Meetings "Downtown"

A request to meet senior or specialized personnel at a regional office may indicate your bank has called in the "big boys" to intervene because of existing concerns.

Strong and Direct Signals

When these signals are made, management must act quickly and decisively, including making back-up plans to ward off what are probably going to be imminent severe steps by the bank.

A "No" Answer

Banks are in the business of lending money and supporting "good" customers. Accordingly, when a bank says "no," it is a statement that they are unhappy with the request or the business.

Reductions in Authorized Lines of Credit

Usually when a bank limits an authorized line of credit, this step is taken to attempt to limit its exposure. There is often a correlation with its current assessment of the industry, the particular business' performance, or the value of its security.

Reduction of Margins/Security Coverages

If the bank reduces margins or security coverage, it may be attempting to bring the borrowings in line with its security in order to minimize exposure.

Requests for Higher Rates or Administration Fees

Higher rates or administration fees can sometimes mean that the bank perceives the level of risk in your account has increased and so it will attempt to balance its risk and reward by increasing rates and fees. In particular, the fees may be levied to compensate for the staffing cost of closer monitoring and head office internal reporting that has been put into effect.

Some banks have been known to increase fees to such an extent that the customer will indirectly get the message to take his business elsewhere.

Suggestions to Refinance at Another Bank

Since this is inconsistent with all banks' business development policies, a bank which suggests you refinance elsewhere can only be saying that the bank does not consider your account to be of good quality.

Inability to Refinance at Another Bank

If you are unable to refinance at another bank, this may be the hard knock, "second" opinion that the quality of your account at this time is not perceived to be attractive.

Open Descriptive Statements

"Non-performing," "non-revolving," "under-margined," or "over-trading" may be terms used by your bank in trying to explain a changing relationship. These euphemistic expressions need to be clarified. Ask for a direct explanation of the bank's current assessment of your account.

Cheques Returned "NSF"

Since a chain reaction with suppliers might occur, a bank usually does not send back cheques on a commercial account frivolously. NSFs reflect a very serious situation.

SIGNS

WARNING

- If your bank is sending subtle signals through requests or other actions, address any outstanding matters immediately to restore a positive working relationship with your bank.
- Analyse moderate signals of your bank's uneasiness and develop a proactive financing strategy to reposition the business.
- If the bank's signals are strong and direct, waste no time! Develop and implement a plan to create cash and stave off imminent action by the bank.

The questions in Quick Check 2.2 are typical of those a bank or other lender will review to anticipate a negative trend or deteriorating circumstances in a company. Of course, the purpose is to avoid further deterioration which might lead to a loan loss. These questions are helpful for critical self-assessment when management senses troubles ahead.

Early Warning Signs

Quick Check 2.2 **A Bank's Early Warning Questionnaire**

A positive answer to any of the questions below may not in itself suggest a pending liquidation situation. However, if a pattern begins to emerge, i.e., there is a positive answer to a number of questions (say, five or more), then you are almost certainly experiencing operating difficulties sufficient to warrant investigation by the bank.

1. In the last three months, has the account been in an excess (or overdraft) position?
2. Was the excess taken without request?
3. Has the average loan balance (hard core) increased over the last six months?
4. Has the turnover (deposits and cheques) on the bank account increased or decreased by more than 10% per month over the last three months?
5. Have there been requests during the last three months from the Directors for their guarantees or other personal securities to be released?
6. Have there been delays in the receipt and deposit of funds?
7. Has it been necessary to return cheques?
8. Has the frequency of returned cheques inwards (i.e., from customers) increased over the last few months?
9. Are cheques being issued in round amounts, thus possibly indicating partial payments to suppliers?
10. Have there been delays in the production of agreed figures or information, e.g., cash flow?
11. Has the company been attempting to raise financing elsewhere?
12. Has there been any change of key personnel?
13. Is the company pursuing a policy of expansion by acquisition?
14. Where a debenture is held, are the covenants being breached?
15. Where a budget and/or cash flow is being monitored, is there any material divergence from the forecast figures?
16. Are profit margins being eroded?
17. Has there been a significant increase in preferential creditors?
18. Is there any evidence that time is being taken from creditors or debtors being called in early, indicating a need to accelerate cash flow?

   Carefully review and understand the current state of your banking relationship to anticipate potential problems.

DEVELOP AN ACTION PLAN

Understand Your Bank's Point of View

Once you realize your bank is uneasy (hopefully not panicking!), it is vital to understand the bank's psyche so that you can develop a strategic approach for improving the bank's confidence in you while staying the risk of their taking severe action.

Most banks will acknowledge a reluctance to take formal action. Past experience tells them that there is considerable aggravation and burden on their time and frequently the results are less than satisfactory for the bank. Skeletons always tend to surface during formal proceedings.

> **Carefully consider the signals and circumstances in your banking relationship to anticipate troubled waters.**

When banks establish that the business condition or the security coverage is not deteriorating, they will usually procrastinate and postpone taking severe action. To support this attitude, it is important to make sure the lines of communication do not break down and the bank continues to have confidence in the integrity of management. Thus, the bank will likely be looking for a basis to do nothing!

Know the Fundamental Principles of Relationships with Banks

The following points emphasize the essence of a lending relationship — money is owing, the lender is entitled to a return of the money, and the lender is well secured and has an abundance of statutory support in its arsenal.

- The bank and the owner/manager sit on the same side of the fence.
- The business' owners cannot realize on their equity investment unless the creditors have been paid.
- The bank and the owner/manager are both better off if formal proceedings can be avoided.
- With the minefield of unexpected problems, the inherent costs of 10-20% of the available proceeds, and the usual shrinkage of assets, the bank is typically worse off in the event of formal insolvency proceedings, as will certainly be the owner/manager.
- A co-operative rather than adversarial approach is generally better for both the bank and the owner/manager.

Typically, a legal fight with a bank in an insolvency proceeding does not lead to a constructive result. The few court cases won by debtors in recent years are indeed isolated and should not be generally considered as a strong basis for considering legal action.

In most situations, the reality will be that the money is owing to the bank and that there is default in payment.

TIP

SNAP

Only consider a legal struggle with your bank if you have solid legal advice as to the unreasonableness of the bank's position and a legal basis for attacking their position. If you do proceed, have a solid backup plan to ensure the business can survive the inherent cash crunch.

TEN STEPS FOR DEALING WITH A CONCERNED BANK

STEP 1

Enhance Lines of Communication with the Bank

Be open and forthright with the bank — avoid surprises. Unexpected surprises can lead a bank to panic!

Establish a co-operative attitude, and solicit joint solutions to the obvious problems and concerns.

STEP 2

Maintain Credibility

A fundamental principle of finance is that credibility generates confidence. Confidence is the cornerstone of any successful banking relationship. As previously stated, good communication helps to establish credibility, as long as it is not fractured by deceit, dishonesty, or deception.

Always tell your banker both the good news and the bad news, and certainly always the truth.

STEP 3

Act Quickly and Decisively

The owner/manager must communicate to the bank a clear understanding of the problems and a commitment to do something about them.

Inaction by the management often leads to action by the bank. Assess the problems and present a credible Action Plan.

Consider a consultation with an experienced person in your weak functional area, e.g., a marketing professional or a financial consultant.

STEP 4
....

Engage Experienced Professional Advisors

You may need to consult experienced legal and financial specialists to help develop an objective and realistic assessment and Action Plan. The emphasis should be on business, not legal, solutions.

STEP 5
....

Conserve Cash

Flexibility is enhanced through a reservoir of cash. Thus, consider the remedial actions outlined earlier in this chapter.

STEP 6
....

Back Up your Action Plan

If you have been drawing a generous salary, bonuses or dividends from the business, tighten your belt and reduce your take. This may also involve selling or mortgaging personal assets in order to cover personal living expenses. If you have other sources of funds, invest in the business and demonstrate your commitment. A new infusion of capital from the owner/manager will instil considerable confidence and go a long way towards ensuring creditors adopt the proposed action plan.

STEP 7
....

Work Co-operatively with Banks and Creditors in Developing your Action Plan

When banks and creditors play a role in the development of an action plan, they are more likely to support it. They may also be able to suggest new ideas and alternatives. Developing the action plan in isolation may waste valuable time and lead you down a path to nowhere.

STEP 8

Respect the Priority Position of Creditors

Credibility may be destroyed by considering actions which favour certain creditor groups at the expense of others. Develop a plan which is fair and equitable to all creditors.

STEP 9

Contemplate the Inconceivable

When on the brink of insolvency proceedings, management and shareholders must be prepared to do the inconceivable; often the "crown jewels" must be sold to generate cash in order to salvage the remainder of the business. No possible actions are sacred at such times; pride must be put aside.

STEP 10

When All Else Fails

In the final analysis, if none of the foregoing is feasible, the next prudent step is to develop your own "wind-down" plan and present this recommendation to the lender as a more cost effective and expedient liquidation approach. If necessary, it may be required to work closely with bank designates in a monitoring role, rather than in a receiver's role.

Experience has shown that the owner/manager is much more successful in liquidating business assets than a receiver. This additional return of proceeds may reduce the personal exposure on guarantees.

TIPS

INSIDER'S

Four Key Approaches to Business Recovery in Troubled Times

1. Maintain a high level of communication and credibility with lenders.

2. Act decisively to develop a co-operative action plan.

3. Be prepared to underpin your plan with your tangible support.

4. Work co-operatively with your bank and all creditors and bring their contributions into the package of solutions in your Action Plan.

THE GOING GETS TOUGH: WORKING THROUGH THE TECHNICAL ISSUES

Not only is it advantageous to assess the bank's attitude and its probable course of action, but you should also carefully *review your documentation* and legal position to underpin your Action Plan. You should *consult your lawyer* now.

Personal Guarantees

If there are personal guarantees outstanding, it may be prudent for the owner/manager (company officers/guarantors) to co-operate fully to ensure:

- the existing security documents are valid and enforceable
- new security is provided over all unencumbered assets
- funds collected are directed to pay down the lender's loans.

SIGNS

WARNING

In the months before calling a loan, lenders will often tighten their security position.

- Lenders may request new guarantors (such as a spouse) be added or collateral mortgages on personal assets be pledged to support existing guarantees.
- Difficult decisions must be made as to the realistic prospects for survival in contrast to the dismal issue of "throwing good money after bad."

Lenders may attempt to reduce the amount of credit available by changing margin requirements.

- Examination of underlying loan agreements or term sheets and the inherent covenants will determine if the lender has breached its contractual obligations.

When concern mounts, a lender will often suggest that it would like to have an independent review of the business by a consultant.

- In somewhat colloquial jargon, this review may be called a "look/see" or a "quick and dirty." In realistic terms, the function of the consultant will be to review the operations, assess the strengths and weaknesses, and attempt to determine its continued viability. In many instances, a positive report can ensue, with a resulting renewal of support by the lender.
- However, the opposite may also occur. If the lender has decided on this approach, resistance or a lack of co-operation will not serve the business' best interest.

However, consideration must be taken as to whether any of these actions might be challenged by an unsecured creditor as a fraudulent preference, under the Bankruptcy and Insolvency Act, if they occur within three months of bankruptcy. On the other hand, this type of situation might encourage a lender to keep the business afloat to allow its security to "season" (i.e., to become effective).

The Consultant's Report

In these situations, owner/managers must make sure that they will have opportunity to review the draft report before presentation to the lender, and that the company will be provided with a copy of the final report.

A consultant's report may lead to one of the following consequences:

- If viability and security seem reasonable, the lender may allow the business to work out its problems over a period of time.
- If some level of concern still exists, the lender may wish to appoint a "monitor" to review the cash flow and financial condition on an ongoing basis.
- If the prognosis is negative, the lender may proceed to the appointment of a receiver.

Current practice among lenders is to not appoint the consultant as the receiver because of an obvious conflict of interest.

Legal Recourse

If a demand is made for payment, current case law has established that the lender needs to provide reasonable notice and time to pay.

Has there been reasonable notice and time to pay?

In the event of liquidation by a secured lender, review legal aspects of the action, but in most instances be prepared to cooperate.

Consider current common law precedents in respect of improvident realization, breach of undertaking, or lack of seasoning of security.

Revitalize and Reactivate

Again, stand back and take a deep breath. Hopefully this chapter has provided you with some fresh oxygen and you're ready to revitalize and reactivate. The key things to remember are:

- Make an early and realistic assessment of your financial and legal positions.
- Develop a co-operative action plan that will allow the business to recover.
- Strive to rebuild a solid financial relationship with your bank and lenders.

TIP

Remember the quote from the Introduction: "At the pleasure of the Bank...". It is probable that the bank's funds are repayable on demand, a legal position which gives them latitude if there have been defaults.

RECAP

We have evaluated:

- the warning signs from your bank that tell you they are not entirely happy
- the degrees of seriousness of those warnings
- the situation from the lender's viewpoint
- what you can do to improve that view
- ten steps to help deal with the situation.

When the Chips are Down...

From indiscretions of youth through to medical catastrophes, sometimes past situations haunt the borrower's financial future. Often these matters have nothing to do with the borrower's past business performance, moral obligation to repay debts, or prospects for operational success in the future. You may have simply had a run of bad luck.

WHY ME?

Too often bad times interact. A financial reverse happens at the same time as you're coping with a marital break-up and health problems. These are all reverses that can be mastered individually, but when they combine they can temporarily defeat even the strongest among us.

How do you deal with special circumstances which affect either your personal finances or the business itself?

That's Life

Does your present life or past record include one or more of these real life situations?

- litigation, i.e., lawsuit
- bankruptcy or formal insolvency proceedings
- divorce
- medical problems
- bad credit history
- a history of pretty awful decisions
- flashy taste.

When You Need Financing, These Are Downers

All of these circumstances will weaken your financing application and certainly dampen the lender's enthusiasm for considering your request. But if you view the tests that life throws you as opportunities to renew your determination and focus, you can succeed.

Honesty Is the Best Application

When you have to discuss a current or past difficult situation with a lender, you need to be candid and honest. As technologies afford us little privacy, there's little point in trying to hide the facts, even when, at first blush, the lender will not view your difficulties as endearing qualities.

Were you at fault? Were you a victim? What have you gained from the experience? What are you doing to rehabilitate or rectify your financial condition?

Based on this information, the lender will evaluate if you represent a greater risk — and, therefore, whether the loan should be denied.

TIPS

SNAP

Whether you have past or present difficulties that affect your desirability as a borrower:

- Be prepared to help the lender investigate the problems or issues objectively.

- Be candid and direct: openness will develop credibility; appropriate explanations and documentation will help understanding.

LITIGATION

Liability gives new meaning to the fashion of deep pockets. An extraordinary number of lawyers and almost as many insurance adjusters make their living settling claims. North American businesses have higher odds of being sued over an unresolved matter or dispute than businesses elsewhere. We live in the most litigious business community in the world. Aren't we lucky. Well at least you are not alone.

Just about everyone faces a lawsuit at some point. Even if you are eventually found "innocent," a considerable amount will have to be spent just defending yourself. Even if you are only "accused" and the matter does not go to litigation, your financial reputation may still be severely damaged.

So, How Was It?

Whether your financial statements are scarred with the extraordinary costs of defending yourself or you have limited your costs by settling out of court, the lender is entitled to a full explanation. If you explain the matter clearly and objectively, the lender will be better able to understand the impact of the litigation on the business' finances.

By being forthright, you can move the application process beyond the legal situation so that the positive aspects of your financing proposal will be considered and emphasized.

Tackle the Lender's Fear of the Unknown

A lawsuit arouses a lender's fear of unknown risks. If you provide quality documentation, the lender can more effectively meet the responsibility to assess the financing request. Whether you were at fault or not, the lender has to look at the potential result of the litigation on the business.

> **Provide lender with complete details of the resolution of a law suit.**

Be prepared to provide the lender with:

- copies of the statement of claim
- your statement of defence
- other supporting materials, particularly independent collaborative data.

If the court's summation made you look good, get a copy of the transcript to give to the lender; the per page cost is relatively nominal. Alternatively, prepare a well-documented outline of the claim and your defence. Provide copies of invoices, receipts, and other documents to show how the business was affected.

Lawsuit Pending?

Wait. The timing's not right. If you have a lawsuit that is pending at the time of application, the best thing to do is wait until the matter is resolved.

Most lenders will not proceed with a financing application if there are litigious matters against the company or principals which are unresolved or under appeal. They'll wait for the judgment. Of course, other routine matters which occur in the normal course of business and which do not threaten the overall financial condition should not interfere with the financing application once the lawsuit is behind you.

Once the lawsuit is resolved, the lender will be interested in how your company handled it. Your response will indicate how you and the company will respond if a similar dispute arises in the future.

BANKRUPTCY

Bankruptcy and other formal insolvency proceedings will certainly pique a lender's interest.

> **Bankruptcy is about money, not morals.**

If you have this in your personal or your company's track record, remember: legitimate bankruptcy cases do not involve morals — they are about money. Bankruptcy is not usually about an *unwillingness* to repay money, but rather the *inability* to pay money. Hold your head up high and use what positives you can salvage.

On the Brighter Side

In fact, borrowers who have had a previous bankruptcy may actually be a lower risk for lenders. These borrowers have a wealth of experience in dealing with difficult situations, better preparing them for the economic risks associated with operating a small business. Surviving these tough circumstances adds to the borrower's management and financial education.

From a business standpoint, bankruptcy is often a legitimate strategy. It's a way to deal with overwhelming liabilities or a dire situation. However, from the lender's point of view, parties who have sought protection under bankruptcy laws represent high risks.

Why? Many lenders do not understand the technical aspects of bankruptcy.

Obviously bankruptcy proceedings can be and are abused, but recognition must be given to its legitimate use in circumstances which threaten individuals and businesses. Some lenders are shortsighted and quick to judge. Look for a lender who will evaluate your case according to its own particular circumstances.

A Costly Strategy

Bankruptcy is usually the debtor's most logical decision. But it is a very costly strategy. Many businesses receive poor or limited advice and seek bankruptcy prematurely without understanding other remedies or recognizing the long-term consequences. Once the decision is made to go the bankruptcy route, the debtor will live with it for many years.

Bankruptcy proceedings are designed to protect individuals or businesses from their creditors in circumstances where the liabilities exceed the assets. This protection is intended to prevent a particular creditor from unfairly collecting a debt at the expense of other creditors or beyond the debtor's realistic ability to pay. Bankruptcy protection can help debtors by providing them the time they need to reorganize their affairs in order to pay off debts without undue interference from creditors.

Climb the Mountain

If there's bankruptcy in the business' or your personal track record, getting that financing application approved will be a challenge but not an insurmountable one.

Countless circumstances lead a party to seek the protection of a bankruptcy court. Without doubt, many parties are forced to choose this strategy as a result of events beyond their control. But you can overcome the stigma of bankruptcy and obtain new financing for starting over. Chances are better if the bankruptcy was an individual case rather than a business case.

A Matter of Public Record

If you have been involved in a bankruptcy case (personal or business), the lender will discover this fact very early in the application process through a simple credit check. It is better to disclose the facts before the lender reads this information in a credit report.

Don't try to hide the facts — the lender will find out.

As a strategy, try to interest the lender in the business financing transaction before referring to the bankruptcy. If the lender is not comfortable with the attributes of the deal before learning about the bankruptcy, you will never get its full attention on the application.

Be wary and be prepared. Credit reports include information about prior connections with any bankruptcy. In addition to personal bankruptcy cases, the credit report records any business in which the borrower was an owner, shareholder, or partner. Although you may have had no control over the events leading to a business bankruptcy, you must be prepared to explain the circumstances of the case.

Because the proceedings of a bankruptcy case are a matter of public record, the lender is able to obtain a copy of the case file to verify the dates, creditors, debts, and final results of the case. In other words, a fictional or biased account of the bankruptcy case could permanently destroy credibility with the lender when the truth is revealed.

Write Your Story

Tell your bankruptcy story, and provide a written version for review purposes. Because the loan officer will probably have to relay the information in writing, it is far better that you provide a detailed account as the basis for the financing report rather than have the loan officer transcribe hastily written notes from your discussion.

Document the circumstances thoroughly and substantiate any difficulties which led to seeking bankruptcy protection. If you were not at fault, prove it by using affidavits from other parties, accident reports, medical records, pictures, newspaper articles, and any other information available to support these claims.

If the bankruptcy experience was due to imprudent management rather than tragic circumstances, the truth is equally as important. Depending on how much time has lapsed, how much money was lost by the creditors, and how you have managed in the post-bankruptcy period, the lender may still consider the loan application.

DIVORCE

A divorce can be a disaster for a small business owner. Because the family law process can be strenuous for the individuals involved, you could have months of under-performance in your business responsibilities. The financial settlement can be very disruptive if you are forced to buy out your spouse or share the business ownership interests.

Because of the many and very stressful issues in divorce cases, the vengeful actions of one party may create liabilities for the other party. Alternatively, one party may refuse to pay legitimate liabilities, allocated through the equalization process, which are in the joint names of both parties. Divorce can ravage a borrower's credit history and ability to borrow money.

Divorce-in-Progress

If the divorce is not yet finalized, consider waiting until the process is over before making a business financing application. If you are in the midst of resolving the emotional and complicated issues of a divorce, the anxiety of seeking credit is compounded. Wait until you can focus on the business at hand — one major negotiation at a time.

Protect Your Credit History

As divorce is probably the most abused excuse used by persons with bad credit, the borrower has to earn credibility, for example by showing how the bad credit was created through the irresponsible actions of others.

Your best defence is to pay off any unpaid accounts, whether individually or jointly held. Focus on protecting a good credit history and later pursue the other party for recovery of these sums.

> **Protecting your credit is your most important concern.**

To limit your liability exposure, close the joint credit accounts when the divorce process first begins and notify creditors that you are not responsible for future liabilities created on a joint account. While you cannot escape joint and several liability on existing balances, a notice can prevent a creditor from holding you liable for subsequent charges.

If you discover you have a negative credit report information as a result of the divorce, contact the credit reporting agency and provide a statement detailing the situation. The credit bureau is obligated to include this explanation in all future inquiries.

Explain, but Don't Emote

Once you are through the divorce process, you will need to work on providing an explanation to the lender about any impact the divorce has had on the business and your personal financial situation. Document this explanation with copies of bank records, financial statements, and a copy of the final divorce settlement.

Do not discuss the emotional inter-personal aspects of the divorce. Not only are they irrelevant, but your stories may be wrongly interpreted as an indication of how you personally handle a difficult situation and could be detrimental to your financing application.

MEDICAL PROBLEMS

It's not hard to imagine what could happen to the economic status of a business if the owner/manager were to become ill for an extended period. There are many possible consequences and many of them include serious financial damage.

It isn't fair that after battling a disease or injury to save one's life, the principal of the business has to battle for the survival of the business. Once the borrower's health recovers, it could indeed be hard work to lead the business through to a recovery.

Focus on Economic Health

Be prepared to provide appropriate documentation to communicate and confirm the medical situation to the lender. The lender will want to know how the illness or injury affected or may affect you personally (i.e., your energies, any limitations and strategies for overcoming these) and the impact on the business' operations. While you should expect compassion for these situations, you must be prepared to accept the burden of proof.

> **Outline the facts of your medical problem/condition to the lender.**

As the real issue is economic health, the discussion should focus on the financial details. Rather than outlining all of the details of the medical treatment and procedures, limit the personal information to a generic description of the medical condition.

BAD CREDIT HISTORY

Compounding several of the problems mentioned above is the trickle-down effect each has on the borrower's personal credit history. If your cash flow has been interrupted by any of life's curve balls, your reason and cash reserves may well have been exhausted. Of course, payments to creditors will have slowed down. Eventually, you must deal with the problem since a record of slow credit payments is one of the most troublesome problems in the eyes of the lender.

It is critical to manage both business and personal credit closely to keep your payment history clean and avoid perpetuating negative entries into a credit record. Lenders focus on a number of aspects in the credit report, including the total amount of credit outstanding, payment history, and any public records which indicate the unsatisfactory conduct of business or personal affairs.

Manage the Process

Understanding how to manage this process cannot repair a previous poor credit record, but modifying current and future performance can improve your situation and put an end to the poor performance reflected in your recent credit report.

Again, it is better to be upfront with negative information. If you have a bad credit record, tell the lender why. Often bad credit is not the result of poor management or lack of responsibility, but rather circumstances which affect the borrower's ability to meet those responsibilities consistently.

To earn the lender's confidence, you must be able to demonstrate that those circumstances have been improved to a degree and they will not interfere with your ability to make payments on the financing being requested.

Clean Up Your Act

Here are some strategies for making a new start:

- Pay off as much credit as possible by using savings, having a yard sale, taking back recently purchased merchandise, liquidating assets, borrowing money from the business, collecting outstanding debts, or even drawing down the cash surrender value of a life insurance policy. Get cash (without borrowing more) to pay off these accounts as fast as possible. Rather than reducing all the accounts, pay off the ones with the lower balances. It is better to have five past due accounts than ten past due accounts.

> **Follow new strategies to reestablish a good credit record.**

- After the small debts are cleared, set priorities for the big debts. Pay off non-tax deductible debt, debt with high payments or debt with higher interest rates first. Making payments on these accounts as the initial strategy will give you more flexibility in the future.
- Manage your payments so nothing goes beyond 30 days past due, even if it means hand delivering a payment. Payments less than 30 days delinquent are not reported to the credit bureau.
- If your cash shortage is temporary, limit the number of creditors

who will receive late payments. If you have five invoices, do not make the one for $500 on time and be late on the payments to four others who expect $125. Pay the four $125 accounts on time and be late only on the one $500 payment.

- Slow down payments where you can. The credit bureau does not usually receive reports of late payments from such liabilities as public utilities, telephone companies, long distance suppliers, cable operators, merchandise buying clubs, and private note holders. Slowing payments to these accounts will not affect a public credit record and may help keep it clean. But keep this strategy in check. If you get too far behind on utility bills, you risk having the service disconnected and having to pay a fee to restore it.

BAD DECISIONS

"To err is human;" however, you may have noticed that some mistakes are far more costly than others. In a dynamic economy, owner/managers are constantly making strategic decisions with long-term implications. Sometimes errors will be made.

Small business owners often wear the hats of chief executive officer, chief financial officer, chief operating officer, advertising agent, transportation specialist, tax expert and computer prodigy. Newspapers, magazines, cable features, sit-coms, talk shows, books, videos and the Internet all make business look so easy. So how can anyone make a mistake?

We live in an age of overwhelming ideas and communications. Today's eighth-wonder-of-the-world is tomorrow's obsolescent trash. More decisions are demanded than ever before, but remember: we are still limited to one brain.

> **Use an error in judgment to illustrate what you have learned from the mistake.**

First, you're forgiven. We all make occasional bad business decisions. Your decision was based on the best possible information and options at the time. Or maybe it wasn't. Regardless, move forward.

Show What You Learned

Document the error for the lender and submit this with your financing request. You want the loan officer to see things in the right perspective. Again, by being upfront about errors and more importantly, lessons learned, you can sway the lender to factor your candour into an assessment of the actions you took to overcome the mistake.

If your request qualifies under the other criteria necessary for financing, a previous error should not prevent your success.

FLASHY TASTE

Like a flashy office and an even flashier car? Elaborate trappings call into question management's judgment and prudence. Is it a wise consumption of limited capital? If the office looks more like a living room than a place of business, does it mean the owner/manager is spending too much time relaxing there and not enough knocking on doors and working at the real business activity?

If these elements are already in place, all you can do is tone it down. In other words, leave the Porsche behind when you take the lender to lunch. Borrow a modest vehicle for the occasion. Better still, return the car to the leasing agency, store the computer games, make your office more functional and cut back on unnecessary frills.

Don't send the wrong signals. In today's pragmatic business world, lenders and investors are not impressed with flash. Indeed, they're wary.

SO IT WASN'T GREAT; GET ON WITH IT

If you've made a mistake, own up.
If you've had bad times, look forward to better times.
If you've overdone it, tone it down.
Be forthright.
Accept that you cannot hide your past.

The lender is going to find out about that problem sooner or later so it is better that *you* present your case. Don't hide it and risk the lender uncovering it, perhaps not fully understanding the real situation and immediately jumping to a negative conclusion.

Good business breeds success and successful financing. This book is for winners, not whiners.

RECAP

We have discussed:

- the specific situations that may cause problems with a lender
- the cost of litigation and its effect on the business

- the legal and financial aspects of formal proceedings for bankruptcy
- the emotional strain of divorce and legal problems that may arise
- the effect of medical problems and possible neglect of the business
- the reflection of a poor credit record
- just plain bad decisions and an extravagant business lifestyle.

Term Loans—The Cornerstone of Long-Term Funding

Next to bank operating lines of credit, a term loan is the most important and fundamental form of financing for many businesses. It can be the cornerstone of long-term funding, particularly for the acquisition of long-term assets (fixed assets).

Once only the domain of large business, term loans are now available to small businesses through many and varied members of the financial services industry. In the last decade, the competition has heated up and interest rates are better than ever as more players try to attract the small business market.

WHAT IS A TERM LOAN?

If you're a home owner, you're likely very familiar with mortgages. Term loans are somewhat similar to mortgages in that they are both loans for a fixed and defined term (usually 5 to 10 years) and both have a fixed charge or encumbrance on specific fixed assets (usually land, buildings, equipment).

But term loans also have many different elements that go beyond a mortgage loan. Understanding the fundamental differences between mortgages and commercial term loans will help you know what you're looking for when seeking a term loan. The chart below compares mortgages and term loans:

Mortgage	Term Loan
secured by a registered real estate mortgage	may be secured by a debenture and/or security agreement with a fixed and floating charge on machinery, equipment, vehicles as well as real estate

Mortgage (cont'd)	Term Loan (cont'd)
focused on security value of assets	additionally focuses on the management and cash flow
conventionally restricted to 75% of value	may be to as much as 100% of value of the security; may include amounts for working capital and other business financing requirements
typically blended payments	may have very flexible payment terms (straight line, stepped, skipped, cyclical, or blended)
usually has a fixed interest rate for its term	interest rate may be either fixed or floating, or perhaps even with an option to change the basis at certain times during the term
the major covenants and under-takings are to repay principal and interest and to insure and maintain the assets	usually has other underlying conditions (often referred to as negative covenants) covering a variety of circumstances
usually closed or limited to pre-payment and lenders are often reluctant to provide further funding prior to maturity.	allows for prepayment and pro-vides for supplemental financing in the future.

TIPS

Although a conventional mortgage loan may bear a lower rate of interest (say 1/4 to 1/2% lower than a term loan), consider the limited flexibility it provides in view of the future opportunities to expand the business or your ability to respond to a downturn.

A Historical Perspective

Prior to World War II, the only financing small- or medium-sized businesses could find were primarily bank operating loans that were secured by accounts receivable, conventional commercial mortgages on real estate, and owners' capital. There was little flexibility in the amounts or terms of these loans. Hence business growth and development was constrained.

While large business had the advantages of accessing the financial bond market for long-term debt financing and stock markets for equity capital, small business could not access these sources that would enable them to expand.

Recognizing this limitation, the Government of Canada incorporated The Industrial Development Bank (now the Business Development Bank of Canada). Its express purpose was to make long-term funding available to small- and medium-sized businesses, on reasonable terms and conditions. Initially, its mandate was as a lender of last resort; this limitation has now been lifted. The majority of its loans were what we would now call term loans.

More Options for Small Business

The founding of the Business Development Bank of Canada sparked the fire which marked the development of a vibrant sector of the financial marketplace.

A 1986 study commissioned by the Federal Business Development Bank revealed that only Credit Unions, Financial Corporations, and the Business Development Bank of Canada (formerly FBDB or IDB) had a term-lending focus on under $1 million rather than the mid-market size of $1 to 5 million. The study's findings are illustrated in Figure 4.1 which shows the term-lending market share of various types of financial institutions in 1986 (conventional commercial mortgages are excluded).

Figure 4.1	Term-Lending Market Shares	
	Loans Less Than $5 Million	Loans Less Than $1 Million
Schedule 1&2 Banks	68.1%	62.7%
Trust Companies	1.9	0.4
Credit Unions	7.5	9.6
Financial Corporations	11.2	14.4
Business Development Bank	6.4	8.1
Other	4.9	4.8
Total	100.0%	100.0%

TERM-LENDING TODAY

Today, small businesses can obtain term loans from domestic banks, foreign banks, trust companies, private syndicates, and in limited cases, insurance companies and pension funds. But before you go out looking for this source of financing, you need to be aware of three significant trends in the long-term lending market that have developed in the past decade:

- competition
- interest rates
- bought deals.

Competition

The entry of several new institutional groups into the financing marketplace — including insurance companies, pension funds, trust companies and some Schedule 2 banks — has made today's lending market far more competitive than it was ten years ago.

Every small business should have an SBL to facilitate its early growth.

With the restructuring and renaming of the Business Development Bank of Canada, this federal financial organization was given an expanded mandate to provide term loans to small business and in many instances, to syndicate loans with private sector lenders. Also, the modifications to the federal Small Business Loan program (SBL), particularly the increase in amounts from $100,000 to $250,000, have made these term loans, "government guaranteed" to banks, and an integral source of term financing. A standard premise is that every small business should have an SBL at the early stage of its development.

This sector is expected to continue to be extremely competitive, particularly in light of the changes in the financial services industry in the last decade. With the fallout of some institutions and the consolidation of others, the remaining competitors are leaning towards the larger transactions, to the detriment of the small- to medium-sized borrower. Although this trend may make it harder for owner/managers to find term loans, there are still many opportunities out there and what's more important, the options are becoming more focused on meeting the needs of small business.

Interest Rates

The increased competition of the '80s meant interest rates for term loans were then lower than ever before. In the '70s and early '80s, it was not unusual to see fully secured loans to good quality credits priced at Prime + 2% or more, but this became rare. From a risk perspective, if a lender felt it needed Prime + 2% or more to compensate for risk, it was inclined to look at the deal more closely. Either the lender would not do the deal at all or would minimize the risk by combining a lower interest rate with a participation in the equity of the borrower (shares or cash flow participation). In the mid '90s, rates have increased in terms of spreads (the margin over the cost of funds to the lender), although overall interest rates in the economy have declined.

Increasingly, small business can negotiate "fixed rate" term loans. The stability that a fixed rate offers is very attractive, although it is usually at a premium over what would be paid on a floating rate basis.

> **Fixed rate term loans have a comfort zone.**

However, the fixed rate is comforting to those who have vivid, perhaps firsthand, memories of the extremely high interest rates of the early 1980s.

From the lender's perspective, particularly the insurance companies', fixed rate transactions match up well against their fixed liabilities (annuities, etc.) and generally provide a better spread over the cost of money than their standard mortgage loans.

When the interest rate is fixed, the interest becomes one of the few expenses which the business can accurately forecast for the 5 or 10 years of the term of the loan.

As the concept of borrowing on a fixed rate basis is now widely accepted by business, the demand for these loans continues. The decision to opt for a fixed rate is a function of the prospective borrower's perception at the time of funding: Are the present rates high or low and in what direction will they go in the foreseeable future? A recent study indicated that borrowers in the last few years saved money if they chose a floating rate.

Bought Deals

In the 1980s, the "bought deal" concept was introduced to the term lending market as well as to the equities market. The "bought deal" generally means that the "lead lender" commits to the entire financing and sells off a major portion of the loan to another institution.

With bought deals, everyone wins. Lead lenders (or original lenders) are motivated to generate a bought deal as they can realize substantial fee income from a relatively small pool of capital while still participating in a large number of transactions. The institutions to whom these deals are syndicated (often pension funds, etc.) are happy because they can participate with a minimum amount of effort and expense in terms of marketing and credit analysis. They also take comfort in sharing the risk with other institutions. The borrower is happy because it receives a commitment faster than could be expected than if it had to approach several different institutions directly. The lead lender acts as a conduit to a much larger pool of funds.

If we assume the need to raise term financing of $1,500,000, then the lead lender provides a financing commitment for the total. Before closing, the lead lender subdivides the loan, and "lays off" $500,000 each to two other institutions, perhaps at an interest rate of 1/2% lower, so that the lead lender retains this extra 1/2%.

SOURCE OF TERM LOANS — BANKS OR TERM LENDERS

If an analysis of your financing model shows that a portion of the financing should be a term loan, you then face another critical decision: Should you have all your business' financing in one place? Or should you have one lender for operating requirements and another for long-term requirements?

There are advantages to each approach. The several factors to consider are summarized below; these are presented from the perspective of whether a term loan should be from the bank that's providing the operating loan or line of credit.

Sometimes when the operating loan lender becomes disenchanted, the term lender will assist the borrower to obtain a new operating loan lender, particularly through the expression of confidence from the term lender.

One Lender or Two?

Advantages of One	Disadvantages

Advantages of One
- one institution to deal with
- one set of security
- avoids disputes over which lender takes which security
- makes the total account more important to one institution

Disadvantages
- at time of cut-back of credit, either by change of policy or personnel, no immediate alternative available
- bank will not have same level of competitive pressure
- uses higher levels of total credit at one financial institution with requirement for higher authorizing levels
- bank could act faster and in a unilateral fashion to liquidate the business in event of financial difficulty
- although structured as term payments, may in fact be due on demand; commitment is often qualified as "at the pleasure of the bank"
- may not have fixed interest rates available, or in any event, only a limited pool of fixed rate funds
- term lenders typically offer longer amortization periods
- term lenders are often more flexible on personal guarantees

Maintain Flexibility

In operations, you likely adhere to the prudent policy of having more than one source of supply for your key purchasing requirements, for example, raw materials. Since cash is such a vital commodity, it also makes sense to have more than one source of supply for financing.

This principle was strongly reinforced during the recessionary period of 1990 to 1993 when there was clear evidence of significant and abrupt changes in some lending attitudes and policies. During that time, many owner/managers experienced the bank's "pulling the plug" and many of those businesses subsequently went down the drain. Some of the bank's actions included:

- cancelling or reducing existing lines of credit
- increasing margin requirements
- wiping out overdraft accommodation
- freezing out certain industry segments (the most notable were real estate and restaurants).

TIP

- Don't put all your financing in the bank's proverbial basket.
- Maintain flexibility.
- Keep your deals separate.
- Deal with a bank for operating funds and a term lender for long-term funds.

Look for the Best Deal

Today's market offers several interest rate alternatives. Look for the one that best suits your cash flow and your plans for the future.

Interest rate alternatives include:

- floating rate
- fixed rate
- interest rate caps, and
- interest rate floors.

You will even find variations and combinations of the above.

Floating Rate versus Fixed Rate Debt

For short-term loans, fixed rates usually provide significant reductions in interest costs. Fixed rates for longer periods are generally more expensive than floating rate debt, but in some instances, the premium may be worth it. A fixed rate can be a form of insurance. It guarantees a fixed cost of borrowing. Your company can also benefit from the ability to predict results more accurately as well as avoid the vagaries of rising interest rates.

Look for options. Some institutions will provide floating rate interest with an option to convert to fixed rate on a predetermined basis and often at defined times.

Interest Rate Caps (Ceilings)

An interest rate cap is an instrument which permits a company to place an upward limit on its interest rate without having to lock it in over the long run. Similar to a fixed rate, it acts as a form of partial insurance.

Figure 4.2 illustrates how a company can insure itself against interest rate rises.

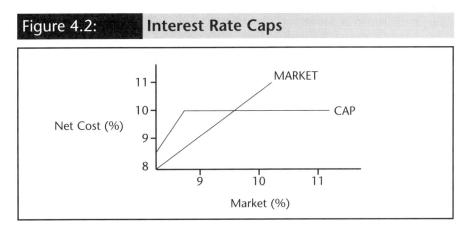

Figure 4.2: **Interest Rate Caps**

In this illustration, the company is protected against market rates rising above 10%, the level of the cap. However, the effective rate the company pays under the cap option is more than under the alternative before market rates reach 10%, since it must pay a fee at the origination of the deal. This cost differential is shown in the spread between the two graphs. Should rates surpass the 10% threshold, the financial institution reimburses the company in the form of a cash payment.

Interest Rate Floors

In some instances, an institution will require a minimum rate (floor). The interest rate floor is often used to offset the provision of an interest rate cap.

Assess Your Options

Today's financial service institutions offer many other risk management products. The astute owner/manager should be familiar with as many as possible.

- Look at all the available financing options and sources. There are many different ways to structure your financing.
- For term loans, for example, if half your loan is fixed rate and half is floating rate, you'll balance your risk — you'll always be half right and half wrong!
- Get familiar with the various options available in the financial marketplace and carefully assess each in terms of the suitability for your particular business.
- Consider your present and future cash flow as well as your long-term goals for the business.
- Carefully assess all of the terms and covenants, consulting with your professional advisors, to be certain that the business is capable of fulfilling each of the terms at the origination of the term loan and later as the continuing operations unfold.
- Before you accept the offer of finance, thereby creating a binding contract, renegotiate any questionable provisions.

COMMITMENT LETTER

The Commitment Letter at Sample 4.1 outlines a term financing program to fund a plant expansion and contains the typical conditions and provisions you might encounter.

RECAP

We have evaluated:

- the alternatives of a commercial mortgage or a term loan
- interest rates historically
- sources for loans and how to find the best deal
- advantages of fixed or floating rates and rate caps
- and looked at a sample "Offer of Finance."

Where to Go ...For Term Loans

Small Business:
- Banks
- Business Development Bank of Canada (BDC)
- RoyNat
- Community Development Funds

Larger Business:
- Penfund
- Canadian Corporate Funding (CCFL)
- Mutual Life
- First Treasury
- Commercial Capital

Sample 4.1 Commitment Letter

26TH FLOOR, 40 KING STREET WEST
TORONTO, ONTARIO   M5H 1H1
TEL: (416) 933-2730   FAX: (416) 933-2783

SAMPLE ONLY

<u>CONFIDENTIAL</u>

April 9, 1998

Rolling Wheel Automotive Inc.
450 Mercedes Avenue
Toronto, Ontario
B1K 1N1

Attention: Messrs. John Doe and William Right

Dear Sirs:

<u>OFFER OF FINANCE</u>

We are pleased to offer you financing in the amount of $700,000 to be allocated to the following program:

Purpose		Source	
Construct Building Expansion	$190,000	RoyNat - Loan A	$450,000
Refinance Existing Bank Loans	$135,000	RoyNat - Loan B	$250,000
Purchase New Equipment	$300,000		
Additional Working Capital	$ 75,000		
	$700,000		$700,000

Program changes may only be made with our prior written approval.

| Sample 4.1 | Commitment Letter (cont'd) |

Rolling Wheel Automotive Inc.   Page 2

REPAYMENT					
No of			Payment Months		
Payments	Amount	Frequency	From	To	Total

LOAN A

59	$ 3,750	Monthly	June 15/98	Apr. 15/03	$221,250
1	$228,750	Once	May 15/03		$228,750
					$450,000

LOAN B

59	$ 4,100	Monthly	June 15/98	Apr. 15/03	$241,900
1	$ 8,100	Once	May 15/03		$ 8,100
					$250,000

If disbursement is delayed, we may, at our option, extend the dates for scheduled principal repayments.

INTEREST

LOAN A

Interest will be calculated and payable on the 15th day of each month. The interest rate in effect to the 15th day of each month will be RoyNat's average cost of short-term funds plus 2.75% per annum. Once disbursement commences, we will advise you monthly of the interest rate in effect and the amount payable on the 15th of that month. Our average cost for the latest monthly period was 5.30% per annum.

LOAN B

Interest will be calculated and payable on the 15th day of each month. The interest rate in effect to the 15th day of each month will be RoyNat's average cost of short-term funds plus 3.50% per annum. Once disbursement commences, we will advise you monthly of the interest rate in effect and the amount payable on the 15th of that month. Our average cost for the latest monthly period was 5.30% per annum.

In addition to the above interest, you shall pay bonus interest fees of $5,000 per quarter for twenty (20) quarters.

Sample 4.1   Commitment Letter (cont'd)

Rolling Wheel Automotive Inc.

Page 3

INTEREST RATE REDUCTION

The interest rate on Loan A of $450,000 will be reduced by ¼% per annum upon receipt and satisfactory review of your audited annual consolidated financial statements for the year ending December 31, 1999, showing a Cash Flow (after tax net profit plus depreciation plus amortization plus deferred taxes), of 1.50 times the total of next year's principal payments due to RoyNat plus a $25,000 Capital Expenditure allowance.

SECURITY

This financing will be secured by our standard Debenture as follows:

1. A first fixed charge on all fixed assets, including land and buildings, now owned or hereafter acquired.

2. A floating charge on all other assets, subject only to a prior floating charge of approximately $300,000 in favour of your Bank, which will permit you to deal with these assets in the ordinary course of business or give security to your Bankers by way of an assignment of Trade Account Receivables and Trade Inventories.

3. The guarantees on our standard form of John Doe and William Right for $50,000 each. The guarantees will each be reduced by $25,000 upon receipt and satisfactory review of your audited annual consolidated financial statements for the year ending December 31, 2000 showing a Cash Flow (after tax net profit plus depreciation plus amortization plus deferred taxes), of 1.50 times the total of the next year's principal payments due to RoyNat plus a $25,000 Capital Expenditure allowance. A similar reduction on the same basis will be available for 2001.

4. The guarantee on our standard form of Little Wheel Productions Inc. for the full amount of the loan supported by a collateral Debenture, secured by a first charge on all its fixed assets, including equipment and vehicles and inventories of replacement parts now owned or hereafter acquired, together with a floating charge on all other assets subject only to a prior floating charge of approximately $300,000 in favour of its Bank, which will permit you to deal with these assets in the ordinary course of business or give security to your Bankers by way of an assignment of Trade Account Receivables and Trade Inventories.

INSURANCE

Insurance appropriate to the risks involved will be maintained by you, with loss payable to RoyNat Inc. as mortgagee. If requested, the policies are to be provided to us.

We require assignments of insurance of $100,000 on the life of John Doe and $100,000 on the life of William Right, together with the policies.

Sample 4.1 Commitment Letter (cont'd)

Rolling Wheel Automotive Inc.   Page 4

ACCEPTANCE

This Offer and the attached Schedule are open for acceptance until April 17, 1998. If, for any reason, you are unable to accept this Offer by this date, then the Offer is cancelled, unless it is re-negotiated on terms and conditions acceptable to us. A commitment fee of $8,375 is earned and payable at the time of acceptance.

Thank you for the opportunity to participate in your long-term financing requirements. We appreciate your business and look forward to receiving your acceptance.

Yours truly,
ROYNAT INC.

James G. Webster
Director of Merchant Banking

JGW/jl
Attachments
g:\offeroffinance\rollingwheelautomotive.doc

Accepted this _____ day of _____ 1998 on behalf of Rolling Wheel Automotive Inc.

Name: _____

Title: _____

Sample 4.1 Commitment Letter (cont'd)

SCHEDULE "A"

To OFFER OF FINANCE dated April 9, 1998 in the amount of $700,000 made by ROYNAT INC. to Rolling Wheel Automotive Inc.

WARRANTY

By your acceptance of this Offer of Finance, you warrant that all information which you furnish is true and correct.

DISBURSEMENT

1 Our funds are to be disbursed not later than October 15, 1998 and extension of that date is subject to our approval.

2. Our funds will be disbursed after:

   a) completion of legal documentation, satisfactory to our solicitors
   b) satisfaction of the insurance requirements
   c) satisfactory confirmation of Program expenditures
   d) the other funds, if any, required to finance the Program have been provided, and
   e) satisfaction of the following contingent conditions:

      i. evidence of a bank operating line for Little Wheel Productions Inc., for at least $300,000
      ii. a fixed cost contract for the building expansion totalling no more than $190,000 satisfactory to RoyNat Inc.
      iii. evidence of firm prices for the equipment to be purchased under the Program totalling no more than $300,000; no disbursement of the new equipment financing proceeds will be available until the building expansion is fully completed and funded
      iv. you will provide an environmental assessment report by a firm satisfactory to RoyNat, confirming the status of your facilities, namely that they are in compliance with all applicable environmental/pollution legislation, Federal or Provincial, together with evidence of all necessary pollution control permits if necessary; the cost of the environmental assessment report and any expenses deemed necessary to bring the operations within the guidelines of applicable law, will be for your account

3. Disbursement may be withheld if, in our opinion, a material adverse change in risk has occurred.

Sample 4.1 Commitment Letter (cont'd)

SAMPLE ONLY

Rolling Wheel Automotive Inc.   Page 6

STANDBY FEE

A standby fee of 2% per annum on the amount undisbursed will be calculated and payable on the 15th day of each month commencing October 15, 1998. We may, at our option, deduct these fees from our disbursements.

PREPAYMENT

LOAN A

Prepayment in whole or in part may be made upon payment of three months interest on the principal amount prepaid. Partial prepayment will be applied in reverse order of scheduled repayment.

However, you may prepay without penalty in each year, from the date of initial disbursement, an amount not exceeding 10% of the balance outstanding at the date of prepayment, non-cumulative.

LOAN B

Prepayment in whole or in part may be made upon payment of three months interest on the principal amount prepaid. However, upon full prepayment you shall also pay the present value of all remaining bonus interest payments. Partial prepayment will be applied in reverse order of scheduled repayment.

CANCELLATION

This Offer of Finance, when accepted, will be a binding contract. If you are unable or unwilling to carry out the contract, you will pay to us as liquidated damages an amount equal to three months interest on the amount contracted at the rate that would be applicable on the date of cancellation, as well as any other fees or charges accrued to that date.

CONVERSION OPTION - LOAN A ONLY

We shall, within sixty (60) days of receipt of your written request to convert this financing to a fixed interest rate, confirm to you:

1. the rate that will apply
2. the effective date of the conversion
3. any extension of the term of the financing that we may require
4. and the prepayment conditions that will apply following conversion

Sample 4.1 Commitment Letter (cont'd)

If you wish to proceed with the conversion on these terms, you must accept our Amending Letter. If you do not accept our Amending Letter, your conversion request will be considered as withdrawn.

Following conversion, interest at the fixed rate will be calculated and payable on the 15th day of each month.

UNDERLYING CONDITIONS

1. You and your associated companies, namely Little Wheel Productions Inc., will maintain consolidated working capital at not less than $100,000 and a ratio of 1.25:1 which will be increased by not less than $25,000 in each fiscal year to 2000 inclusive to the greater of $150,000 or a ratio of 1.50:1.

2. (a) voting control now vested in John Doe and William Right may only change with our prior written approval
   (b) voting control now vested in Little Wheel Productions Inc. which in turn is controlled by Rolling Wheel Automotive Inc. may only change with our prior written approval

PRE-AUTHORIZED PAYMENT SYSTEM

By your acceptance of this (Conditional) Offer of Finance, you authorize RoyNat Inc. to draw monthly cheques or prepare debits, by paper or electronic entry, in amounts sufficient to cover payments on the loan and you authorize and instruct your Bank to honour those cheques or debits. However, if RoyNat requests payment by cheque of amounts due to it, you agree to pay those amounts in this manner. Please attach your cheque marked "VOID" to this Offer. You also agree to renew this authorization if you change your Bank or branch or account.

FINANCIAL STATEMENTS

Your audited consolidated annual financial statements must be provided within ninety (90) days after the end of each fiscal year.

You will also cause Little Wheel Productions Inc. to provide its annual audited financial statements within ninety (90) days after the end of each fiscal year and its unaudited semi-annual financial statements within forty-five (45) days after the end of the half year. All unaudited financial statements will be approved by the signature of an Officer of the Company.

ATTACH SAMPLE CHEQUE MARKED "VOID"

CHAPTER 5

Mezzanine Debt — The Next Step for Term Financing

When you've exhausted your avenues for secured financing, mezzanine debt financing is often the next logical source for term financing. As a newer financing structure, this type of term loan is an excellent way to get more debt financing, with reasonable operating flexibility, than would otherwise be possible. It is sometimes, and perhaps more aptly, referred to as participating debt, junior debt, subordinated debt or even quasi-equity. You may be familiar with a U.S. term for this type of financing — "junk bonds."

WHAT IS MEZZANINE DEBT?

Lenders who offer mezzanine debt are willing to accept a higher level of risk. Notably, these lenders are often more flexible than more traditional lenders and may even provide a lower rate of interest in return for a share in the success of the business. The target rate of return to the lender is the normal term debt rate of interest, with the addition of some factor that reflects the additional risk the lender is accepting or other benefits the borrower will acquire.

This type of loan is typically based on fixed asset security but may also be related to working capital financing based on current asset security. Importantly, lenders will tailor mezzanine debt to the individual transaction so as to minimize the risk of borrower's default. In customizing the loan transaction, the lender might offer to:

- take a subordinated position to the traditional term lender
- advance more funds than would be available under traditional criteria

- reduce or defer interest, or
- tie payments to interest only with no principal repayment, or provide long terms such as 8 to 10 years, often as a function of cash flow.

LESS EQUITY REQUIRED

Mezzanine debt does not eliminate the need for equity but it does reduce the amount required. Accordingly, it also reduces business risk.

A usual criterion for mezzanine debt is an established and predictable cash flow which can be relied on, instead of a solid security base. Usually security is secondary, and subordinated to the primary or senior debt.

This is the type of term loan an owner/manager should seek when planning for such things as:

- a leveraged buyout
- ownership succession
- a major plant expansion
- an acquisition, or
- a rapid, but temporary, growth phase.

While these circumstances are the more typical situations for mezzanine debt, the financial community has welcomed the principle of bonus-type returns and has adopted the structure of mezzanine debt for many other circumstances where it has met their requirements. For example, mezzanine debt is periodically used to carry out a turnaround or a restructuring.

> **Mezzanine debt allows financing without ownership dilution.**

SHARING IN YOUR BUSINESS' FUTURE SUCCESS

While these lenders take a more passive role than that of an investor and may convert much of the yield to a pre-tax cost, they do participate in your business' future success. Depending on the nature of the transaction, the lender may structure the loan repayment for sharing in your future prosperity in a number of different ways. For example, the lender may require:

- a percentage of net cash flow, pre-tax income, or gross revenue
- a fee
- nominal cost common shares, or
- warrants or options to purchase common shares or the right to convert debts into common shares.

Cash Flow

Cash flow participation is structured on the expectation that cash flow steadily increases so that a low net return in the early years is more than compensated for by higher returns in later years. The advantages to borrowers funding on this basis is that your cost varies with your ability to pay and the bonus is treated as interest (and is therefore tax deductible). Most significant, this approach doesn't involve equity dilution.

TIP

SNAP

The structuring of participation payments to allow tax deductibility requires expertise. The owner/manager should not attempt this financing strategy without first seeking professional advice from a tax professional.

Percentage of Financial Results

The per cent return established may be related to the bottom line — net cash flow or pre-tax income. However, many lenders will tend to base this type of return solely on gross revenue. The latter approach is simple and easy to calculate and allows for far less debate about matters such as proper expenses.

Fees

To make the loan transaction extremely simple, the lender may even take an approach of charging only a periodic fixed fee (monthly, quarterly or annually) to achieve its desired rate of return.

Simplicity is the keynote in structuring a deal.

Nominal Cost Common Shares

When the loan involves the lender's purchasing nominal cost common shares, this participation is based on increases in the borrower's book or market value. Usually, the lender will be party to a shareholders' agreement which has predetermined put/call provisions. Nominal cost common shares preserve the borrower's cash in the early years and assures that the interests of the lender parallel that of the shareholders.

Warrants or Options

Issuance of warrants or options gives the lender the right to acquire shares in the borrower's business or convert its debt position to shares at a specified price at some future date. This right is usually tied in with some form of liquidity that enables the lender to receive value for the warrants without having to purchase the stock.

WHERE TO FIND MEZZANINE DEBT LENDERS

Unlike the United States where a public marketplace has evolved (often referred to as "junk bonds"), mezzanine debt in Canada is primarily a private placement market. The primary source is pension funds due to their substantial accumulated treasury funds, the inherent lack of cost base for these funds and, of course, their long-term perspectives. While some insurance companies are candidates for the same reasons, they have traditionally preferred mortgages. Trust companies and banks are beginning to take a more active interest as competition and sophistication for corporate financing increase.

> Mezzanine debt is like junk bonds.

In Canada, the most active participants are:

- for larger sized companies — the banks and fund managers such as Penfund and Canadian Corporate Funding and
- for the smaller borrowers — RoyNat and the Business Development Bank.

Few institutions are equipped to deal with the extensive business analysis at the front end and the close monitoring required throughout the term of a typical transaction. As a result, many deals are structured and placed through financial intermediaries.

BENEFITS OF MEZZANINE DEBT

The overall economy is an important factor. Mezzanine debt is attractive in an expanding economy where growth permits cash flow increases and allows the company to retire the mezzanine debt. However, in a recession, mezzanine debt presents more risk for both the lender and borrower.

The key benefits of this type of funding are the limited term and defined costs, but don't underestimate other ways mezzanine debt can benefit the company:

- Often a mezzanine lender will actively participate in the company's Board (this participation can add important expertise, objectivity and networking contacts for a company).
- The company shareholders can retain a higher proportion of ownership.
- It is less expensive than equity financing.
- The "return" to lender is usually paid out of pre-tax earnings, thereby reducing taxes otherwise payable.
- Leveraged buyout (LBO) and management buyout (MBO) transactions can be completed with higher leverage than would normally be possible.

TIPS

INSIDER'S

- Mezzanine debt is ideally suited to a leveraged buyout because the business being acquired will have an established track record and an ability to enhance financial leverage.
- Management buyouts are even more attractive to these lenders because of the continuity of management coupled with their proven track record and their increased commitment as a result of becoming owners of the business.

A WORD OF CAUTION

Most mezzanine deals do not provide for prepayment indemnities because the lender is usually quite anxious to receive a prepayment since it reduces the amount of its funding at risk. However, typically the lender structures the deal so that the participation feature carries on throughout the contracted term, on the premise that the majority of the risk occurs in the early stage of the loan.

UNDERSTANDING THE LENDER'S PERSPECTIVE

The lender's financial return is comprised of:

- return of principal
- interest spread (mark-up) on funds loaned
- participation revenue or ongoing fees, and
- upfront fees.

In assessing your application, the lender will estimate the timing of each of these elements and develop a financial model to compute its Internal Rate of Return (IRR). Whether the deal is acceptable, of course, depends on the lender's forecast of an acceptable return in relation to the risk.

Given the above, the lender's most important yardsticks for an attractive mezzanine debt deal are:

- a proven management team
- shareholder commitment
- an established historical cash flow
- stability within the industry
- minimal capital expenditures
- a clear market niche, and
- the existence of competitive barriers, including trademarks or patents.

The lender will typically complete a comprehensive business evaluation. Some aspects will be objectively based on factual data while others will be subjectively analyzed, based on intuition. A comprehensive and credible business plan will both assist the lender and enhance its interpretation of the opportunity.

THE BUSINESS DEVELOPMENT BANK FOCUSES ON EMERGING BUSINESSES

The BDC changed its name from FBDB in 1995 and adopted a more aggressive approach to support and finance young emerging businesses with mezzanine-type programs.

Working Capital for Growth

Under this program, the BDC provides working capital loans to small- and medium-sized businesses that have identified new opportunities for growth or expansion. BDC loans "top-up" financing from conventional lenders.

Who is eligible?

Eligible borrowers include existing small- and medium-sized Canadian businesses which have identified new or expanded markets for their products and demonstrate:

- past earnings record with good future prospects
- proven management capability
- a solid business plan that outlines the steps being taken to expand the operations and/or improve corporate viability.

What projects qualify for financial support?

Qualifying projects which enable firms to expand or develop new markets for their products include:

- financing larger inventory and accounts receivable
- launching new products
- developing/tapping new, international markets
- research and development.

What are the terms and conditions?

The maximum loan available under this program is $100,000. The amount is based on an analysis of the firm's cash flow requirements, inventory levels and receivables.

The repayment schedule is flexible and tailored to the needs of the business. In some cases, principal payments may not be required in the first year and subsequent payments may be adjusted to fit the firm's cash flow.

The maximum amortization is seven years.

Applicants must demonstrate support from current lenders, growth potential and a past earnings record with good future prospects.

Business counselling is also a part of this program and helps business owners manage expansion effectively.

Micro Business Program

The maximum size of these loans is $25,000 and the owner operator must take a training program specifically designed for his or her business. There is a cost to the training program and it must be paid by the entrepreneur.

Patient Capital®

Many early stage companies operating in the new economy are having difficulty finding appropriate financing on reasonable terms and conditions to support growth. While these companies may offer an innovative product or service with major market potential, their revenues are minimal and tangible security is lacking.

Although venture capital may seem appropriate for these firms, it is not always available for early-stage companies in the process of marketing their product. And, many entrepreneurs are reluctant to share the ownership of their companies with outside investors.

Patient Capital® is a type of financing which provides firms with long-term capital under flexible repayment terms without ownership dilution. The principal repayment can be postponed and interest capitalized for up to three years until the company begins to generate revenues and has the capacity to pay.

Who is eligible?

Eligibility includes Canadian-owned, commercially viable small- and medium-sized businesses which clearly demonstrate:

- a high-quality, experienced management team
- superior products or services
- excellent growth potential
- an expanding economic sector.

How much can you borrow?

Loans range from $50,000 to $250,000. Follow-up financing can raise this to $500,000. Partnerships with other lenders/investors are encouraged. The charge for this product is usually a base interest rate plus a royalty on the firm's sales. Loan amortization will normally be from six to eight years.

Venture Loans®

Although originally introduced in the late 1980s, Venture Loans® are now actively promoted by the BDC. These loans are a type of mezzanine financing, with a smaller loan size focus than those offered by the private sector.

Who is eligible?

These loans are available to Canadian businesses incorporated under a federal or provincial charter (limited partnerships are not eligible) that:

- demonstrate a commitment to the long-term growth and development of the business

- have a high quality, well-rounded management team experienced in planning, operations, marketing and administration
- have proven earnings and a substantial level of financial commitment by the major shareholders
- lack the collateral required for normal long-term borrowing.

What kinds of projects qualify for Venture Loans®?

The following types of activities are eligible.

- modernizing or expanding facilities
- improving productivity or competitiveness through the acquisition of new equipment
- acquiring working capital in support of rapidly expanding sales
- initiating management buyouts (where the major beneficiaries are not the withdrawing shareholders)
- implementing marketing plans for additional products or services
- developing export markets.

What are the terms and conditions?

The loan size ranges from $100,000 to $1,000,000. A rate of interest is charged as well as a royalty on sales or premium linked to the performance of the business. Payment of interest, royalty and repayment of principal are worked out according to a schedule tied to the amount of cash flow clients need to operate their businesses comfortably over the term of the loan.

All formal Venture Loans® applications must be accompanied by a fee equal to a small percentage of the amount of the application; the fee is returned if the loan is not approved.

THE MANAGEMENT BUYOUT

In an MBO, the purchaser can often finance the deal with a nominal amount of equity contribution (as low as 5% of the purchase price in strong circumstances). The key factor is the purchaser's substantial personal commitment. This is sometimes demonstrated through investing a significant portion of his or her personal equity and providing back-up personal guarantees.

REAL LIFE: The Successful MBO Takes Planning and Sacrifices

The four senior managers of Bestaste, a well-established kitchen equipment company, determined it was time to own the company. It was in a good market position and with their hard work, the future looked even more prosperous.

The following list of assets being acquired summarizes the financial profile of the proposed transaction. Although these amounts are expressed in millions, the principles are consistent whether the dollars are smaller, or indeed, larger.

Assets being acquired:

	($ mill.)
Current assets	
Accounts receivable	$ 3.8
Inventory	1.6
Prepaids	.1
	5.5
Fixed assets	
Land and building	2.2
Equipment	1.9
	4.1
Goodwill	.4
	$10.0

Sources of financing:

	($ mill.)
Assumption of accounts payable	$ 2.5
Bank, line of credit	2.0
	4.5
Senior Debt - Term loan, secured	2.5
Mezzanine Debt	
Term-lender, subordinated loan	1.0
Venture capitalist, convertible	
subordinated debt	.4
Vendor's note, subordinated	.6
	2.0

Equity

Venture capital, common shares	.3
Management investment, common shares	.7
	1.0
	$10.0

To structure the deal, they combined various sources of financing, each interrelating with the other. The bottom line is that the four senior managers successfully put together a deal wherein they ended up investing, as a group, just 7% of the needed funding to own 80% of a what is now a major corporation!

Here's how they did it:

The Bank

The bank provided a line of credit of only $2.0 million in view of the substantial financial leverage in the business. Although the bank had been approached for a larger line of credit, using traditional margins of:

	($mill.)
Accounts receivable - 75% of $3.8	$2.8
Inventory - 50% of $1.6	.8
	$3.6

The bank insisted on more equity in the structure, which resulted in the raising of venture capital funds:

	($mill.)
Common shares	$ .3
Convertible subordinated debt	.4
	$ .7

and the term-lender's subordinated loan of $1.0, a total of $1.7 of additional pure equity and/or quasi-equity.

Senior Debt — Term Loan

This loan was fully secured against the fixed assets and represented approximately 60% of the asset value.

Mezzanine Debt — Term Lender

10% interest payable monthly, plus annual payment of percentage of gross revenue in excess of stipulated base. Participation payment could only be drawn if working capital ratio (the ratio of current assets to current liabilities) exceeds 1.25 : 1.00, based on restrictions imposed by the bank. (The 10% interest equates to the normal rate for a fully secured term loan.)

Mezzanine Debt — Venture Capitalist

10% interest payable monthly. Subordinated to all senior debt and to the term-lender's subordinated loan. Convertible to 10% of common shares on fully diluted basis, at option of holder, within three years of issuance. The monthly interest payment provided cash flow to the venture capitalist, and the debt position, although subordinated, provided less risk.

Vendor's Note

Interest free, repayable only from a defined percentage of annual net profit earned over a three-year period.

Venture Capital — Common Shares

This additional amount of pure equity made the senior debt holders more confident in the deal and the financial base of the company. The venture capitalist received 20% of the common shares for providing this additional leverage to facilitate the overall structure of the deal.

Management Investment — Common Shares

The management team of four senior managers pooled their personal resources. Some even raised money by taking second mortgages on their residences. Overall, the four accumulated $700,000. Their equity contribution represented only 7% of the total assets being acquired yet their astute financing strategy allowed them to own 80% of the company and its assets of $10 million.

TIPS

SNAP

Contemplate mezzanine debt as a less-costly alternative to venture capital.

- In a closely held entrepreneurial business, consider the lender's participation in the form of bonus interest to maximize your company's net after-tax return and increase your leverage position.
- If your business is expanding and growing fast and you anticipate a public offering of shares within three to five years, negotiate for the participation to be in the form of shares (issued or warranted) to maximize reported profits and expand the current list of shareholders with the names of credible financial institutions.

RECAP

We have looked at:
- the structure of mezzanine debt
- the advantages of the lower equity requirements, but the need for an assured cash flow
- where to find mezzanine debt lenders
- understanding the lender's needs
- an example of successful mezzanine borrowing.

Where to Go   ...For Mezzanine Debt

Small Business:
- Banks (limited)
- Business Development Bank of Canada
- RoyNat
- Community Development Funds
- Morrison Financial

Larger Business:
- Penfund
- CCFL
- McKenna Gale Capital

CHAPTER 6

Equity — The First Building Block

Equity, or the residual interest of owners or shareholders, is the first building block, and the essential cornerstone of business financing. While it's a major concern for start-ups, most businesses will suffer from a lack of equity capital at some point during their life cycle. And that's when it becomes a very serious roadblock to both growth and progress. It can even be a threat to the company's very survival.

The *Oxford Dictionary* defines equity simply as "stocks and shares not bearing fixed interest." The Canadian Institute of Chartered Accountant's publication, *Accounting Terminology*, more fully defines it as: "the claim or right of proprietors to the assets of an enterprise; commonly used with reference to the residual interest of an owner or shareholder."

Its significance to Canadian business is underscored in a study done for the *Small Business Review* of the Department of Industry, Trade and Commerce, which notes:

> **Canadian businesses need more equity.**

> *Over the long term .... there are higher levels of equity in American businesses (than in Canadian businesses) and the U.S. has a healthier small business sector, more able to withstand economic downturns and interest rate swings.*

To understand equity more clearly in the context of your business, think about the company's liabilities in comparison to equity:

- Liability is a fixed obligation and must be paid back.
- Equity is residual and does not have a fixed repayment requirement.

BEYOND DEFINITIONS

However, these definitions do not fully illustrate the true character of equity. To understand what equity *does*, imagine the root structure of cedar trees growing around the country. Those growing in low-lying land with a high water table have shallow root structures. In the face of a severe storm, many of these cedars will be blown down. On the other hand, cedars growing on high land will have deep and well developed roots and be able to withstand storms. As a result, these cedars will survive and grow to regal heights.

Similarly, when you think of the old adage "a building is only as strong as the first course of blocks in its foundation," equity is the cornerstone in the financing of a business.

Equity is the cornerstone.

These analogies underscore that equity is the linchpin to business strength and vitality — giving it the lifeblood to withstand the "winds" of adversity. Specifically, equity provides:

- the cushion to absorb shrinking asset values in a downturn
- the resilience to withstand operating losses, and
- the leverage to avoid debt carrying costs.

A weak equity base along with an economic downturn or outside calamity can be fatal to a business. Many of these events will result from management mistakes, whether in planning, strategy or execution. However, a solid equity base can also mask these mistakes.

An important aspect of equity is that it reflects the ultimate business risk. In relation to the risk/reward curve, equity is at the extreme end — it takes the greatest risk, and therefore, deserves the greatest reward. Hence, the well-deserved perception: equity is costly!

The cost of debt is measured in terms of interest to be paid: the cost of equity is related to the amount or share of ownership given up. The true cost of a portion of the ownership is not just a pro rata amount of the annual profit and the accumulated retained earnings, but more significantly may be an implicit future per share value.

WHEN DOES A BUSINESS NEED ADDITIONAL EQUITY?

Every business requires a level of equity. Certainly, there must be a significant infusion to start a business on a good foundation. However, in the life of a corporation typically circumstances will change and the corporation will face new situations where additional equity will be needed; for example, the circumstances may be:

- growth, with its inherent need for working capital, that has outstripped earnings

- a management buyout of the company
- a buyout of a retiring or deceased partner
- bridge financing before going public
- a major plant and equipment expansion, perhaps to keep pace with technology
- market expansion through the introduction of new products or services
- a business acquisition
- the need for significant research and development
- restructuring/refinancing of a company depleted by a recession
- the rescue or turnaround of an insolvent company.

DETERMINING THE DEBT TO EQUITY RATIO

The need for equity is often measured in relation to the existing debt, known as the debt to equity ratio. For many businesses, a debt to equity ratio of 1:1 to 2:1 is considered satisfactory. However, the debt must also be evaluated in relation to the profitability, cash flow and product or service cycles; consequently, the ability to service the debt burden is a key factor. An inability to "cover" or service the debt adequately may be a signal of insufficient equity.

> **Banks include all liabilities in determining the debt to equity ratio.**

This ratio is not an absolute, but varies from business to business and from different viewpoints; for example:

- Capital intensive businesses (e.g., manufacturing, resources, processing) require more equity to support the significant financing burden, in contrast to service businesses.
- Cyclical businesses need higher levels of equity to cushion the bottoms of the cycles.
- The past track record of the business is often important. A business with a long history of profitability and prudent financial management can often enjoy a higher debt/equity ratio.

Notably, a bank will include all debt (all current liabilities plus all long-term liabilities) in determining the debt to equity ratio for its purpose, whereas a long-term lender/investor will typically only include the long-term debt.

CAN YOU WORK WITH ANOTHER SHAREHOLDER?

Additional equity can essentially mean that you are bringing another "partner" or shareholder into the business. It could be an informal investor or "partner" as the shareholder, or it could be an institution or experienced venture capitalist as the shareholder. The list below sets out the pros and cons of having another shareholder.

Accentuate the Positive

Having another shareholder can have the following positive results:
- adds financial and management depth
    - increases credibility of company
    - brings knowledge of financing and sources
    - adds discipline of business planning
    - builds additional negotiating strength
    - brings input from other business backgrounds
    - provides contacts in business community
- generally makes further funds available, if needed
- improves position of senior lenders to company, and margin coverage of operating lines if additional equity funds invested
- enhances objectivity — an outsider looking in
- increases importance of Board of Directors, with
    - periodic review of business plans
    - discipline of reporting in writing
    - more formal accountability
- should solve problems arising from being under-capitalized
- can mark the first step to going public, by establishing working relationships and accountability to other shareholders
- provides financial help in case of incapacity of owner, and perhaps contacts for urgent assistance
- aids in estate planning; for example, the incumbent shareholder can liquidate some of his investment to the partner and establish a successor in the business.

But Look Out For Negatives

The following negative outcomes could result from having another shareholder:
- the corporation can no longer be used as a storehouse of personal assets
- the owner/manager can no longer manage with complete and arbitrary discretion which could restrain corporate activities
- documentation of management actions will need to be tighter
- the owner/manager will have to abide by a shareholders' agreement
- certain matters will require unanimous shareholders' approval

- Carefully evaluate the downsides to having a "partner" in your business.
- Assess the pros and cons in relation to your specific situation.
- Realistically evaluate your management style, your open-mindedness and your ability to be flexible, as these factors will be essential to an effective working relationship.

- the owner/manager must report to other shareholders, even if they only hold a minority position
- company management and outside shareholders will need to have compatible styles and objectives.

SOURCES OF EQUITY

A business requires different types of financing as it progresses through the many stages of growth. These types will come from many varied sources. Similarly, there will be different sources of equity financing in relation to its growth stage as a business. The chart at Figure 6.1 summarizes many of the usual sources of equity.

Figure 6.1 Growth and Equity Sources

SOURCES OF EQUITY

GROWTH OF BUSINESS

| Personal Assets / Close Friends / Relatives |
| Angels |
| Government Programs |
| Industry |
| Venture Capital |
| Strategic Partnering |
| Initial Public Offering |

Carefully Assess Potential Sources of Capital

Within these broad categories, there are many potential sources of capital, each with varying inherent costs, characteristics and problems. Each source should be considered cautiously, with a full understanding of the implications and a careful evaluation of the advantages and disadvantages.

Also, it is important to understand the many sources of referrals for potential equity investors:

- government industry departments
- local Chamber of Commerce
- area industrial development department
- entrepreneur clubs
- professional advisors (lawyer, accountant)
- suppliers
- banker.

Sources of Capital

Private Sources and Angels
- clients of professional advisors
- employees
- private individuals
- suppliers
- customers
- recently successful entrepreneurs

Government
- provincially sponsored business development equity corporations
- grants or subsidies
- forgivable or performance loans
  (Chapter 7, "Government Programs", gives more details about these programs and ways these funds can be accessed.)

Industry
- significant competitors, suppliers or customers
- major companies seeking vertical or horizontal integration

Foreign Investments
- investors immigrating to Canada
- Schedule 2 banks

Private Placements
- large block placements of equity, often to institutional investors

such as insurance companies and pension funds, and usually sourced through intermediaries such as investment dealers and brokers

Venture Capital
- institutional pools such as pension funds, trust companies and insurance companies
- corporate holding companies
- private investment syndicates

Internal
- retained earnings
- sale/leaseback of fixed assets
- turf financing, by the sale of certain rights

PRIVATE SOURCES OF EQUITY

As an entrepreneur, your initial sources of equity are usually self-generated — your personal assets, and your close friends and relatives. Generally these sources:

- can be unsophisticated
- have low levels of expectation, and
- are typically patient.

The terms "patient money" or "love money" are often, and aptly, used to describe these sources. Well-funded individuals who often invest equity into smaller businesses to help "kick start" their development are often called "angels." Angels were originally unique financiers of Broadway plays, where investments were usually seen to be of a high risk.

Making a Deal Work

Beyond listing a number of potential sources of private capital, how do you structure a deal that will work? Where do you actually find the investor willing to risk his or her money by making an investment?

To illustrate the creative sourcing and structuring which must take place, the following outlines of some successful "real world" deals may help you generate ideas for similar strategies.

Tapping People Power

One significant source of private equity funding is to tap "people power" through the syndication of small individual investments.

REAL LIFE 6.1: People Power

A haute couture women's fashion manufacturer had been selling from his plant and now wished to set up stylish retail outlets, but had no cash to pay for $150,000 of leasehold improvements.

He sold preference shares of $3,000 per unit with a standard dividend rate to a group of female customers, along with a discount card to buy at 50% off retail. Not only did he raise the cash, but he also acquired a new "sales force"; typically these customers would bring friends to "their" store.

––––––––––

A new real estate brokerage firm needed additional equity of $150,000 for leasehold alterations.

The firm offered "Royalty Units" at $10,000 each to friends and associates, with repayment and investment return being a fixed percentage of commission revenue earned and collected over three years.

––––––––––

A group of interested investors needed to raised $500,000 for an art production project.

They sold $25,000 units to be repaid pro rata from 20% of the revenue earned from sales of the art.

––––––––––

A group of entrepreneurs in a far northern community needed to raise a substantial amount to invest in a local business that needed capital for expansion.

They bought $5,000 shares in a provincially subsidized small business development corporation to raise $150,000 equity for investment into the local business. The investee business provided important jobs and economic activity in their community and, hence, was of indirect benefit to the other local businesses.

––––––––––

A group of successful entrepreneurs, the senior management team of a local business, wanted to invest in needy businesses where the synergy of their experience and expertise could be advantageous.

They pooled their profit-sharing bonuses to provide a capital fund of $300,000 for investment in the needy businesses. These "angels" play an important role in recycling money within a community.

Tapping Hard Work and Sacrifice

Equity isn't always cash; sometimes it is "sweat equity."

REAL LIFE 6.2: Sweat Equity

A management team needed capital for a new technologically based start-up.

They worked for two years without salary to launch their project, an economic value in excess of $500,000 and, indeed, a source of "contributed capital."

In a Big-Business Context

While these cases demonstrate funding for small- and medium-sized business, an interesting and equally creative parallel occurred in the financing of the Toronto Skydome.

- A group of corporate investors were syndicated at $5 million each for approximately $150 million of equity capital, through an investment vehicle known as Dome Consortium Investments Inc.

> **Big business uses the same approach to financing.**

- Government grants of $60 million were obtained from the Province of Ontario and Metropolitan Toronto.
- Some of the "turf" was sold through prepayment of 10-year leases on private boxes and club seats.
- The balance of the financing came from a conventional bank loan, with specific covenants on priority payment.

As a sweetener to the equity investment, each syndicate partner held an exclusive preferred-supplier status.

Securities Laws

The foregoing fundings are considered to be private placements. An important consideration is that there must also be recognition of the provincial securities legislation in the province where these investments are sourced. Typically, there is a "seed capital," "private placement" or "exempt purchaser" exemption from prospectus requirements into which such a placement can fall.

Creative Sourcing and Structuring

In all of these examples, the common factor is creativity in both the source and structure of equity placements. In most cases, conventional institutional equity investment or venture capital was not available — these were, in many instances, deals put together as a last resort.

It is also important to recognize that most deals permitted the leveraging of further term-debt, bank, or government funding to fulfill the total financing packages of the companies. Hence, this private equity became a solid foundation upon which to build the entire financing structure.

Informal Venture Capital: "Angels"

To better understand the prospects and potential targets for informal venture capital, studies show that the "angel" investor typically has the following characteristics:

- is an entrepreneur who has, or has had, a successful business
- is well-educated
- is pragmatic or has a specific knowledge of the industry
- has funds to invest, from capital on hand and from a portion of earnings
- becomes a venturesome venture capitalist, with majority of investments in early stage businesses
- is inclined to syndicate, usually with an average of two co-investors
- deals in small amounts, in the range of $25 - 50,000
- provides cash investments as well as guarantees
- is a patient investor, with a typical realization period of five years or more, and
- prefers simple structures and documentation.

The Advantages of Working with an Informal Investor

Working with informal investors rather than institutional investors can be very advantageous; for example, they:

- invest their own money so can make decisions quickly without having to rationalize investments to a board of directors

> There are many advantages to working with an Angel.

- can invest small amounts
- don't need a current flow of cash from the investment since they do not have overhead to pay
- are often familiar with the industry they are investing in, and can frequently bring important backup knowledge to the business
- are entrepreneurs themselves and can understand early stage businesses
- do not measure returns strictly in financial terms
- in some cases, know the entrepreneur or act on the advice of a lead investor comfortable to them, and
- do not rely on this investment as it is not their primary occupation and, hence, they will usually not take an active role in day-to-day affairs of the business.

GOVERNMENT PROGRAMS

Governments often "share the risk" in significant business start-ups or expansions by providing performance loans or non-repayable contributions (grants) as a tool of economic development. From a financing perspective, these funds have the characteristic of equity to the business.

A company was acquiring new technology for Canada, involving a unique process and the related specialized production equipment, at a cost of $1.0 million. Governments supported this program with funding that had the essence of equity, as follows:

Federal - Grant	$400,000
Provincial - Interest free loan	200,000
Guarantee of private sector loan	125,000
	$725,000

The balance of the funding was arranged from the private sector, generally by leveraging the existing assets of the business.

INDUSTRY SOURCES OF EQUITY

Suppliers to a business are often an untapped source of equity capital.

REAL LIFE 6.3: Industry Sources of Equity

A supplier of major equipment for a new plant knew the entrepreneur from his past employment and had confidence in the prospects.

He bought 1/3 of the shares in the company for cash to help fund the capital requirements of this start-up business.

––––––––

A company which had been through a period of substantial over-expansion and faced a downturn, found the need to restructure its finances.

Analysis showed that five out of 300 creditors represented 70% of the unsecured debt, and failure of the business would have been catastrophic to them. When approached with these hard facts, the group of five provided leadership by converting their unsecured debt to equity in the form of redeemable preference shares with a nominal dividend rate, plus a sweetener of a small common share equity position.

––––––––

The installation of equipment and set-up of a substantial plant needed additional equity to complete the project.

Each of the contractors involved reinvested $25,000 of their contract through a provincial equity corporation to provide the additional equity capital that was needed to finish the project.

––––––––

A processing company needed a large volume of specialty chemicals for the start-up of a plant.

They approached the supplier and received a "donation" of the initial supply of chemicals in return for prospective future consideration. This was a source of equity in the form of "contributed capital" to the business.

Strategic partnering (or joint venturing) between large and small businesses will often facilitate the development and exploitation of leading-edge technologies by the smaller entrepreneurial enterprise, while the large corporation often provides the necessary cash infusion as equity in return for its share of the pie. In addition, the large corporation will usually provide other specialized resources, such as marketing and production.

REAL LIFE 6.4: Strategic Partnerships

A corporation which had developed an innovative new production material as an offshoot from its new product development business assessed that the commercialization of this new material had immeasurable potential, but that the expansion was far beyond its cash and staffing resources.

A strategic partnership with a major public company provided these resources and enabled the small Canadian company to tap international markets and enjoy the fruits of this new technology.

EQUITY FROM FOREIGN INVESTMENTS

Non-residents will often be special purpose investors in a Canadian company if the right match can be uncovered. Certainly, globalization of trade will enhance the opportunities for globalization in finance.

REAL LIFE 6.5: Foreign Investors

A company which supplied a service to the automotive industry needed $500,000 of equity to reduce its debt burden and to expand its operations.

They raised the entire amount through minority equity funding from a Japanese corporation, where the principal purpose behind the investment was the right to promote that they were partners in a Canadian company in this industry — a strategic advantage to them in their marketplace.

————

A group of immigrant investors wanted to obtain visas to settle in Canada.

They bought a minority investment in a company on reasonable terms and conditions, with the express motivation of obtaining a visa. The Immigrant Investor Program sponsored by the federal government is established to sanction and facilitate this type of financing support for Canadian corporations.

An easy way to tap this foreign source capital is to contact any one of the large professional firms (lawyers, accountants, management consultants), most of which have people specializing in foreign client interface. Some firms actually prepare a monthly list of new Canadian investment opportunities that is circulated to their network with foreign investor clients and prospective Canadian investee clients.

Another way to tap potential foreign investors is to contact any of the Schedule 2 chartered banks for their contacts. Both they and their clients want to establish themselves in Canada on a long-term basis, and what better way than to encourage an investment in a new Canadian business.

TURF FINANCING

Turf financing is the sale of certain rights to a new process/product up front. It can often provide early stage capital to reinvest into development of the new process/product.

REAL LIFE 6.6: Turf Financing

A company with worldwide patent rights to a new product needed substantial capital to finalize prototype development and market introduction of the product throughout North America.

The company sold the Australian and European rights for $1,000,000 each. The $250 million North American market was more than this company could expect to exploit.

––––––––

A company developing unique software for a particular Canadian service sector needed $500,000 as equity to foster its primary product.

They pre-sold the rights to the same software for application in another service sector for $500,000.

- Review the many informal sources of equity capital before considering institutional or public sources.
- Consider the terms of each source.
- Informal sources will often be more flexible, less costly and offer more "value-added" features than formal sources.

VENTURE CAPITAL

Venture capital is another form of equity that is similar yet distinctively different from the other sources already discussed. As investors, venture capitalists look to earn a return based on a capital gain from an increase in the value of shares in the company, rather than interest or dividends. The largest gains are made from selling the shares at the highest value over cost in the shortest time frame.

A popular myth in Canada is that there is an extreme shortage of venture capital. Indeed, there is no shortage! But from the perspective of the venture capitalist, there is a shortage of good deals.

In 1990, financial industry experts estimated that there was between $500 and $750 million in investment capital available in the industry. Based on the annual level of investing, that amount represented two to three years of funds for investment. By 1997, the capital available for investment was estimated to be in excess of $7 billion, which represents almost four years of funds for investment at the current per annum rate of investment. Over 50% of these funds is in the hands of labour-sponsored venture funds.

Venture Capital Goes Where the Action Is

The venture capital industry in Canada, and indeed, in most parts of the world, is often misunderstood. To a large extent, we are discussing institutional venture capital — significant pools of capital formed for focused and specialized investing, and often professionally managed. (This discussion excludes the provincial small business equity corporations.)

> Venture capital goes to where the action is — it does not create the action.

Venture capital goes to where the action is — it does not create the action.

TIP

SNAP

Obtain the *Annual Statistical Review and Directory* of the Canadian Venture Capital Association (Tel. (416)487-0519; Fax (416)487-5899; Web www.cvca.ca) to short list the priorities and focus of each venture capitalist member.

A number of the key factors prevailing in this industry include:

- the venture capitalist's primary focus is capital gains, not current income
- the investor seeks an unsecured minority position
- the venture capitalist is loath to invest in early stage businesses, preferring the less risky, quick turn returns from LBOs (leveraged buyouts)
- although the optimum may be a quick turnover, many deals take five to seven years to mature properly
- the investment fund often spreads its risk, over a number of deals in diverse sectors
- venture capital is not a substitute for the owners' personal equity, but rather a supplement
- losers tend to surface before winners
- only two or three deals out of a hundred that pass through the door are consummated
- the experienced venture capitalist does not waste time on doubtful prospects; in most cases, applicants that fail to meet the venture capitalist's criteria will receive a quick rejection
- investment results often fall into a 2/6/2 syndrome; that is, of deals completed, two are quick bankruptcies, six are the "living dead" or "walking wounded," and two are "superstars"
- investors look for overall long-term returns of at least 20% per annum compounded; to achieve these results, individual deals need to be priced to achieve 30 - 40% per annum, based on the ultimate disposal and selling price of the shares
- as the company grows and expands, several rounds of equity financing are often required
- deals can be completed in from four weeks to four months, depending on the degree of preparedness of the company management

- an experienced investment officer can properly manage six to eight active investments
- the exit or disposal strategy should be contemplated at the outset
- many deals are completed through syndication; that is, two to five investors join together for a piece of the pie, working with a lead investor.

Makings of a Successful Venture Capital Deal

INVESTOR'S PERSPECTIVE

Venture capitalists invest in people first and products second, and then only after a rigorous examination of the business and its management, a process called due diligence.

As minority investors, venture capitalists carefully scrutinize the entrepreneur — the person who can make or break the deal. What do they look for? Venture capitalists often describe their key criteria for a good deal as:

> **Venture capitalists invest in people.**

- a strong management team with a demonstrated commitment to the business
- a product in the forefront of its technology
- competitive market niche, and
- a focused business plan.

If your company is highly rated in all of these areas, the venture capital investment can likely help the business penetrate North American and even international markets, earn above average profits and significantly increase sales and profit levels in a short period. It's these kinds of results that will generate the capacity for the venture capitalist to dispose of its investment at a significant gain.

COMPANY'S PERSPECTIVE

The company seeking venture capital must carefully evaluate a prospective venture capitalist. In the same manner that you would hire an employee, the investor must also be a good fit for your company. Remember, a venture capitalist will be a new shareholder, indeed a partner, in your business.

There are clearly many positives from having this investor join your business. However, these can only be achieved if you are careful in selecting that investor. In evaluating a prospective venture capitalist, consider:

- Personal Chemistry
  Venture firms are small (two to ten people) and tend to acquire personality. Is this personality a good match for you? Is it comfortable?
- Value-added Assistance
  Does the venture firm have relevant experience to assist the company's board and management in formulating strategies?
  Is it familiar with geographic territories in which you may operate?
  Does it have the contacts that can assist with joint venturing, marketing contacts/agreements, licensing?
  Are there strong relationships in other sectors of the financial community?
  Can it help to locate and attract new senior management?
- Deep Pockets
  Most investments require follow-on funding before full maturity. Will it have additional funds available in its capital pool in the future?
- Reputation
  Check references. Ask if you can contact some of the venture capitalist firm's previous investees (including ones gone bankrupt). Some of the questions you will want to ask include:
  - Did the investor attend and make a useful contribution at board meetings?
  - When the company needed further funding, were they reasonable and fair in their dealings?
  - What was the investor's demeanour when the business turned sour?
  - Were they able to establish valuable contacts for the business?

TIPS

INSIDER'S

- Venture capital is a financing source for the exceptional company that requires additional capital to achieve its strategic objectives. You should be well prepared for a thorough screening during the due diligence phase.
- Establish plans for an exit approach at the time of the investment. This approach will be a significant factor in establishing strategic goals for the enterprise.

Sample 6.1 is a commitment letter from a venture capitalist that illustrates the typical structure, terms and conditions of a venture deal.

Sample 6.1 Commitment Letter

VenGrowth Fund

The VenGrowth Investment Fund Inc.
145 Wellington Street West
Suite 200
Toronto, Ontario
M5J 1H8

Telephone 416-971-6656
Facsimile 416-971-6519

Mr. John President
Exciting Electronics Limited
1200 Main Street
Port Perry, Ontario
M1B 1H8

September 1, 1998

Dear Mr. President:

Re: Offer to Finance

This letter sets forth the terms and conditions under which The VenGrowth Investment Fund Inc. ("VenGrowth") would provide financing for Exciting Electronics Limited ("Electronics" or the "Company"). The proposal is for a total investment of $3,000,000 by means of shares and warrants.

The funds will be used to acquire new manufacturing equipment and provide working capital.

The financing program is as follows:

Application of Funds

Acquisition of equipment	$3,500,000
Working capital	500,000
	$4,000,000

Source of Funds

VenGrowth	$3,000,000
New Term Loan	1,000,000
	$4,000,000

The terms and conditions of the financing are as follows:

Preferred Shares:

Issue Size:	20,000 preferred shares, for aggregate price of $2,000,000.
Issue Price:	$100.00 per share

Sample 6.1 Commitment Letter (cont'd)

Dividend:	8% payable quarterly in arrears.
Redemption Rights:	The preferred shares can be redeemed at the company's option on or before August 31, 2003.
Voting Rights:	One vote per preferred share.
Liquidation Preference:	The preferred shares rank ahead of the common shares upon liquidation.
Covenants:	Company activities requiring preferred shareholders' consent:

- redeem or otherwise acquire share capital;
- distribute assets;
- issue a class of shares in preference or on an equal basis to this issue of preferred shares;
- amend articles of incorporation;
- amend bylaws;
- issue or guarantee debt;
- non-arms length transactions;
- any reports provided to the Company's bank are to be provided to the preferred shareholders if requested.

Warrants:

Issue Size:	1,000 warrants entitling the holder to purchase 1,000 common shares at the exercise price for each one warrant held.
Exercise Price:	$1,250.00 per share.
Exercise Date:	The warrants are exercisable anytime prior to August 31, 2004.
Exchange Rights:	The warrant holder may tender any of the preferred shares held against the exercise price of the warrants.

Common Shares:

Amount:	$1,000,000.00
Number of Shares:	1,000 (25% of shares outstanding after giving effect to this common share issue).
Price/Share:	$1,000.00
Voting Rights:	One vote per common share.

Sample 6.1	Commitment Letter (cont'd)

Shareholders' Agreement:

The Shareholders' Agreement will contain standard terms including, but not limited to:

i) Board of Directors:

The Board will be composed as follows:
- two representatives of existing shareholders;
- a new independent outside director selected by existing shareholders;
- a new independent outside director selected by VenGrowth;
- a representative of VenGrowth.

ii) matters requiring Board approval:
- annual operating budget;
- annual capital expenditures budget;
- capital expenditures in excess of $50,000.00;
- annual compensation plans;
- declaration or payment of dividends;
- incurrence of debt other than in the normal course of business;
- transactions outside the normal course of business;
- issuance of guarantees;
- non-arms length transactions.

iii) Right to Sell:

VenGrowth will have the right to participate, on a pro rata basis, in the event of the sale of shares by the existing shareholders of Electronics.

iv) Right of First Refusal:

VenGrowth and the existing shareholders of Electronics will have mutual rights of first refusal in the event of a sale by the other.

v) Pre-emptive Rights:

Each shareholder will have a pro rata right to participate in future financings.

Sample 6.1 Commitment Letter (cont'd)

vi) Put:

In the event that Electronics is not listed on a recognized stock exchange by August 31, 2003, VenGrowth will have the right to require Electronics to purchase all the common shares owned by VenGrowth (ie: the "Put"). The price per share will be the greater of: eight times the average earnings per share for the fiscal years ending June 30, 2002 and 2003 or fair market value as determined by the Company's auditor. Both VenGrowth and the Company have the right, at their cost, to use a third party business valuator to determine the Put price in the event the above fair market value is not acceptable to either party. Such third party valuator will be selected by representatives of the Company and VenGrowth who are C.A.'s and act independent from the Company and VenGrowth.

vii) Call:

The Company would have the right to call the common shares for repurchase on or after August 31, 2004.

The shares will be repurchased at fair market value as determined above.

viii) Information Clause:

- audited financial statements within 90 days of fiscal year end;
- monthly financial statements within 20 days of month end with management comments on variances from budget;
- Board approved annual budget 30 days prior to fiscal year;
- any reports provided to other lenders.

Directors' Indemnification:

The Company will indemnify VenGrowth and its nominee with respect to the nominee's action as a director. The company shall use its best efforts to secure Director and Officers liability insurance.

Sample 6.1 Commitment Letter (cont'd)

Fees:

A commitment fee of $15,000 shall be paid to VenGrowth by Electronics upon acceptance of this Offer to Finance. The commitment fee will be refunded to Electronics in the event that VenGrowth's Investment Committee fails to approve the proposed transaction by September 30, 1998.

Legal Costs:

Any legal or other professional expenses incurred with respect to this proposed transaction are for the account of Electronics.

Conditions Precedent:

Prior to the closing, the following items will be reviewed and resolved on a basis satisfactory to VenGrowth in its sole determination.

1. Completion of legal documentation on a basis satisfactory to VenGrowth and its legal counsel;

2. Completion of VenGrowth's due diligence;

3. Approval of this investment on a basis substantially as set forth herein by VenGrowth's Investment Committee by September 30, 1998.

4. During the period from acceptance of this Offer to Finance, until the closing of the investment outlined herein, the business will be operated in the normal course and there shall be no material, adverse change in the operations of the business, financial position or financial performance of the company.

In the event that the conditions precedent are not fulfilled, VenGrowth reserves the right not to proceed with this proposed transaction and shall not be liable for any damages or for any expenses incurred by any party.

Confidentiality:

This Offer to Finance is to be treated strictly as confidential by all parties hereunder. It is not to be distributed to any individuals, corporations or any other parties without the written consent of VenGrowth.

Please confirm your acceptance of the terms and conditions outlined above by signing and returning the enclosed copy of this letter. This offer,

Sample 6.1 Commitment Letter (cont'd)

if not accepted on or before September 8, 1998, will expire at the close of business on that date.

We are pleased to be able to make this proposal to you and look forward to a long and mutually beneficial association.

Yours very truly,

THE VENGROWTH INVESTMENT FUND INC.

_____

R. Earl Storie, C.A.
Managing Director

The undersigned hereby confirms acceptance of the terms and conditions outlined above.

EXCITING ELECTRONICS LIMITED

_____

Authorized Signing Officer
Date:

EMPLOYEE SHARE OWNERSHIP PLANS

Employee participation in the ownership of their corporations through the acquisition of shares is an important trend in business today. As a source for new equity capital, an employee share ownership plan (ESOP) provides many benefits to both employees and the company. This financing strategy is not limited to public companies; even a small private corporation can create an ESOP. Of course, the many public companies that offer ESOPs provide the added advantage of liquidity of their stock.

An ESOP can be approached in various ways; for instance, the company can allow employees to acquire shares of stock through:

> **Ensure an ESOP provides for cash flow, liquidity and governance.**

- profit sharing participation
- stock options
- purchase plans through payroll deductions.

Is an ESOP a Viable Financing Strategy for Your Company?

For the ESOP to be an attractive incentive for employees, the company's plan needs certain key attributes:

- Cash Flow
  The plan should provide for annual distribution of a specified portion of the profits, by way of dividends.

- Liquidity
  The plan should provide for buy-back at current value for the shares, should the employment cease for any reason whatsoever.

- Governance
  Designates of the employee group should be represented on a functioning Board of Directors.

Everyone Benefits

For the company, an ESOP can mean that:

- cash is generated that can be invested in the company
- the company can pay part of its employees' wages in the form of stock and also deduct this as an operating expense for tax purposes

- the company may attract highly skilled employees that it might otherwise be unable to afford
- the possibility of strike action and work stoppages are significantly less
- ownership helps to improve the quality of a company's products, since employees take greater care in the production process.

When employees "own" a company, their pride of ownership helps to:

- stimulate their loyalty and reduce turnover
- increase productivity
- significantly reduce absenteeism
- encourage workable suggestions to improve company operations and efficiency
- reduce wastage in supplies and material.

But ESOPs Are Not Entirely a Bed of Roses

In the planning stages of an ESOP, a company needs to carefully weigh the potential downside of this financing strategy and make allowances where possible.

- If a number of employees leave at one time, this could produce a significant drain on cash resources as the company may have to re-purchase the stock (this is normally the case with agreements where shares are not listed on a stock exchange).
- When the company faces a declining market or a poor economy, employee morale may also decline.
- Legal and accounting costs associated with implementing an ESOP may be high.
- Unions are usually hostile to employee stock ownership plans.
- If only some of the employees are offered the opportunity to participate, then discontent may arise amongst those who have been excluded.
- The company may focus too much on the short term or may make unrealistic compromises of fixed asset renewal and research and development expenditures.
- Management becomes more accountable to workers for their actions and must be prepared to improve their communications with them.

- The rules for ESOPs vary by jurisdiction, for instance:
  - there may be a maximum reduction that can be applied against other income
  - the plan may have to be administered by a trustee
  - it might be necessary to have some means of financing the purchase of the shares, either in the form of loans or through salary withholdings
  - common shares may have to carry full voting rights, or the employee's investment in the company may be limited to annual and lifetime amounts.

REAL LIFE 6.7: The Employees Buy Out the Company

A group of factory employees wanted to carry out a leveraged buy-out of a division of a multi-national corporation.

They invested $10,000 each through a provincially subsidized small business development corporation to raise $280,000 and bought a minority position in the new company. Key terms in the shareholder agreement were the annual payment of 30% of the profits as dividends, and a guaranteed liquidity through the automatic buy-back of the shares, if at any time the employee ceased to be employed by the company, for any reason whatsoever.

In putting together this type of group, it is important to have at least one or two in the group with "deep pockets" — those who would be able to invest additional funds to cover overruns or downturns.

KNOW THE FUNDAMENTALS OF EQUITY FINANCING

Equity is typically the most difficult form of financing to raise. Entrepreneurs are often very passionate about giving up a portion of their ownership interest and what they perceive to be a fraction of their independence and control.

Regardless of which equity financing source or sources you pursue, here are some fundamentals that can help you make the right move for your particular company and for you as an entrepreneur. Remember:

- Your business is NOT unique. The basic principles of return on investment prevail in all enterprises.
- Separate your personal affairs from that of the company.

- Do not wait until it's too late to start looking for equity as management may be seen in a negative light.
- Get the "team" together at the beginning: lawyer, accountant, advisors. Are your regular people experienced in this area of corporate financing?
- Before you search for outside equity, check with the "team" as to any legal, accounting or financing moves you should make before you begin.
- Work closely with your advisors in structuring the proposal and in preparing your financing presentations. You must understand every word and figure in your company's presentation and be able to answer all questions.
- Be familiar with normal provisions of shareholders' agreements (outlines and checklists of shareholders' agreements are available from many consultants, lawyers or accountants).
- Communicate your intentions to your bank and your major customers and suppliers. Equity sources will call them to ask about you and your company.
- Do not give out misinformation; be candid and forthright.
- Don't get fancy in your structuring and don't propose "in vogue" financing structures.
- Be prepared to explain your own financial circumstances — outside investors want to be convinced that you are sufficiently financially committed to the company.
- Proceeds should not be used to "bail out" any of the principal owners of the company; outside investors want to see their money at work in the company.
- Understand the point of view of the sources of outside equity money, and understand what they want to get for their money. Don't bother sources with deals that they obviously won't want.
- Don't attempt to set deal terms until the source indicates a willingness to negotiate; but do determine the basic deal points early rather than waiting until the last moment.
- Understand the significance of the documents you will have to sign; for example, loan agreements, shareholders' agreements and so on.
- Tell prospective investors if you are talking with others.

TIPS

INSIDER'S

Angels, government, industry, foreign investors, venture capitalists — whatever your financing source:

- Do not take your proposal to too many places at the same time. It will quickly become "shop worn" and no one will take you seriously.

- Seek professional advice every step of the way, but remember that your advisors are not the business decision makers for the company.

RECAP

We have analysed:

- the meaning of equity
- the debt to equity ratio
- when a business needs more equity
- the pros and cons of bringing in a partner
- the various sources of equity: angels, business, governments, venture capital, turf financing
- making the new deal work
- sweat equity as an alternative to cash investment
- possibilities of an ESOP.

Where to Go   ...For Venture Capital

- ACF Equity Atlanta Inc.
- Bank of Montreal Capital Corporation
- BDC–Venture Capital Division
- Fonds de Solidarité des Travailleurs du Québec
- Helix Investments (Canada) Inc.
- Horatio Enterprise Fund
- Investissements Novacap Inc.
- MDS Capital Corp.
- Penfund Partners
- Priveq Financial Corporation
- Royal Bank Capital Corporation
- RoyNat Inc.
- Saskatchewan Opportunities Corporation

- TD Capital
- Trilwood Investments Ltd.
- VenGrowth Funds
- Ventures West Management Inc.
- Working Ventures
- Working Opportunity Fund

Government Funding — Backing Winners

In today's fast-moving environment, you can't afford to overlook the potential for financing through government programs. This source can be time-consuming and paper intensive, but it could be the means for you to find those additional funds you need to gain competitive advantage or get moving on a new market opportunity.

Businesses used to view government programs as "bail-outs" — they helped keep plants open, save jobs and retain products and sales. Not so today. Governments, like everyone else, want a bigger return per dollar spent. In their view, business failure is simply part of the natural process of the free enterprise system. Today's government funding backs the winners!

Take note that the term "grant" is disappearing from the government vocabulary. It's replaced by the term "contribution" — either repayable or non-repayable — and generally the price is right.

A SOURCE FOR ASSISTANCE AND INCENTIVES

For several years, various levels of government have promoted assistance and incentive programs. Past federal and provincial governments focused on devising new programs primarily to influence the development of various sectors of the economy. New programs continue to be introduced as governments change and likewise their social, economic and political priorities. In recent years, the top priority of all governments, and thus government funding, has been job creation and training.

> In recent years, the top priority of all governments, and thus government funding, has been job creation and training.

The most significant change in this source of financing stems from budgetary problems and ongoing changes in philosophy: government assistance has changed from handing over the hard cash to offering an advisory role. This approach is most evident in the areas of human resources and international trade.

It is important to distinguish between "assistance" and "incentive." A government will often provide an incentive for a business to do a project and often in a variety of forms. It may provide a grant for undertaking a project because the business may otherwise not proceed with the project. It is up to the business, therefore, to convince the bureaucracy that, while worthwhile, the project is risky or may not achieve the threshold return on investment. Of course, you can't start the project until approval has been received from the granting authority, otherwise it would contradict your apparent requirement for the incentive.

> **Governments are looking for a "return" on their money.**

On the other hand, assistance programs do not require that a project go ahead just because of the program. Essentially those programs are predicated on need and that can usually be demonstrated only by a sound and methodical business plan.

Supporters, Not Leaders

Governments are reluctant to take a leading role in a financing structure, but rather usually supplement and complement funding from the private sector. Governments often provide funding assistance to share the risk in situations where the risk would otherwise be too high for private funding.

While government funding may sometimes fit the definition of term debt or of equity, most frequently it has the characteristics of mezzanine debt. Mezzanine debt, discussed in an earlier chapter, is defined as:

> *A term debt that accepts a higher level of risk, offers more flexibility, and/or offers a lower rate of interest in return for a share in the success of the business.*

Most government funding closely parallels this definition. Instead of sharing in the success of the business, the government program will anticipate appropriate benefits to the economy as its upside payback.

In playing the same role as mezzanine debt, government funding typically finances the shortfall between senior debt and equity. In many instances, the government funding will supplement the equity of the business. However, it is important to recognize that it "supplements," not "replaces," equity. Generally, there must be a reasonable level of equity in the business.

Forms of Government Funding

Government funding may take many forms, including:

- cash grants
- subsidies (either capital or operating)
- relief and incentives under The Income Tax Act
- reduced interest rates
- loan guarantees
- provisions of loans of "last resort"
- management assistance, or
- cash funding (repayable and non-repayable contributions).

Playing on a Level Field

You need to be keenly aware of the rules of the game. For example, certain guidelines come into play to ensure that governments take a secondary role in a company's financing picture:

- Stacking
  It is standard policy that all government funding from all sources, whether federal or provincial, be restricted to no more than 50% of a project.
- Equity
  Certain funding statutes specify that a project may have no less than 20% equity. In fact, 30% to 50% equity is the usual standard applied in practice.
- Return on investment
  Business normally assesses capital expenditures by evaluation of return on investment. So it is with government funding, except that assistance is also evaluated against a social rate of return. Consideration is given to the discounted cash flows to be generated by the project and the investment per job created. Many government agencies have a guideline for the amount of funding per new job created, often in the range of $15,000 to $20,000 per job.
- Government Priorities
  Governments are increasingly sensitive towards labour and environmental issues. Keep in mind that an important consideration for a government funding program will be a clean report from

related labour and environmental ministries. This may be the time when all outstanding work orders and concerns are brought forward and become the pre-emptive "shopping list" of the labour and/or environmental ministries.

LEVERAGING WITH GOVERNMENT FUNDING

Canadian businesses frequently have too high a level of debt, and therefore have little resilience at the time of a business downturn or high interest rates. The debt servicing cost is then high and consumes too much of the available cash flow.

Government funding focuses on sharing the risk with entrepreneurs; however, it also lowers the risk. A frequent approach in government programs is to provide for repayment of the principal contributed, and to abate all, or a portion of, the interest cost. Furthermore, principal repayments may be tied to available cash flow.

Consider the annual debt servicing alternatives for a business requiring a capitalization of $1.0 million.

Figure 7.1:	Debt Servicing Alternatives			
	Alternative 1		Alternative 2	
	Financing	Debt Service	Financing	Debt Service
Owners' Equity	$ .4		$ .4	
Senior Debt, at 10% (1)	.4	$80,000	.4	$80,000
Secondary Debt, at 14% (2)	.2	68,000	—	
Government Funding (3)	—		.2	25,000
	$1.0	$148,000	$1.0	$ 105,000

With government funding, the company's annual saving in debt servicing is $43,000 (approximately 30%). Also, consider the total over the term of the funding. This represents a significant reduction of the financial risk in this business!

TIP

When searching for financing, investigate the availability of government funding which has the characteristics of mezzanine capital to strengthen the business' leverage.

WILL YOUR PROJECT QUALIFY?

Any project that is expected to create jobs may qualify for assistance. Specific business activities that may be received favourably include:

- industrial research and product development
- financing the business
- restructuring specific industries
- marketing products
- exploitation of technology
- training and upgrading the workforce
- industrial engineering opportunities.

In addition to "cash funding" programs, governments are continually changing the tax structure to try to redirect the economy. Obviously, governments realize that a healthy business sector can soften many of the tough social problems they have to face.

The amount of available cash is, however, limited. Therefore, any business or individual hoping to partake of any of the programs must be well organized and methodical in its approach.

Obviously, governments realize that a healthy business sector can soften many of the tough social problems they have to face.

A recent Ontario study indicated that most government assistance funds go to larger companies. The reason? Small businesses appear to overlook or are apprehensive about the paperwork involved with getting government assistance. Yet, government funds can make a big difference in whether a business is successful or not.

Business Activities

Many government programs are available only for manufacturing businesses. Service businesses, unless they are involved in tourism, are generally not eligible for assistance. The fact that more jobs have recently been created in the service sector than any other sector of the economy may mean that this area may now receive more attention from governments. From time to time, other sectors are given government priority, such as the textile industry, oil and gas exploration, farming and fishing.

Your company may be eligible for assistance if it's involved in or contemplating the following:

- manufacturing a product that is or could be exported
- planning to manufacture a product that will abate imports
- acquiring new capital assets for manufacturing
- improving present products
- restructuring for international competitiveness
- closing a financing gap
- using considerable energy
- requiring or currently employing workers that need training or retraining
- establishing a new production facility
- planning to increase productivity through improvement, modernization and expansion of existing manufacturing operations.

TIP

As a first step to assessing whether your business qualifies for government funding, carefully consider your objectives and business circumstances.

PREPARING A SUCCESSFUL APPLICATION

Be prepared for a lengthy process. As is obvious from Figure 7.2 of the government funding process, considerable time is required to go through these various steps. From the government's viewpoint, these steps are essential for ensuring the proper stewardship of taxpayers' money as well as compliance with the focus and priority of each program.

Figure 7.2: Government Funding Processing Stages

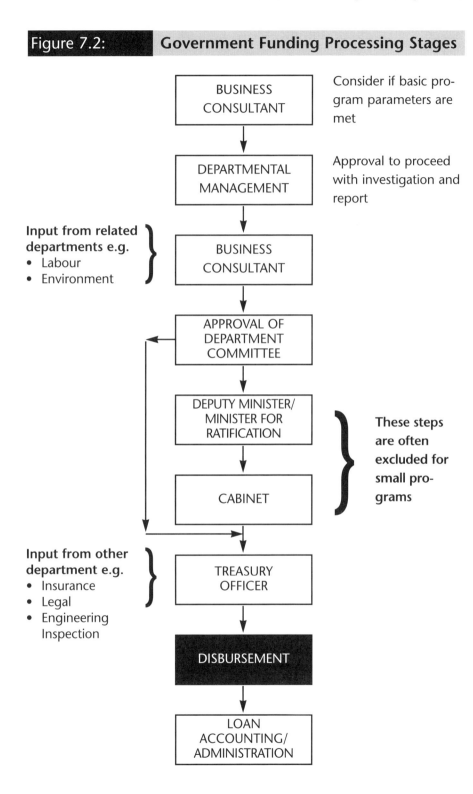

Avoid the Common Pitfalls

Most government officers will agree that delays are often a result of the applicant's providing incomplete data. To succeed in your funding quest, you need to understand both the information required for government programs in general and the specific requirements of a particular program. The latter you can gain at your first meeting with the government business consultant.

Make sure your application gets the consideration it deserves! Here are some general guidelines that can help you avoid the common pitfalls.

- Read the guidelines carefully
  If you just scan the printed materials for many programs, you may leap to the conclusion that your business won't qualify. Read the guidelines carefully and keep in mind that most programs are much more flexible than is suggested in the print materials.

- Understand the criteria for the program
  Ensure that the application includes one or more of the factors outlined above as key issues from a government perspective. This provides the appropriate Return On Investment (ROI) or payback to government and society in general.

- Plan the timing of your application

  Do not proceed with program until you have approval or a waiver.

  Approach the relevant government agency early, and certainly before you make any financial commitments. If you must proceed with the project before you receive approval of government funding, request a waiver in writing from the agency.

- Tailor your proposal appropriately
  Your presentation must emphasize your ability to carry out the project successfully and the benefits it will bring locally and/or nationally, including:
    - employment
    - increase in exports / abatement of imports
    - use of domestic manufactured goods and resources, and
    - spin-off to other businesses and industries.

- Talk to the right people
  Always speak to the appropriate officials and explore the possibility of eligibility. If you can communicate the important benefits of

your project's receiving funding, the program administrator may feel compelled to exercise some discretion and find a way to establish eligibility.

NOTHING'S PERFECT

Even though government assistance and incentive programs can help launch a new business venture or put an existing one on a more solid footing, there are some drawbacks to using them.

The Approval Process

You usually need government approval before you can start a new project, otherwise you may disqualify yourself for assistance. To that end, you may need to demonstrate that your company conforms to all government regulations in economic, environmental, and social areas. Some projects, for example, have to be inspected and approved by the Ministry of the Environment. All this could take a long time.

The approval process itself can also take what seems like forever, and even after a project is approved, the actual disbursement of the funds can take a long time also. You have to be prepared for such delays and should always plan to work around them. For example, you might consider arranging bridge financing with a bank or other financial institution.

Additional Costs

It's likely you will incur additional costs you haven't planned for. For example, expenditures for a project often have to be audited and reported on. This means paying the expenses of appropriate professionals, such as accountants and lawyers.

As well, the program may require a holdback of 5% to 15% of the government funds until certain requirements are met, such as completion of the project, engineering certification of operation, and final summary and audit of costs.

Success Can Spell Repayment

If the financing program involved funding for the fabrication of a prototype, the subsequent sale of the prototype or commercial production from it may force repayment of the government funds.

Once in operation, there will be a significant amount of required ongoing reporting to the government on matters such as sales levels generated, new employment, and results of commercialization of technology.

Confidentiality

Confidentiality of information may be of some concern. All dealings with the government are supposed to be confidential. The number of persons involved in dealings at the various government levels, however, makes enforcement difficult, and the Access to Information Act can provide public access to your information.

The Government Maze

You may encounter frequent staff turnover in the government departments you deal with. Employee transfers, attrition, and promotions may mean different people will be handling your file. All this increases the chance of your paperwork being interrupted and slows down the completion of your application.

Restrictions

Some of the programs may have restrictions (negative covenants) that prohibit changes in voting control of the business or disposal of assets.

TIP

SNAP

When you are dealing with government programs, you need to do your homework. Make sure you know and understand what you may be up against so you can modify your approach and tactics appropriately. This will help ensure that your application isn't lost in the shuffle.

DEALING WITH GOVERNMENT OFFICIALS

Here are some helpful pointers to keep in mind when dealing with government officials:

- Study the organization
  Learn the basic departmental structure so you can identify the key people who may be reviewing and/or approving your project.

Organization charts are often available through reports published by government agencies. If this information is not available, you can often identify the key people by making telephone inquiries.

Once you know who's in charge, start at the top. You may be shunted down, but at least the senior people will know about you and your project. If you can inspire enthusiasm for your project at senior levels, you will find the response at the lower levels more positive.

- Find out how the approval process works
  If you understand the approval process, you will be in a much better position to overcome objections as they arise.

- Allow plenty of time and be patient
  Realize that the approval process sometimes requires an abundance of patience. Allow the government officials plenty of time to grant approval.

- Be prepared to answer all questions
  Even when you have prepared a comprehensive business plan, you will still be faced with many questions. Be prepared to provide additional detail for the individuals assessing your proposal. Recognize that they must justify the project and be convinced that it makes economic sense. Answer all questions thoroughly and promptly.

- Do not involve politicians
  Generally, politicians are not the pipeline to government participation. Most government departments are administered by civil servants who report to deputy and assistant deputy ministers, all of whom have probably been on the scene longer and will be there long after the politician departs.

- Do not compromise your judgment
  One final guideline when contemplating government funding: do not compromise solid business judgment in the pursuit of a few dollars of government assistance. This often comes in to play in respect of funding to locate in "economically depressed" regions of the country. After set-up in these remote areas, businesses frequently are constrained from profitable operations because of transportation difficulties, lack of skilled labour, the problem of

attracting management to remote communities, and shortage of back-up services.

Ensure that a sound business evaluation has been made of the feasibility of amending a business plan in order to meet the qualifying criteria for government funding.

TIP

When seeking government funding, keep in mind the truism of all financing:

"If you want a quick answer, it's NO! A YES takes a little longer."

SOURCES OF INFORMATION

With up to 900 federal and provincial services and products available, keeping up with current changes can be a formidable task.

Unlike income tax changes which come once or twice per year, usually at federal budget time with specific information following afterwards, information on changes to government programs is usually sporadic, emanates from a multitude of ministries, and can take many forms.

Canada Business Service Centres (CBSC)

The federal and provincial governments have responded to business' problems in getting all of the information about programs and have introduced "one stop shopping for information on government programs" through the establishment of the Canada Business Service Centres (in Quebec, Info Entrepreneurs).

> Each CBSC offers access to almost 900 federal and provincial services and products, tailored for local clients.

Located in each province, these centres are designed to give new entrepreneurs and established small- and medium-sized businesses the information they need to make informed business decisions. Each CBSC offers access to almost 900 federal and provincial services and products, tailored for local clients. By phone or in person, you can find out about starting a business, ongoing support for business improvements and expansion, regulatory requirements, financial assistance programs, taxation, and trade and export opportunities.

Information is provided to each CBSC by numerous federal departments including the Business Development Bank of Canada and provincial ministries related to business and economic development.

Local CBSCs ensure that nationally sponsored program information is modified for its province and local government contacts are developed for client referrals. New information is being added rapidly as more departments and levels of government join the initiative. Data is updated regularly to ensure accurate and timely information is passed on to clients.

Information by Phone

Basic information can be retrieved by touch-tone phone 24 hours-a-day, 7 days-a-week. An interactive voice response system, provides recorded messages about frequently asked questions dealing with business operations, loans for small businesses, GST and other topics.

During regular business hours, information officers are available to answer basic questions and to direct callers to resource people in various government departments.

Information by Fax

Documents can be faxed to you 24 hours-a-day, 7 days-a-week by calling the Faxback line (by voice) and by following the instructions. It is best to start by requesting a master catalogue that describes all the catalogues that are available and then progress to more detailed information from the choices on the master catalogue.

Information via the Internet

The Internet address is: cobsc@cbsc.ic.gc.ca

Information in Person

Most of the CBSCs are open to the public and provide similar information to walk-in clients as that available by phone.

Information in Publications

There are many publications that provide some useful guidance about government programs, such as:

- *The Canadian Business Financing Handbook*, published by the Canadian Institute of Chartered Accountants (CICA)
- *Export Assistance Programs*, published by Royal Bank of Canada
- *Industrial Assistance Programs in Canada*, published by CCH Canadian Ltd.

- *Government Programs and Services*, published by CCH Canadian Ltd.
- *Government Assistance for Canadian Business*, published by Carswell
- *Sources of Successful Small Business Financing in Canada*, published by Entrepreneurial Business Consultants of Canada
- *Handbook of Grants and Subsidies*, published by Canadian Research and Publication Centre
- *The Canadian Reference Directory on Business Planning and Funding*, published by The Canadian Sources of Funds Index Ltd.
- *Canadian Industrial Incentives Legislation*, published by Butterworths.

These publications offer a good overview of all the programs available at the time of their publication and the pertinent administrative details of the programs. The books (or relevant chapters thereof) are usually organized functionally by the type of project the assistance covers (e.g., exporting or research and development). Unfortunately, updating is sporadic and programs change so frequently that a publication can be obsolete before the printing process is finished.

Information from Other Sources

Other sources of information include:

- senior officers in the various employment and immigration offices who can advise you about training programs that may be available for upgrading a workforce
- the blue pages of the telephone directory where you will find telephone numbers for various government departments and service centres.

TIPS

SNAP

To research the availability of appropriate government funding for a project and develop a short list for further follow-up:

- contact the Canada Business Service Centres
- review the many publications available
- contact one of the database services.

PREPARING A BUSINESS PLAN FOR GOVERNMENT FUNDING

A well-prepared business plan is a cornerstone to every financing program, whether in the private or public sector. However, government priorities and accountability bring in certain unique requirements which need to be addressed in order to ensure a timely processing of an application.

> **Consider the unique facts of a business plan focussed on government funding.**

In addition to the information normally included in a business plan, the following should also be considered in preparing a business plan for government funding.

History
- a significant chronological outline of the evolution of the business
- details of previous government funding received.

Location
- detailed outline of the proposed site
- advantages and disadvantages of operating from this site (with specific cost savings premiums)
- reasons for moving from existing site
- any other feasible alternative sites
- availability of the following infrastructure in the proposed community:
  - housing
  - schools
  - hospitals and medical facilities
  - recreation facilities
  - sewer and water capacity
  - fire and police protection
  - business support services
  - retail establishments.

Also outline any plans to contribute towards the foregoing infrastructure improvements or expansion.

Financial
- develop forecasts to reflect the incremental steps of the project; i.e., the increase in key aspects such as:
  - employment
  - sales, distinguishing export and domestic

- capital expenditures
- net income and net cash flow.

Employment

- provide a breakdown of proposed employment levels, including management
- outline the jobs by classification, duties and wage rates
- indicate the location and sourcing of personnel to fill the new positions
- calculate the number of shifts and equivalent person years of employment forecast for three years
- identify availability of required skills
- outline any training programs to be initiated
- determine if any employment levels drop at other plant sites as a result of this project.

Marketing

- analyze forecast sales by units of output and by nature and location of markets served
- outline basis for forecast volume levels
- summarize major competitors, and consider impact of new project on competitors' businesses.

Production

- describe the types, quality and sources of raw materials.

Capital Expenditures

- justify any purchasing of equipment from foreign suppliers, rather than from domestic sources.

RECAP

We have checked through:

- the attitudes of federal and provincial governments to financial assistance to business
- the various forms of assistance
- requirements to qualify
- preparing the application and business plan
- how to avoid the pitfalls
- the approval process
- sources of information.

Where to Go   ...For Government Program Information

Location of Canada Business Service Centres

Yukon
Canada/Yukon Business Service Centre
201-208 Main Street
Whitehorse, Yukon
Y1A 2A9
Tel.: (867) 633-6257
Toll Free: (800) 661-0543
Fax: (867) 667-2001
Info-FAX: (867) 633-2533
Info-FAX: (800) 841-4320
Internet:
http://www.cbsc.org/yukon/index.html
E-mail: perry.debbie@cbsc.ic.gc.ca

Northwest Territories
Canada/Northwest Territories Business
Service Centre
P.O. Box 1320
8th Floor Scotia Centre
Yellowknife, Northwest Territories
X1A 2L9
Tel.: (867) 873-7958
Toll Free: (800) 661-0599
Fax: (867) 873-0575
Info-FAX: (867) 873-0575
Info-FAX: (800) 661-0825
Internet:
http://www.cbsc.org/nwt/index.html
E-mail: yel@cbsc.ic.gc.ca

British Columbia
Canada/British Columbia Business
    Service Centre
601 West Cordova Street
Vancouver, British Columbia
V6B 1G1
Tel.: (604) 775-5525
Toll Free: (800) 667-2272
Fax: (604) 775-5520
Info-FAX: (604) 775-5515
Info-FAX: (800) 667-2272
Internet: http://www.sb.gov.bc.ca/small-
bus/sbhome.html
Bookstore: dixon.glen@cbsc.ic.gc.ca
Website Comments:
hartley.len@cbsc.ic.gc.ca
Business Start-Up:
olson.dave@cbsc.ic.gc.ca
Trade and Markets or Export/Import:
marcarenhas.carm@cbsc.ic.gc.ca
Statistics: yee.judy@cbsc.ic.gc.ca

Alberta
The Business Link
Business Service Centre
Ste. 100, 10237-104 Street
Edmonton, Alberta
T5J 1B1
Tel.: (403) 422-7722
Toll Free: (800) 272-9675
Fax: (403) 422-0055
Info-FAX: (403) 427-7971
Info-FAX: (800) 563-9926
Internet:
http://www.cbsc.org/alberta/index.html
E-mail: buslink@cbsc.ic.gc.ca

Saskatchewan
Canada/Saskatchewan Business Service
Centre
122-3rd Avenue, North
Saskatoon, Saskatchewan
S7K 2H6
Tel.: (306) 956-2323
Toll Free: (800) 667-4374
Fax: (306) 956-2328
Info-FAX: (306) 956-2310
Info-FAX: (800) 667-9433
Internet:
http://www.cbsc.org/sask/index.html
E-mail: saskatooncsbsc@cbsc.ic.gc.ca

Manitoba
Canada Business Service Centre
330 Portage Avenue, 8th Floor
P.O. Box 2609
Winnipeg, Manitoba
R3C 4B3
Tel.: (204) 984-2272
Toll Free: (800) 665-2019
Fax: (204) 983-3852
Info-FAX: (204) 984-5527
Info-FAX: (800) 665-9386
Internet: http://www.cbsc.ic.gc.ca
E-mail: manitoba@cbsc.ic.gc.ca

Ontario
Canada - Ontario Business Call Centre
Toronto, Ontario
M5V 3E5
Tel.: (416) 954-INFO (4636)
Toll Free: (800) 567-2345
Fax: (416) 954-8597
Info-FAX: (416) 954-8555
Info-FAX: (800) 240-4192
Internet:
http://www.cbsc.org/ontario/index.html
E-mail: cobcc@cbsc.ic.gc.ca

Quebec
Info entrepreneurs
5 Place Ville Marie
Niveau Plaza, Suite 12500, Plaza Level
Montreal, Quebec
H3B 4Y2
Tel.: (514) 496-INFO (4636)
Toll Free: (800) 322-INFO (4636)
Fax: (514) 496-5934
Info-FAX: (514) 496-4010
Info-FAX: (800) 322-4010
Internet:
http://www.cbsc.org/quebec/index.html
E-mail: info-entrepreneurs@bfdrq-
fordq.gc.ca

New Brunswick
Canada/New Brunswick Business
   Service Centre
570 Queen Street
Fredericton, New Brunswick
E3B 6Z6
Tel.: (506) 444-6140
Toll Free: (800) 668-1010
Fax: (506) 444-6172
Info-FAX: (506) 444-6169
Info-FAX: (800) 401-3201
TTY: (800) 887-6550
Internet: http://www.cbsc.org/nb/index.html
E-mail: cbscnb@cbsc.ic.gc.ca

Nova Scotia
Canada/Nova Scotia Business Service Centre
1575 Brunswick Street
Halifax, Nova Scotia
B3J 2G1
Tel.: (902) 426-8604
Toll Free: (800) 668-1010
Fax: (902) 426-6530
Info-FAX: (902) 426-3201
Info-FAX: (800) 401-3201
TTY: (800) 797-4188
Internet: http://www.cbsc.org/ns/index.html
E-mail: halifax@cbsc.ic.gc.ca

Prince Edward Island
Canada/Prince Edward Island Business
   Service Centre
75 Fitzroy Street
P.O. Box 40
Charlottetown, Prince Edward Island
C1A 7K2
Tel.: (902) 368-0771
Toll Free: (800) 668-1010
Fax: (902) 566-7377
Info-FAX: (902) 368-0776
Info-FAX: (800) 401-3201
TTY: (902) 368-0724
Internet:
http://www.cbsc.org/pei/index.html
E-mail: pei@cbsc.ic.gc.ca

Newfoundland
Canada Business Service Centre
90 O'Leary Avenue
P.O. Box 8687
St. John's, Newfoundland
A1B 3T1
Tel.: (709) 772-6022
Toll Free: (800) 668-1010
Fax: (709) 772-6090
Info-FAX: (888) 772-6030
Internet:
http://www.cbsc.org/nfld/index.html
E-mail: St. Johns@cbsc.ic.gc.ca

Source: Canada Business Service Centres,
1997.

Leasing — A Workable Financing Option

With more than 10% of all business equipment now being lease-financed, leasing is a rapidly growing, multi-billion dollar industry across North America. Despite several regulatory changes in 1989 which affected leasing, there is continued optimism for growth in equipment leasing in Canada.

Virtually all types of business equipment are leased. Recently, new leases in Canada exceeded $4.5 billion. Lease receivables now stand at a total in excess of $12 billion.

THE LEASE AS A FINANCING OPTION

When compared to traditional sources of financing, the bottom line benefits of leasing can be very attractive:

- The rates are usually fixed
  A fixed rate protects your business' budget for a specified period of time. Because rates are usually fixed for the duration of the lease, often three to five years, the company's cash flow and budgeting are protected from rate fluctuation. Over 90% of all leases transacted in Canada are fixed rate leases.

- Payment schedules are flexible
  The term, payment and purchase option of a lease are flexible. A lease can be structured to fit your company's operating budget or cash flow cycle. Structuring the rental payments to meet the specific needs of your company can be very beneficial to your cash flow and business cycle. Figure 8.1 shows four types of lease payments.

Figure 8.1:	Types of Lease Payments
Type of Payment	**Description**
Stepped payments	A "stepped payment" which increases to coincide with increasing projected revenues.
Seasonal payments	Seasonal rental payments to match seasonal use of equipment or seasonal revenues.
Decreasing payments	Decreasing rental payments where increasing maintenance costs make rapid equipment depreciation necessary.
Higher purchase option/ lower rental payments	By negotiating a higher purchase option, lower rental payments can be assessed over the term, provided the purchase option is a reasonable estimate of the then fair market value of the equipment.

- Budgeting is simple
  Rentals can be structured from the outset of the lease to match the useful life of the revenue-producing asset. This can be particularly beneficial for equipment that will eventually become technologically obsolete.

- Working capital and credit availability can be preserved
  Leasing can provide up to 100% financing, thereby preserving working capital and your operating line of credit.

- Usually no additional collateral is required
  Typically, it is not necessary to pledge other assets, such as accounts receivable or inventory. Also, there usually are minimal, or indeed no, restrictive covenants of the type usually found in loan agreements.

- The documentation is straightforward
  Lessors usually provide simple, standardized lease documents using forms such as the Equipment Lease Agreement and Lease Application. Completing the transaction is simple and cost effective.

- Costs can be deducted over the term of the lease
  The lessee can deduct 100% of the lease payments as a business expense. Deducting the entire rental payment often may be more advantageous than expensing the interest costs of a loan and the asset's capital cost allowance.

Understanding Leases

The *Handbook of the Canadian Institute of Chartered Accountants* (the *CICA Handbook*) defines a lease as the conveyance by a lessor (owner) to a lessee (user) of the right to use an asset usually for a specified period of time in return for rent. The lessor owns the asset and deducts the capital cost allowance (CCA) for tax purposes. The lessee rents the asset and deducts the rentals for tax purposes (unless a Joint Election is taken, discussed later).

Bank-owned Leasing Companies

A bank-owned leasing company typically leases moveable business equipment; however, the federal Bank Act limits the type of equipment bank-owned leasing companies can lease. Generally, the restrictions are that banks or bank-owned companies:

- cannot lease consumer household property; they can lease only commercial transportation equipment
- can lease only specialized commercial vehicles with a gross vehicle weight capacity of at least 21 metric tonnes or approximately 46,300 pounds, i.e., no automobiles or light trucks, unless they qualify as specialty vehicles
- cannot lease real property, land or buildings.

TWO TYPES: CAPITAL LEASES AND OPERATING LEASES

For accounting purposes, the *CICA Handbook* also divides leases into two categories: capital leases and operating leases. Both capital and operating leases can be true leases signifying that the lessor can deduct the capital cost allowance and the lessee can deduct the rentals for tax purposes.

A Capital Lease

A capital lease (also called a financial or a full pay-out lease) is a contractual agreement that transfers substantially all the benefits and risks of ownership of property to the lessee. The lessee's payments cover the lessor's capital outlay and provide a return to the lessor.

In a capital lease, the lessee usually:

- carries the maintenance and insurance
- carries the acquisition and the payment obligation on its financial statements
- has a fixed option to purchase the equipment at a specified time
- has fixed rental payments.

In other words, the total amount the lessor receives during the lease term (including the option price) is equal to the equipment cost, plus profit. The lease term is usually related to the estimated useful economic life of the equipment being leased.

An Operating Lease

An operating lease is a lease in which the lessor does not transfer to the lessee all the benefits and risks incidental to ownership of the asset.

The present value of the minimum lease payments is usually less than 90% of the original equipment cost. The amount of the original equipment cost which is not recovered during the term of the lease is an exposure remaining to the lessor and is commonly described as "residual risk."

Because the federal Bank Act precludes bank-owned leasing companies from taking a residual value greater than 20% of equipment cost on a specific transaction, in certain instances, a creditworthy third party (usually the equipment supplier) may assume the residual risk of the leasing company.

In an operating lease, the lessee:

- may not need to assume ownership risks and benefits
- does not carry the acquisition and payment on the balance sheet
- sometimes has a fixed option to purchase the equipment.

An operating lease is not capitalized on the lessee's financial statements, although it is recommended that the lessee disclose the future minimum lease payments. Minimum lease payments are those payments (usually rentals), not including taxes and executory costs, which the lessee is contractually obligated to pay the lessor.

TO LEASE OR TO BUY?

In making the lease/buy decision, carefully analyse:

- the after-tax savings of leasing compared to owning
- all relevant costs such as sales tax, legal fees, installation costs, and removal costs
- an appropriate discount rate used in the present value analysis
- the documentation, structuring, financing and other qualitative considerations
- the impact on balance sheet ratios.

Figure 8.2 compares the two situations: taking a term loan to buy equipment versus leasing the equipment.

CCA

CCA, or capital cost allowance, is the annual depreciation expense allowed by tax authorities as a charge against taxable income. An important factor in leasing is the half-year convention which allows only one-half of CCA to be deducted by the owner of the asset in the year of acquisition (except for certain class 12 property). Consider reviewing the principals of CCA and the leasing benefits with your accountant.

BEFORE YOU SIGN — UNDERSTAND THE TERMS

Although the lease documentation is relatively straightforward, the typical prepared forms are characterized by an abundance of "small print." Review the wording carefully to ensure you fully understand the terms and the contractual rights and obligations.

> **Carefully understand the "small print."**

The Contract

The three types of lease contracts are:

- equipment lease (or short form lease)
- master lease agreement
- customized agreements for large and complex leases.

Equipment Lease

The Equipment Lease, used to document most standard lease transactions, is a one-page form on which information about the lessee, the supplier of the equipment, and the equipment itself is specified. It also outlines the number and amount of rental payments negotiated, as well as the legal terms and conditions of the lease contract.

Figure 8.2:	Leasing versus a Secured Term Loan	
	Loan	**Lease**
Ownership of the asset	Borrower owns the asset	The lessor owns the assets
	Bank has a collateral security interest	The lessee uses and maintains the asset, and needs no other collateral
Tax treatment of the payments	Borrower deducts the interest part of the payment, and claims depreciation (CCA)	Lessee deducts as an expense the entire rental payment but not CCA unless a joint election is made allowing the lessee to deduct CCA and notional interest at the prescribed rate in lieu of rental payments
	Bank considers only the interest portion as taxable income	Lessor treats entire lease payment as taxable income, but can partially offset income with the CCA
How repayment relates to ownership and taxes	Bank recovers investment through interest and principal payments	Lessor recovers investment expense through • the rental payments • the purchase option • CCA
The "rate" which is quoted	A loan has an interest rate	A lease has an implicit rate

Master Lease Agreement

The Master Lease Agreement enables a lessee to periodically acquire equipment without having to complete a new lease agreement each time. It serves as an umbrella document and sets out the general terms and conditions for the lease contract. As each new piece of equipment is added to the lease, a separate Rental Schedule is completed.

> **Consider a Master Lease Agreement if you lease a number of similar assets.**

Customized Lease Agreement

A customized lease agreement provides the lessee with an opportunity to custom-tailor a lease, provision by provision, to specific needs. These are used in large-ticket transactions where the equipment is specialized or requires particular maintenance or financial terms and conditions, e.g., aircraft. These customized agreements may be costly to develop and the legal fees for their development are usually paid for by the lessee.

In addition, it is possible to have an Agency Agreement which simplifies administration. This document conveys the right to a lessee to purchase several pieces of equipment in the name of the lessor and under the Provincial Tax Exemption Licence of the lessor. It helps lessees acquire several units of equipment over time without completing separate lease agreements. The agreement gives the customer control of the transaction, flexibility in purchase timing, and more cost-effectiveness as the lease transaction size increases.

Figure 8.3: Terms and More Terms

Lease Term	What It Means
Full term	The number of months from the commencement of a lease until maturity
Term to option	The number of months from the commencement of the lease to the date the option to purchase can be exercised
Extended or stretch term	The number of months from the purchase option date until maturity date.

The *option to purchase* may be exercised after a specified number of payments have been made. At that point, the lessee has the option to purchase the asset at a predetermined price.

The *option price* will normally be a fixed sum, expressed as a percentage of the initial equipment cost. This price should be a reasonable estimate, made at the inception of the lease, of the fair market value of the equipment at the time the option is to be exercised. (Otherwise, the lease could be viewed as a sale.)

The *maturity date* is the specified date on which the lease matures (i.e., all rental payments are completed).

Sometimes it may be necessary to terminate the lease (aside from the completion of all payments). *Termination* can take place when any of the following conditions occur:

• the lessee exercises a purchase option
• the asset is involved in a total insurance loss
• the lessor allows the lessee to purchase the asset at a mutually agreed-upon price and date during the term of the lease.

Settlement value, also known as the Casualty Value or Stipulated Loss Value, is a percentage of the original cost of the asset being leased. The settlement value indicates the minimum amount the lessor would require from the lessee to terminate the lease and still maintain its economic yield on the lease, if it became necessary.

Don't Forget the GST!

Lessors are required to collect the 7% GST on rental and purchase option payments for leases. Under the GST, leasing of personal and real property is not considered to be an exempt financial service. The normal application of the input tax credit rules will apply to both lessors and lessees.

Be Wary of Apples and Oranges Comparisons

For marketing purposes, lessees may offer convincing comparisons of the costs associated with a lease and a loan. When assessing your particular situation and the credibility of the sales pitch, keep these key distinctions in mind:

• The "implicit" or "lease" rate is not the same as a borrowing cost or an interest rate.
• In a lease, the full amount of the rental payment is expensed for tax purposes.
• In a loan, only the interest portion of the payment is deducted for tax purposes and capital cost allowance is claimed on the cost of

the equipment (but CCA is reduced to one-half in year of purchase).

- As an alternative to deducting rental payments, a lessee can file a Joint Election to exercise an election to claim CCA and notional interest in a lease.

REDUCING TAXABLE INCOME WITH A JOINT ELECTION

The joint election can benefit both the lessor and the lessee. Rather than trading the CCA to the lessor in exchange for the ability to fully expense the lease rental, the lessee can lease the asset and elect to retain the CCA, as if an owner, in order to reduce taxable income.

> **Consider if a joint election will save tax.**

The Joint Election is available under the following conditions:

- the lessee and lessor are dealing at arm's length
- the lessor is a Canadian resident or a non-resident who conducts business in Canada through a permanent establishment in Canada
- the leased property is non-exempt from the new rules and hence is defined as specified leasing property
- the lease is in respect of tangible property with a fair market value greater than $25,000
- the term of the lease is more than one year.

When a lessee chooses the joint election, the following rules apply for the purpose of computing the lessee's income:

- the rentals are not tax deductible
- the lessee is deemed to have acquired the property from the lessor at a cost equal to its fair market value
- the lessee is deemed to have borrowed the money from the lessor for the purpose of acquiring the equipment in a principal amount equal to its fair market value
- the interest is deemed to accrue on the principal amount of borrowed money at the prescribed rate in effect, compounded semi-annually.

To decide whether the joint election will provide an economic, after-tax advantage, you need to complete a present value analysis comparing the rental payment deductions to the CCA/interest deductions.

Whether the joint election is tax efficient for a potential lessee depends upon its tax rate, structure of the lease, and the Capital Cost Allowance rate associated with the asset to be leased. The lease term, start date, and purchase option are all important considerations. Generally speaking, the longer the term and the higher the purchase option and CCA rate, the greater the likelihood that the Joint Election will produce after-tax advantages for a lessee.

BE TAX CAUTIOUS: SOMETIMES A LEASE IS CONSIDERED A SALE!

In certain circumstances, a lease transaction may be deemed to be a sale. Revenue Canada considers that a transaction is a sale rather than a lease if any one of the following conditions exists:

- The lessee automatically acquires title to the property after payment of a specified amount through rental payments.
- The lessee is required to buy the property from the lessor during or at the termination of the lease or is required to guarantee that the lessor will receive the full purchase option price from the lessee or a third party (except where the guarantee is only in respect of excessive wear and tear caused by the lessee).
- The lessee has the right during or at the end of the lease to acquire the property at a price which at the beginning of the lease is substantially less than the likely fair market value of the asset at the purchase option date.
- The lessee has the right during or at the end of the lease to acquire the asset at a price or under terms or conditions which at the commencement of the lease would cause a reasonable person to exercise the option.

Tax Consequences of a "Sale"

If a lease transaction is deemed to be a sale, the lessee is considered to have acquired the asset; the purchase price is deemed to be the fair market value of the asset. Any difference between the total of the lease payments and the fair market value is considered to be interest income for the lessor and interest expense for the lessee. So, if your lease rental is viewed to be a sale rather than a lease, your outlays for the asset will be considered to be blended payments of interest and principal as opposed to rental payments. However, if the lease is deemed to be a sale transaction, the lessee is entitled to claim CCA and the associated interest expense.

TIPS

INSIDER'S

Leasing equipment, rather than borrowing to purchase, is the more cost effective option when:

- the CCA rate of the asset in question is low (i.e., 30% or less)
- the lessee is currently paying taxes (the higher the tax rate, the greater the potential benefit)
- the term of the lease is short (i.e., five years or less) or, in the case of certain exempt property (trucks/trailers and railway cars), where longer term tax-oriented leases are structured
- 100% financing is sought
- the equipment to be leased is highly susceptible to technological obsolescence.

REAL LIFE: To Lease or to Buy — Which Is Best?

The Smartpik Company needed a new large widget production line. The equipment cost is $25,000. Presently the company's combined federal and provincial tax rate is 40%. ABC's incremental, weighted average, after-tax opportunity cost of capital is 10% and its after-tax cost of debt is 4.90%. In order to meet projected sales, the equipment must be in place no later than January l.

Before deciding whether to buy or to lease, management carefully analysed the costs and benefits of each approach.

To Lease: Lease payments are $6,261 annually in arrears for five years. Although the lease contains a fair market value purchase option, it will not be exercised.

To Buy: If ABC purchases the asset, a $5,000 down payment is required. The balance of $20,000 will be financed over five years at 9% interest with payments of $5,009 annually in arrears. The equipment represents the company's only Class 8 (20%) property. A pre-tax residual value of $1,000 is expected by the user-owner at the end of year five when the asset can be sold for proceeds of $1,000.

Lease Alternative

	0	1	2	3	4	5
Lease Payments	0	6,261	6,261	6,261	6,261	6,261
Tax Saving at 37%	0	(2504)	(2504)	(2504)	(2504)	(2504)
NET CASH COST	0	3,757	3,757	3,757	3,757	3,757

Buy Alternative

	0	1	2	3	4	5
Down Payment	2,000	0	0	0	0	0
Loan Payments	0	5009	5009	5009	5009	5009
Interest Related Tax Saving	0	(640)	(531)	(413)	(286)	(148)
CCA Related Tax Saving	0	(1,000)	(1,800)	(1,440)	(1,152)	(922)
Net Residual Value, after tax (a)	0	0	0	0	0	(4,286)
NET CASH COST	2,000	3,369	2,678	3,156	3,571	(347)

(a) After-tax residual value is computed as follows:

Residual value of asset		$ 1,000
Less: Original Capital Cost	$25,000	
Less CCA Claimed	15,784	
Pool Balance		9,216
Terminal Loss		$(8,216)
Tax Benefit at 40%		$ 3,286
Residual Value		1,000
Net Residual Value		$ 4,286

To evaluate the lease and buy alternative, present value analysis is employed. In the example presented, two discount rates are assumed.

- After-tax cost of capital at 10%;
- After-tax cost of borrowing at 4.9%.

Present Valuing (PV) the net-cash cost of the lease and buy cash flow alternatives produces the following results:

Discount Rate	P.V. Lease Alternative	P.V. Buy Alternative	Difference
After-tax cost of capital (10%)	$14,240	$14,871	$(630)
After-tax cost of debt (4.9%)	$16,309	$16,055	$254

If the after-tax cost of capital (the higher discount rate) is used as the discount rate, the leasing option is more attractive.

When the lower discount rate is used (after-tax cost of debt), the advantage shifts to the buying option.

There is no standard solution to the lease versus buy analysis. Whether a lease is preferable to buying depends upon the particular circumstances of the potential lessee, the type of asset being acquired, the qualitative advantages of leasing, and the selection of the appropriate discount rate for present value analysis purposes.

Because of the complexities of these calculations it would be appropriate to review this lease versus buy decision with your accountant.

TIPS

INSIDER'S

- While most lessors prefer new equipment, it could be advantageous to consider a sale/leaseback for previously acquired equipment.

- The purchase option price is usually determined as a reasonable pre-estimate of the then fair market value at the date of the option.

- A lease is separate from the operating line of credit but, if material, could affect the available cash flow from the business, thereby reducing the amount of the line of credit otherwise granted by a banker.

- In certain instances, a bank will establish a separate credit facility for leasing.

RECAP

We have looked at:

- the statistics of leasing
- financing advantages of leasing
- capital leases and operating leases
- the terms of a lease
- Joint Elections and CCA
- leasing or buying — do the calculations.

Where to Go   ...For Leasing

- Banks
- Newcourt
- Commcorp
- Greyvest

CHAPTER 9

Factoring — Another Source of Financing

Factoring is a widely misinterpreted and sometimes little known source of funding for the day-to-day operations of a business.

Essentially, a factoring transaction involves the purchase and sale of an account receivable. The vendor is usually a business with an immediate need of cash. The business has an entitlement to cash in the form of an account receivable, but under ordinary commercial terms, that entitlement may not be realizable for 30 to 60 days or more. By factoring (selling) the receivable to a factoring company (a specialized financial institution), the business is able to realize the cash immediately; the receivable then becomes the property of the purchaser, which will administer it to collection.

> **Everyday credit card purchases are an example of factoring.**

The purchase price in a factoring transaction is usually calculated as the face amount of the receivable, less a small discount. The discount represents the factoring company's administration and financing fee, which it recovers when the receivable is collected at its full face amount.

Although we don't commonly label them as such, many of our everyday transactions are forms of factoring. For example, a receivable is usually factored every time a consumer uses a credit card. The credit card company pays the retail establishment a discounted amount, and assumes the responsibility of collecting the full transaction amount in due course from the cardholder. As well, certain chequing, coupon and guarantee transactions are also considered forms of factoring.

TWO PRODUCTS

In the world of business finance, there are two distinct products associated with factoring:

- the factoring company provides financing to a business to support it through a period of rapid growth or in meeting other strategic objectives; the factoring company receives its payment once the business collects the accounts receivable, or
- the factoring company offers a form of credit insurance, coupled with a package of administrative services.

The first product is often referred to as "invoice discounting."

Because both of these involve accounts receivable management, they are often lumped together under the broad heading of "factoring." In practice, they are actually very different, but the objectives are the same. When applied properly, both of these "factoring" services can add value to the small- and medium-sized business. In some cases, factoring can add immense value by carrying a start-up or small company through extraordinarily rapid growth/expansion for which the business might otherwise be undercapitalized.

This chapter focuses on factoring as a financing tool for small- and medium-sized companies and the criteria your business will have to meet in order to utilize this source.

REAL LIFE 9.1: Factoring Can Be a Tool to Finance Growth

John has just started a business importing widgets, using $70,000 in cash which he had saved from his previous employment. He is confident that his product will be in demand and that he can access high gross margins of 30% or better.

As it turns out, John's assessment is right — too right! In the first week, he receives an order from Company X for $100,000 in widgets, and he is able to fill this order using his $70,000 of start-up capital. After shipping, he invoices Company X for $100,000 and books a profit of $30,000.

However, in the second week Company Y, to whom he had also made a sales presentation, places an order for $135,000 in widgets — and they want the goods right away. John is anxious to fill this order, but he cannot — he's out of cash. His $70,000 of capital was fully deployed in the sale to Company X and his foreign suppliers will allow no credit. It is true that Company X now owes him $100,000, but by normal invoice terms he is not likely to receive payment for 30, 60 or even 90 days.

At this stage, approaching the bank for a conventional line of credit is an unlikely solution to John's problem. In view of the business' limited history and lack of a proven track record, the bank would likely decline his application. In addition, asset margining limitations and other balance sheet ratios which banks normally apply to such credits would likely preclude a favourable response. Even if the bank were inclined to grant the credit, the response and implementation time would be a minimum of two to three weeks and likely more. But John's need is immediate.

John uses factoring to create a "win-win" situation.

- He sells the $100,000 receivable due from Company X in exchange for $94,000 in immediate cash.
- This transaction reduces his profit on the Company X sale from $30,000 to $24,000.
- He now applies the $94,000 in immediate cash to complete the $135,000 sale to Company Y.
- John realizes an additional gross profit of $41,000.

EVERYONE'S A WINNER

In this example, the factoring company receives a good rate of return on funds deployed in a short-term current asset transaction, while John enjoys gross profits much greater than he otherwise would have been able to achieve. Moreover, the very same dynamic could again be brought into play if John receives another order before he has collected from Company Y, and then again after that, providing John with an ongoing source of working capital throughout the high-growth period.

This is what factoring is all about — a method for enabling small- and medium-sized companies to achieve rates of growth which they otherwise could not achieve, due to a lack of operating cash or credit. However, it is not a viable method for those who have sufficient cash or credit resources to take advantage of all available opportunities. And it is certainly not cost effective if it is used in a casual manner to accelerate receivables when there's no opportunity cost in simply waiting for payment. Factoring is only viable when it will help the business seize an opportunity that would otherwise be lost.

TIP

Explore factoring as a means to raise working capital to take advantage of a profitable growth opportunity when you don't qualify for conventional financing.

CREATIVE APPLICATIONS OF FACTORING

While factoring is most commonly seen as a method of financing sales growth, there are situations where it can be applied creatively to achieve other strategic goals.

REAL LIFE 9.2: The Leveraged Buyout of a Partner

Tom and Peter are partners in a business, with Tom owning 60% and Peter the remaining 40%. The business has $1,300,000 in good quality receivables. Under a predetermined formula or agreement, which takes into account other assets and liabilities, Tom can buy out Peter's share upon lump sum payment of $300,000.

Tom factors a portion of the receivables to raise some or all of the $300,000 to close. Tom must be careful to allow sufficient working capital to operate the business after closing. If collections on the remaining $1,000,000 of the receivables will not be sufficient cash flow, ongoing factoring will be helpful in the period following.

REAL LIFE 9.3: Purchase Back of Assets From a Receiver

John ran a business for many years, with a strong clientele and good receivables. Unfortunately, the company borrowed heavily to support a plant and equipment expansion just prior to a devastating recession wherein business dropped off. The result was debt of $4,500,000 which the company could not maintain, and a receivership ensued. While the receiver was in possession of the plant and equipment, John asked if he could rent the assets on a month-to-month basis under a new company. No other source of income for the property being evident, the receiver agreed, and John resumed business with his old clientele, free of the previous debt burden and able to create new, good quality receivables.

After a year or more, the receiver is still unable to sell the property.

John puts in an offer at $1,600,000, which is accepted. A term lender agrees to provide $1,200,000 of the closing amount. John factors $425,000 of receivables in the new company to raise the rest.

As in the previous example, John must be careful to allow sufficient working capital to operate the business after closing. If collections on the remaining receivables will not be sufficient, factoring will be of continuing benefit.

CRITERIA GENERALLY APPLIED BY FACTORING COMPANIES

Unfortunately, not every small- or medium-sized company has access to factoring as a means of financing growth or achieving other strategic goals. Most factoring companies apply a rather restrictive set of criteria in determining whether a potential client's receivables qualify for purchase. The four criteria discussed in the following sections are:

- unconditional rights of payment
- creditworthy payor
- verifiable, and
- controllable receivables.

Unconditional rights of payment only

Factoring companies will generally purchase only "receivables," defined as rights of payment, where the underlying goods or services have been fully performed and accepted by the indebted party so that the money is owed without conditions or set-off.

Creditworthy payor

The indebted party, to whom the factoring company will ultimately look for payment, must be creditworthy, which generally means government and large companies. Most factoring companies refuse invoices in distressed industries or industries such as construction, where collections can be a problem, often because of disputes.

Verifiable

The amount due must be independently verifiable by the factoring company by reference to supporting documentation and, in many cases, through actual contact with the indebted party.

Controllable

The indebted party must be irrevocably instructed by the company selling the receivable that payment is to be made directly to the factoring company. In many cases, the factoring company will want the customer to acknowledge receipt of such instruction to ensure that the appropriate procedures for re-direction of the payment have been effected.

In the real world, a prospective client rarely approaches a factoring company with such a level of understanding of the above factors that an unconditional right of payment from a creditworthy payor, which is verifiable and controllable is immediately offered up for sale. More typically, the client describes in general terms a particular financing or cash flow problem, which the factoring company must interpret and analyse to see whether a factoring solution is available. It is here that factoring companies can differ measurably in practice and procedure. While the four criteria provide the essential framework for analysis, they are more guidelines than strict criteria.

Factoring companies could vary considerably in their attitudes towards your company.

What is meant, for example, by a receivable being independently verifiable? You might think that a review of the underlying purchase order and bill of lading would be satisfactory, and in certain circumstances, it might. But clearly this would be far from sound verification, for all you could tell from such documents is that something was ordered and something delivered. You could not determine whether what was delivered actually complied with the purchase order, particularly as to required and acceptable quality.

Relying on that verification alone, the factoring company could be setting itself up to be caught in the middle of a trade dispute between its client and its client's customer. It would perhaps be better to require an acknowledgement in writing from the customer that the money is owed and will be paid in due course. Often, however, such a requirement will be impractical.

In considering the unconditionality of a payment, the creditworthiness of the payor, and even the controllability of the payment in different circumstances, factoring companies will also apply similar gradations of meaning. Consequently, in order to achieve measurable volumes, factoring companies are generally forced to assume varying degrees of risk in their dealings. Over the years, certain tools have been developed, which are commonly used in the management of such risk. Once again, it is here that individual factoring companies can differ measurably in practice and procedure.

TIP

Review your accounts receivable to establish those accounts that would qualify for factoring, using the suggested criteria.

UNDERSTANDING THE RISK MANAGEMENT TOOLS OF FACTORING

A factoring company will apply certain risk management tools and criteria in evaluating a business' application for financing, including:

- general financial review
- specific due diligence
- recourse
- holdback or reserve
- industry specialization
- collateral security.

Understanding the application of these tools can help you prepare and assemble the necessary background documents and strategies for successfully using this financing source.

General Financial Review

Usually the factoring company will begin its relationship with you, the prospective client, by trying to gain a general understanding of your business and why you need financing at this point. This will normally be followed by a review of recent financial statements, including an aged listing of your company's receivables.

These steps will assist the factoring company in deciding how flexible to be in the application of its general criteria.

Significantly, in conducting its financial review, a factoring company does not hold the client to the standards normally required by conventional bankers. Rather, it will usually look for certain specific indicators that:

- your business has a clearly demonstrated need for the transaction
- your business has some real substance
- your business is not hopelessly insolvent.

The factoring company must also consider:

- Securities
  They will want to determine who might already have a charge against the receivable under pre-existing security, as such creditor's consent to the transaction will be necessary.
- Taxes
  They will also need reassurance that an audit will not determine that taxes are in arrears and therefore the government authorities would be able to issue indiscriminate third-party garnishments of receivables.

> **A factoring company does not advance credit.**

Unlike a traditional lender, a factoring company does not really advance credit to its client. It assumes the risk of credit that the client has already advanced to another, i.e., the client's customer. In theory, once the receivable purchase is completed, it should not matter what happens to the client; the invoice should still be collectible. But in practice, the insolvency or disappearance of the client prior to collection may, for a number of reasons, increase the factor's risk substantially.

As a general rule, the stronger the evidence that a clearly creditworthy party is bound to pay an invoice, the less the factoring company will be concerned about its own client's overall financial strength.

Specific Due Diligence

Along with its general review, the factoring company will conduct due diligence with respect to the specific receivable or group of receivables offered for purchase. This will always include a review of

If you don't have a comprehensive business plan prepared, assemble appropriate financial statements and analyses, and a focused business case to support the opportunity to be financed.

your supporting documentation such as:

- contracts
- original purchase orders
- bills of lading
- invoices.

In some instances, the factoring company may also seek verbal confirmation with your customers' accounts payable departments or require an actual written acknowledgement from your customers that the money is owing, without condition or set-off, and will be paid within a certain time period.

Recourse

A common method used by factoring companies to reduce risk is to retain a right of recourse against your business if, after a certain period of time, the receivable remains uncollected. A factoring company will almost always retain a right of recourse where its ability to verify the transaction is limited or your creditworthiness is deemed weak. The right of recourse will also remain where it is a trade dispute that is interfering with payment or they feel you have misrepresented the receivable.

The concept of "non-recourse" factoring is really more applicable to the activity known as "credit factoring," discussed in more detail below.

Holdback or Reserve

Where a factor feels confident about the overall collectability of an account, but is uncertain that precisely the full amount will be received, or is concerned that payment may take longer than expected, it may require a "reserve" or "holdback." This means that the factor does not advance the full amount of the receivable net of its discount fee, but rather holds back an additional amount to cover a shortfall in payment or interest charges in the event that collection is outside the expected period. Upon collection of the receivable, the reserve or holdback is remitted to the client, less the shortfall or interest charges, if any.

SIGN

WARNING

- Assess the significance of a factoring company which advertises its financing as "non-recourse," meaning that they relinquish the right to ask for payment back from the client: it usually means that it restricts itself to only the highest quality credits (i.e., government and "blue chip") where the obligation is acknowledged unconditionally by the debtor in writing. To say that there will be no right of recourse in such situations is nebulous, since the likelihood of uncollectibility from the debtor is insignificant.

- While some factoring companies have standard holdback or reserve policies, on an industry basis, there is no such thing as a normal holdback or reserve amount. It may be 1% or it may be 50%, or even more.

- It all depends on what is motivating the factor to require a holdback or reserve in the first place.

- Be prepared to shop, compare and negotiate.

Industry Specialization

Factoring companies often develop areas of expertise in specific industries. With a good knowledge of the key players and the detailed "ins and outs" of how a particular industry works, the factoring company will often feel comfortable doing transactions which another might not do or even consider.

Collateral Security

The practice of taking collateral security, such as a real estate mortgage, a general charge against the client's business assets, or personal guarantees in support of a right of recourse, varies greatly among factoring companies. Many are not equipped to implement such security in a cost-effective manner, and thus limit themselves to transactions where they can feel comfortable without such additional security. Some, however, are willing and able to take collateral security in appropriate cases, with the result that there is greater flexibility and the client is afforded a wider latitude in the determination of whether a particular request is acceptable.

DISCOUNT RATES AND FEES

The amount charged by factoring companies for the discounting of a receivable usually ranges between 4 and 10% of the face value of the invoice, with 6% being widely regarded as the norm for invoices due 30 to 60 days from the date of purchase. This means that, in order for factoring to be viewed as a viable option, the client must enjoy fairly good gross margins in its business.

The factoring fee is not in any sense a pure financing charge. By its nature, to be done with any measure of comfort on the part of the factor, the purchase of a receivable is a relatively time-consuming and expensive process, involving ongoing due diligence and management of the collection process. Moreover, marketing to, and standing ready to serve, a relatively narrow segment of the overall business community is also expensive.

If you do have an alternative source of financing, it will likely be in the realm of venture capital or merchant banking. By contrast to factoring, the negotiation of a venture capital or merchant banking deal is a much more time-consuming and tortuous process, and invariably involves a substantial dilution of the borrower's equity (ownership of the business) in favour of the lender. In this sense, although the capital raised may be more "patient," the true overall long-term cost is usually greater than in factoring.

Neither of these alternatives, moreover, is really designed to address short-term working capital needs; generally a relatively large transaction size, for a considerable term of three to five years or more, is necessary before a venture capitalist or merchant banker will even consider a financing request.

TIPS

INSIDER'S

- In searching out a factoring company, first investigate whether or not there is a company that specializes in your particular industry.
- Carefully consider whether additional security is necessary in light of the qualifying criteria of your receivables.
- If necessary, consider shopping for better terms.
- Be prepared to give personal guarantees to demonstrate clearly your commitment to the business.

TIPS

- Do not confuse a discount rate of 6% on invoices factored with a cost of 6% of total sales. You should not factor all of your receivables but rather use factoring selectively only as needed to take advantage of opportunities that emerge from time to time, opportunities where the result would be a net gain after the cost of factoring.

- Do not evaluate factoring on the basis of the gross annualized rate of return to the factoring company. The proper comparison is in the cost-benefit of your doing or not doing the transaction, taking into account the cost of the next best alternative, assuming an alternative exists.

FACTORING STEP BY STEP

The specific steps to complete a factoring financing arrangement are typically as follows:

1. Your business applies to factor, and an agreement is reached in principle.

2. The factoring company completes its due diligence.

3. Both parties complete and acknowledge a financing agreement.

4. Collateral security is executed and registered.

5. Your business verifies and acknowledges its specific receivables to be financed.

6. Your business and the factoring company complete a specific assignment agreement for each receivable (see sample that follows).

7. The factoring company advances the funds.

"NEAR-INVOICE" DISCOUNTING

Obtain funds to purchase materials to complete production.

In certain instances, some factoring companies will provide services related to invoice discounting designed to assist the client in advancing a transaction to the invoicing stage, whereupon the receivable will be factored. Generally, these services are in the nature of supplier guarantees, including the posting of letters of credit on behalf of clients in appropriate circumstances. Samples 9.1 and 9.2 provide typical examples of documentation used in these circumstances. These services might be called "near-invoice" discounting because, in all cases, the client will be near the point of having an unconditional right of payment represented by an invoice, but not be quite there yet.

<u>REAL LIFE 9.4:</u> A Supplier May Guarantee the Transaction

Harry is a Canadian distributor of widgets which he imports from a company in the United States. He receives an order for $100,000 from a creditworthy potential customer. He can purchase these widgets for $70,000, but his supplier is reluctant to ship such a large quantity over the border without having an absolute guarantee of payment.

Harry approaches a factoring company which solves this problem by taking assignment of Harry's purchase order and purchasing (factoring) in advance the ultimate invoice in the standard manner. It then provides the supplier with its written guarantee that payment will be made upon shipment of the goods as ordered. If necessary, this guarantee is rendered as a formal letter of credit naming the supplier as beneficiary.

In completing this type of transaction, the factoring company will want to be careful that its guarantee or documentary credit can only be called upon after the satisfactory shipment of goods as ordered. Due diligence might thus include anything from retaining a knowledgeable agent to inspect the goods to requiring written acknowledgement of acceptance from the ultimate buyer. In addition, the factor may wish to control shipment to ensure that the goods got to where they were supposed to go. How involved the factor actually becomes will depend on the strength of its recourse and level of confidence it has in the client to complete the transaction successfully.

In essence, however, this sort of transaction involves no greater risk than the typical invoice discounting transaction. The factor incurs no cost or liability until it has a corresponding right for a higher amount from the ultimate customer who, by definition, is creditworthy. The difference is that the obligation to pay is made in advance. And, where a letter of credit is used, the mechanism for the factor's payment to its client — or, to be more precise, on behalf of its client — is there in support of that obligation.

Sample 9.1 Standard Form Assignment (General)

1. The undersigned, hereinafter referred to as the "Assignor," for good and valuable consideration the receipt and sufficiency of which is hereby acknowledged, assigns to MORRISON FINANCIAL SERVICES LIMITED, hereinafter referred to as the "Assignee," the Assignor's right to payment for the goods and/or services, hereinafter referred to as "the Goods and/or Services," identified below.

2. The Assignor represents and warrants: (a) that the invoice of the Assignor identified below accurately describes the Goods and/or Services and the amount owing therefor; (b) that the Goods and/or Services were delivered pursuant to an agreement with the person or company named on the invoice, such person or company being hereinafter referred to as the Customer; (c) that the Assignor has in all respects complied with the terms of agreement between the Assignor and the Customer, such that the Customer, at the time of execution of this Assignment, is liable to pay the invoice amount; and (d) that there has been no act or omission of the Assignor which may prevent the Assignee from obtaining the full benefit of this Assignment in accordance with its terms and intent.

3. The Assignor hereby directs the Customer to make payment for the Goods and/or Services directly to the Assignee and a copy of this Assignment executed by the Assignor's authorized representative shall be the Customer's good and sufficient authority for doing so. In the event that payment is made by cheque payable to the Assignor or the Assignor and Assignee jointly, the Assignor agrees that the Assignee may, without further authorization, endorse the Assignor's name upon the cheque for the purpose of negotiating such payment. The Assignor agrees that, notwithstanding the within direction, should payment for the Goods and/or Services be directed to the Assignor, it shall be received and held by the Assignor in trust exclusively for the Assignee. In such case, the Assignor agrees to notify the Assignee immediately upon receipt of the payment and to cooperate in delivery of the payment to the Assignee forthwith. In addition to any other civil or criminal liability which may attach, the Assignee's currently published penalty amount will be charged in the event of a breach of this provision.

4. The Assignor agrees that, in the event that the Assignee, for any reason whatsoever, has not within 60 days after the execution of this Assignment, obtained full payment for the Goods and/or Services in the invoice amount identified below, the Assignee may claim immediate payment from the Assignor of such amount and the Assignor shall be liable for the same. The Assignee's currently published penalty amount will apply where payment hereunder is delayed more than 10 days after demand. The Assignor shall also be liable for interest on the invoice amount at the rate of 2.5 per cent per month (30 per cent per annum) from the date of demand upon the Assignor until payment. The Assignor hereby indemnifies the Assignee against any loss suffered by the Assignee as the result of the refusal or neglect of the Customer or the Assignor to perform in accordance with this Assignment to the effect that the Assignee obtains the full benefit hereof. Such indemnity includes liability for all solicitor and client legal costs incurred by the Assignee to enforce the terms of this Assignment. Upon repayment or indemnification by the Assignor, the Assignee shall forthwith cease to be entitled to payment hereunder and this Assignment shall become null and void.

5. The Assignor hereby expressly acknowledges and agrees that the Assignee does not guarantee the Goods and/or Services, and shall not be liable or in any way responsible for the same.

6. This Assignment enures to the benefit of the Assignee and its assigns.

Assignor.		Customer.	
Inv. No.	Inv. Date.		Inv. Amount.
Purch. Order No.		Delivery Date.	
Cust. Contact.			Tel. No.

_____   _____

Date   Assignor (By Authorized Representative)

For MORRISON FINANCIAL Office Use Only:

Acc't. No.	Acc't. Rep.	Trans. No.	App'd.

Sample 9.2 Standard Form Supplier Guarantee

156 Duncan Mill Road, Suite 17
Don Mills, Ontario, M3B 3N2
Tel: (416) 391-3535
Fax: (416) 391-4843

M Morrison Financial Services Limited

STANDARD FORM SUPPLIER GUARANTEE

Client: _____

Supplier: _____

Supplier Contact:_____ Tel. No.: _____

P.O. or   P.O. or   Invoice
Invoice No.: _____Invoice Date:_____Amount:_____

Morrison Financial Services Limited ("Morrison Financial") hereby guarantees payment to the above-named Supplier ("the Supplier") of the Supplier's invoice identified above to the above-named Client ("the Client"). Payment on the said invoice will be made to the Supplier within_____ days of receipt and unconditional acceptance by the end-user customer of the Client of the invoiced goods and/or services, as installed.

The Supplier should note that this is a credit guarantee only, designed to assure the Supplier of the Client's financial ability to pay. It specifically does not cover a situation where the Client fails to satisfactorily perform all obligations to its end-user customer. The Supplier seeking to rely on this guarantee acknowledges that Morrison Financial is a financing facility only, and is not a partner of or otherwise associated with the Client, and as such, before making payment under this guarantee, Morrison Financial will require from the Client's end-user customer an unconditional acceptance of goods and/or services provided by the Client.

MORRISON FINANCIAL SERVICES LIMITED
Per:

Date: _____ _____
       Authorized Signature

Note: For contract confirmations or any inquiry regarding this Supplier Guarantee, Client or Supplier is asked to contact the following person at Morrison Financial:

Name: _____ Direct Line: (416) 391-_____

TIP

Consider factoring as a selective financing alternative to facilitate business growth "when the bank says no," and as another means of raising short-term capital without permanent equity dilution.

CREDIT FACTORING

The introduction to this chapter notes that there is considerable confusion within the business community about exactly what factoring entails. The reason for this confusion is, in part, due to the fact that certain related but distinctly different services have come to be known as "factoring." Thus far we have discussed factoring in its purest form — the purchase of invoices at a discount — or "invoice discounting," as it is referred to in more specific terms. Now let us examine a different situation.

Consider the position of a clothing manufacturer, whose plant and offices are located in Toronto, but whose product is sold in hundreds of small and large independent retail stores across the continent. Typically, such distribution is effected by the establishment of a network of manufacturer's sales agents to represent the product in each geographic area. The agent in each area, selling from samples, takes purchase orders from retailers wishing to stock the company's product, and transmits them to the manufacturer for shipment. Often a completed credit application form must be submitted with the first order.

> The percentage paid to a guarantee company can be a valuable safeguard.

For the manufacturer in this situation, managing credit risk in any meaningful way is a difficult if not an impossible task. How is it to be determined, with the limited information available, whether a small boutique located hundreds or thousands of miles away is a good credit risk? Yet, requiring cash on delivery is often impractical in the context of selling to retailers. Even determining how much credit a large and well-known company should be granted can be difficult.

For many decades now, there have existed throughout North America and worldwide, companies whose services are designed to assist manufacturers, and others selling at the wholesale level, with this problem. These companies provide, on a selective basis, a guarantee to their clients that invoices for goods satisfactorily delivered will be paid. The principal condition for obtaining this guarantee is that the client must process all of its invoices and collections through the guarantee company. The guarantee company thus becomes the manager of what is collectively a large portfolio of receivables on behalf of its many clients.

The processing of invoices and collections through the guarantee company is considered a fundamental part of the service offered by these companies. It includes:

- maintaining the full receivables ledger
- posting payments
- making collection calls
- following-up on short payments and bad cheques
- providing a range of reports.

More importantly, over time this process allows the guarantee company to develop a very accurate picture of both general payment patterns within the industries serviced, and the payment patterns of particular customers, small and large, within those industries. Using this information, the guarantee company will set limits on whose credit it will guarantee and for how much.

The fees charged by credit guarantee companies are usually set at a percentage of the face amount of each invoice processed. The percentage ranges from 0.75% of the invoice amount to 2%, depending on such criteria as the client's total volume, number of accounts, quality of accounts, and the average invoice amount. Minimum annual fee amounts and special rates may apply. Fees are ordinarily paid on a monthly basis from the amounts remitted to the client after collection.

Because it includes the processing of invoices and collections, the service of providing credit guarantees in this manner has come to be known as "factoring." This is notwithstanding that, unlike with invoice discounting, the central purpose is not the provision of financing. Having a creditworthy party guarantee your receivables certainly makes them more bankable in terms of their being able to support an application for an operating line of credit. But the credit factoring companies operative in Canada today are not generally in the business of providing financing per se. To the extent that they will from time to time loan money against a client's outstanding portfolio of receivables, it is usually done as an accommodation to a valued client.

TIP

If you have complex receivables and credit management, consider "credit factoring" as an effective and viable service.

FACTORING IN THE UNITED STATES

The orientation of credit factors in the United States is discernibly different. Most U.S. companies regard the lending of money against outstanding portfolios of receivables as their principal business and major source of revenue. There are also companies who provide portfolio loans without the credit guarantee, so that recourse remains against the client in respect to any invoice which is loaned against but ultimately proves uncollectible. When receivables management is combined with portfolio lending, whether or not on a recourse basis, we end up with a service which is closely allied to traditional factoring of the invoice-discounting variety and it can serve much the same purpose. But the two types of factoring are nonetheless different, and it is important for the prospective client to understand the differences in order to evaluate which service is more appropriate and which is more likely to be available as a solution to a particular need.

The reason Canadian credit factoring companies have limited themselves when it comes to financing has to do with the substantial difference in the conventional banking practices in the two countries and, in particular, with the practice of Canadian banks, wherever possible, of tying up all available assets as security under broad general security agreements. The parcelling off of receivables or other specific assets to support outside financing activities of the borrower, although achievable, can be a somewhat complex and cumbersome process in this context.

RECAP

We have looked at:

- the two products associated with factoring
- how factoring can be useful for growth and taking advantage of opportunities

- the criteria and risk you should understand
- rates and fees
- examples of standard forms
- some typical cases where factoring enabled a business to grow
- factoring in the U.S.

Where to Go   ...For Factoring

- Interface Financial Group
- Morrison Financial Services
- Riviera Finance
- First Vancouver Finance
- Accord Business Credit
- Refco

CHAPTER 10

Trade Finance — Funding International Imports and Exports

Trade finance has evolved from the trading days in the British Empire, specifically from services offered by confirming houses. While this form of financing has been carried on in Canada for many years, it is still not well known by Canadian businesses.

Today's trade finance companies fund inventory purchases over and above the level of finance provided by a business' primary banker and normally without affecting the lines of credit provided by the primary banker. They fill a specialized niche in the finance industry, particularly for importers, in that they provide a means for a business to expand and improve its profitability, without compromising its working capital, financial strength or ownership.

IS TRADE FINANCE A SOURCE OF WORKING CAPITAL FOR YOUR COMPANY?

Trade finance companies generally target small- to medium-sized, owner-managed businesses with sales volumes of between $1,000,000 and $50,000,000 and involving trade finance facilities of between $200,000 and $5,000,000. These businesses may be manufacturers, wholesalers, or distributors and may purchase their raw materials or end products internationally or on the local market.

Funding Sales Growth

Typically, trade finance is a funding strategy for a company that is experiencing growth in its sales volume and more so, a company with a long trading cycle, especially an importer. Companies in these situations will frequently require funding in excess of their existing operating banking facilities. Often they are unable to utilize the full value of their operating banking facilities because of margin restrictions. These restrictions limit the level of funding available at any time to a percentage of the value of a firm's existing accounts receivable and inventory on hand. Also, debt/equity levels may encumber the availability of bank operating facilities.

Do margin or equity levels restrict the ability to use your operating line of credit?

Because banks include outstanding letters of credit ("LCs") in their facility utilization calculations (even though little or no margining is allowed for these LCs), importers often face cash flow restrictions during the period that LCs are outstanding. The situation can be effectively alleviated by using the trade finance company's LC facility and using the bank operating facility to finance other elements of the operations. Many companies also use trade finance as a means of reducing their dependence on their primary source of operating finance.

How Does Trade Finance Work?

Typically, a trade finance facility will provide two types of funding:

- funds to be utilized for the purchase of inventory, which may be done either through letters of credit or by payments directly to local or offshore suppliers
- an extended credit period of between 30 and 120 days, usually designed to correspond with the business cycle. This longer credit period gives a business the time it needs to purchase and subsequently sell inventory and extend a period of credit to its customers before collecting funds.

The trade finance facility usually operates on a revolving basis. When the company collects funds, some of that is then used to liquidate the trade finance debt and that portion thus becomes available for immediate re-use. A trade finance facility is therefore an additional source of working capital.

The trade finance company pays the foreign or local vendor, up to the maximum stipulated amount, in accordance with the terms of the purchase documentation. This payment is only made upon satisfactory evidence that the client's order has been completed and shipped.

Trade finance facilities are generally secured by a charge (lien) over the assets of the business, ranking behind the charge of the primary lender (usually a bank), plus the guarantees of the owners of the business. A first ranking charge (with the concurrence of the bank) may also be taken over the inventory funded by the trade finance company and the resulting sales proceeds, until collected.

The trade finance cost structure is generally higher than that of the banks providing traditional working capital financing. But as the business activity funded by a trade finance company is incremental business which the company might not otherwise have done, the trade financing will result in a significant contribution to the business' bottom line.

TIPS

INSIDER'S

- For cash flow purposes, trade finance is usually more effective funding than factoring or accounts receivable discounting, both of which require the creation of invoices before the finance facility can be used.

- Venture capital is another alternative, but remember that venture capital is usually a permanent form of financing and is substantially more costly than trade finance.

- Remember too, future profits sacrificed by the current owner in favour of a venture capital partner can often represent significant "opportunity costs."

REAL LIFE: An Opportunity to Be the Exclusive Distributor

The opportunity arose rather suddenly for the Select Office Equipment company. A manufacturer in Italy offered Select the exclusive Canadian rights to distribute their high-quality line of office equipment. Select was their first choice for this contract because of Select's extensive contacts with dealers across Canada, management's previous experience as employees with an international manufacturer and distributor of similar equipment, and their first-hand knowledge of the industry, both retail and service, through Select's existing business.

However, Select would need substantial working capital to finance the long business cycle that would be required. The manufacturer's requirement for letters of credit when Select placed orders for merchandise further compounded the cycle problem.

Select carried out a feasibility study and in-depth financial analysis to document the high profitability of this project; however, when management looked at the bottom line, the required working capital seemed almost beyond its resources.

Select assessed its operating cycle and working capital requirement as follows:

- Place an order for container of machines costing $25,000 F.O.B. Halifax and provide letter of credit from Canadian chartered bank with order. An order would be placed at the beginning of each month to meet forecast sales.

- After manufacture of machines (60 days later), they are shipped from Italy and the letter of credit drawn down.

- In 30 days, container arrives at bonded warehouse in Halifax.

- Average warehouse inventory held equal to 60 days requirements.

- Duties and taxes of 20% of costs paid as machines are withdrawn from bonded warehouse and shipped directly to customer. Invoice as account receivable prepared at time of shipment from warehouse.

- Accounts receivable collected on average within 60 days.

The selling price of the machines was determined by a 100% mark-up over cost, including duty and taxes. Therefore, the line of credit financing of 75% of the selling price would be available.

Select determined that the maximum working capital required to finance purchase commitments, inventory and accounts receivable would occur after month seven as shown on the following table.

Select's Financing Summary

Month	Letters of Credit	Inventory in Transit	Inventroy Warehouse (Bonded)	Accounts Receivable	Total Requirement
7	$25,000				25,000
6	$25,000				25,000
5		$25,000			25,000
4			$25,000		25,000
3			$25,000		25,000
2				$45,000	45,000
1				$45,000	45,000
Total Requirement	$50,000	$25,000	$50,000	$90,000	$215,000

The problems were overcome and the financing put in place through an innovative joint effort of the company's bank and the confirming house. In both cases, the financiers' confidence was enhanced by an appropriate and detailed business plan supported by comprehensive cash flow statements, prepared with the assistance of the company's financial advisor.

The confirming house secured the chartered bank issue of letters of credit by cash advances, and subsequently secured itself by way of warehouse receipts when the goods arrived at the bonded warehouse. The confirming house was paid out using the chartered bank operating line at the time of sale of the goods (creation of accounts receivable) and shipment from the warehouse.

The use of a bonded warehouse deferred payment of duty and taxes until the goods were sold.

Since the major risk occurred at the beginning of the cycle, the confirming house agreed to finance this portion. A letter of credit could only be issued by the banker, and hence, the confirming house would grant a loan each month equal to the required letter of credit. These funds were held on deposit by the banker as security for the letter of credit. On draw down by the supplier of the letter of credit, the funds on deposit were claimed by the bank to settle each account.

When Select shipped goods from the bonded warehouse, the bank would advance required funds against an operating line of credit to pay:

- duty and taxes
- the confirming house's oldest outstanding loans for the basic cost of machines shipped
- Select's operating overheads.

Both lenders had assessed the security value of the inventory as being quite high. Because the equipment was marketable at the retail level without further costs beyond duty and taxes and the retail price was double the company's landed cost, they felt that in a distress situation they could readily dispose of the entire inventory on a discounted job-lot basis at a price equal to cost.

Select's successful strategy illustrates how a potential financing deadlock situation can be resolved with creative sourcing and structuring of alternative financing.

KNOW THE RISKS

In international trade, there are inherent risks to both the buyer and the seller. Figure 10.1 compares the different methods of payment and the correlating risks involved in the most common situations.

Figure 10.1: Trade Finance — Payment Instrument Chart

Method of Payment	When Seller Is Paid	When Goods Are Available to Buyer	Risks to Seller	Risks to Buyer
Cash in advance	Prior to shipment of goods	Upon arrival of shipment	No payment	Goods not shipped Late arrival of goods Goods not as ordered
Confirmed sight letter of credit	By confirming bank upon presentation of correct documents after shipment	Upon payment of drawing under LC and arrival of shipment	Inability to produce correct documents Inability of confirming bank to pay	Goods not as called for in LC

Figure 10.1: Trade Finance — Payment Instrument Chart (cont'd)

Confirmed term letter of credit	By confirming bank upon maturity or discounting of accepted draft	Upon acceptance of draft and arrival of shipment	Inability to produce correct documents Inability of confirming bank to accept or pay draft at maturity	Goods not as called for in LC
Unconfirmed sight letter of credit	By issuing bank upon presentation of correct documents after shipment	Upon payment of drawing under LC and arrival of shipment	Inability to produce correct documents Inability of issuing bank to honour LC	Goods not as called for in LC
Unconfirmed term letter of credit	By issuing bank upon maturity or discounting of accepted draft	Upon acceptance of draft and arrival of shipment	Inability to produce correct documents Inability of issuing bank to accept or pay draft at maturity	Goods not as called for in LC
Documentary sight collection	By collecting bank upon payment of draft by buyer after shipment	Upon payment of draft and arrival of shipment	Failure of buyer to pay, leading to warehousing and insurance expenses	Goods not as ordered
Documentary term collection	By collecting bank upon payment by buyer upon maturity or discounting of accepted draft	Upon acceptance of draft and arrival of shipment	Failure of buyer to pay at maturity Loss of title to merchandise, leading to legal expenses	Goods not as ordered
Open account	By buyer upon receipt of goods or at arranged future date	Upon arrival of shipment	Full reliance on buyer to pay Loss of title to goods leading to legal expenses	Payment risks not applicable

RECAP

We have studied:

- the possibilities of trade financing for your company
- the value of trade financing in the import/export business
- the various financial instruments, their benefits and risks
- the various methods of payment.

Where to Go ...For Trade Finance

- Banks
- Business Development Bank
- Canadian Commercial Corporation
- Export Development Corporation

CHAPTER 11

Franchising — A Jump Start To Expansion

The best way to obtain the benefit of financing is to minimize the requirement for financing. If you want to expand your business quickly, franchising is an imaginative and often very viable strategy for broader distribution and vigorous financing. It's also very attractive to new entrepreneurs who are looking for a lower-risk means of becoming an owner/operator of a business. The success rate of franchises is very good: independent businesses suffer four times the failure rate of franchises.

This chapter explores franchising and its relationship to financing from two points of view:

- the franchisor looking for new opportunities for financing growth
- the entrepreneur considering the purchase of a franchise business, and the means of financing the acquisition.

WHAT IS A FRANCHISE?

Franchising is a complete method of doing business. An often cited definition of franchising, developed by the Canadian Franchise Association (CFA) is:

> *An arrangement under which one party grants to another party the right to operate a business in accordance with prescribed operating methods and procedures controlled by the grantor, which business incorporates extensive use of the grantor's know-how, expertise, and trademarks or other distinguishing marks or names, with the grantor maintaining a continuous interest in the business by advising with regard to its operations, and with the grantor having a continuing right to compensation.*

Current predictions are that some 40% of all retail sales will pass through over 50,000 franchised outlets. At 15% annual growth, sales attributable to franchised units are growing at twice the pace of other retail sales.

Although most common in the retail sector, franchising is also

> **Franchising is where its at in retailing.**

being successfully applied in service businesses, such as travel and personnel agencies, lawn care, accounting and consulting services, and even in manufacturing.

SHARING RIGHTS, KNOWLEDGE, GOODWILL AND MORE

From the *franchisor's* (the company offering the franchises) point of view, franchising is a method of sharing the economic power of ownership of product rights, business knowledge, copyrighted techniques and trademarks, and goodwill — in return for fees and royalties — rather than developing this power on its own, through employees.

For the *franchisee* (or owner/operator), franchising is a relatively low risk means of starting a business. It's a way to access rights, methods, skills and economies of distribution in return for payment of fees and royalties.

WHY IS FRANCHISING A GROWING SECTOR?

Franchises are becoming more prevalent for many financial and other sound reasons. From a financing perspective, franchising offers several distinct features to both the established business seeking expansion and to the individual in a start-up situation.

For the *established business*, franchising can:
- provide a new source of capital and cash flow
- reduce fixed overhead costs per sales dollar
- convert goodwill, an intangible asset, into hard cash
- improve the profitability of marginal units or locations, thereby strengthening market position.

For the *individual* starting his or her own business, franchising can:
- provide greater security for capital invested (the investment often represents a large portion of the franchisee's life savings)
- offer more favourable access to debt financing, which may not be otherwise available to an independent business starting out

- help lenders gain greater confidence in cash flow projections in the business proposal, particularly when there's the track record of the other outlets, as opposed to conjecture.

FOR THE FRANCHISOR: NEW OPPORTUNITIES FOR GROWTH

Franchising is an alternative means of generating growth, without major capital expenditures, financing, and risk. It can open doors to a franchisor which might otherwise not be available; it's a proven way to:

- generate greater sales
- expand the distribution base
- increase market penetration
- decrease capital costs
- develop new profit centres
- increase productivity and efficiency
- improve quality control
- enhance image through name
- reduce labour costs
- increase effectiveness of advertising
- take advantage of new product opportunities
- reduce material and unit costs through volume purchases
- gain input from dedicated franchise operators
- provide a vehicle for international expansion
- accelerate growth
- win favour by introducing opportunities for entrepreneurs at the local level.

Most important, all of these benefits can be accomplished without the franchisor having to make major capital expenditures or take on additional risk.

TIP

Consider franchising your business as a means of pursuing your growth opportunities without the need to raise additional capital.

IS YOUR BUSINESS A POTENTIAL FRANCHISOR?

Consider the many factors which qualify a business for franchising.

The business considering this strategy as a means to expand needs a number of inherent factors in its corporate environment in order to succeed. Key factors include:

- a high level of profitability and therefore a greater than average rate of return
- unique characteristics, usually protected by patents or trademarks
- a concept that's readily portable
- an approach to business that can be standardized
- a solid management team.

As franchisor, you should be able to offer other attractive enticements, such as:

- a registered trademark and a trade name
- a reliable, affordable product or service
- the strength of a national network of independently owned and operated franchises that add strength to, and gain support from, each other
- a complete training program for both the franchisee and the franchisee's staff; it must provide hands-on experience in every operation of the business
- a detailed and readable operations manual, which will guide the franchise through start-up and well into successful operations
- resources and support, with plenty of elbow-to-elbow involvement, for the franchisee and his or her staff, on everything from site selection to decor and inventory to grand opening advertisements
- managerial training, including regional and national meetings and seminars, and assistance in operations and accounting procedures
- guidance in marketing, merchandising and advertising, including everything from selecting retail decor and display ideas to setting up co-operative advertising assistance; often the unique exterior and interior design will be known and so will attract customers to a new outlet
- well-designed communications, including newsletters, publications and bulletins to keep the franchisees informed about the latest activities and trends affecting the business and industry, feature the successful efforts of different franchisees and monitor the competition
- store or territorial expansion with possible development of a multi-store operation in a city or area of the country

- a continuing program of new product development and testing
- purchasing benefits because, as a franchisor, you can assist in obtaining items or buy products in volume and pass the advantage of this buying power to the franchisee
- entrepreneurial opportunity with lower risk and capital requirement
- rigid quality assurance programs and inspections to ensure uniformity and consistently high standards.

DEFINING THE BUSINESS RELATIONSHIP

To be successful, the relationship between the franchisor and franchisee should be win-win, offering advantages for both parties:

- the two parties, the franchisor and the franchisee, have a contractual arrangement that is in force for a specified period of time
- its purpose is the efficient distribution of a product or service — or an entire business concept — within a particular market area
- both parties contribute resources towards the establishment and maintenance of the franchise
- the contract between the parties outlines and describes the specific marketing practices to be followed and details the contribution of each party to the operation of the business
- the establishment of the franchised business creates a business entity which will, in most cases, require and support the full-time business activity of the franchisee
- both the franchisor and franchisee participate in a common public identity achieved most often through the use of common trade names or trademarks; frequently reinforced through advertising programs designed to promote the recognition and acceptance of these within the franchisee's market area.

PLANNING A FRANCHISE OFFERING

Before establishing a franchise operation, your company must carefully plan and assess all costs in order to bring the program to successful implementation. This means you must analyse and review all of these areas in detail:

> **Carefully plan and assess all costs for a franchise offering.**

- capital costs to set up franchisor and each franchise unit
- fees and royalties required from franchisees
- marginal costs to set up each franchisee

- marketing program
- training program, and
- organization and formation.

Capital Costs to Set Up Franchisor and Each Franchise Unit

As a franchisor, you will require physical facilities (office, warehouse, distribution centre, and perhaps plant) plus equipment. Similarly, each franchisee will require an outlet (owned or leased) with relevant equipment as well as staff and supplies to support each operation.

Fees and Royalties Required from Franchisees

Fees, initial and continuing, must be set. Franchise fees are typically charged at the outset, representing a type of capital to the franchisor. Ongoing fees are generally considered as royalties, and represent a distribution of a portion of the profits to the franchisor. Furthermore, expense rebates may be paid to subsidize centrally paid costs, such as national or regional advertising and promotions.

Marginal Costs to Set Up Each Franchisee

Variable expenses will be incurred for marketing support, staff supervision, operating and training manuals, site selection, legal agreements, and accounting systems. Determining these costs will facilitate the calculation of the break-even number of new units required.

Marketing Program

Specific start-up marketing should be considered to kick-off a new franchise location. This may include media coverage (press, radio, local TV), marketing materials as give-aways (pens, key chains, mugs) and an opening reception. In addition, consider national and/or regional marketing and advertising. These campaigns could perhaps be facilitated through co-operative contributions by the franchises.

Training Program

Training is essential for ensuring quality product and service and across-the-board standards. Time and budget commitments must be made for franchisee management and staff orientation and ongoing training. This may involve on-site training at other franchise locations as well as specific management training courses offered through various business development agencies.

Organization and Formation

To the extent that the organization and formation are well planned and implemented at the outset, the franchise operation will be successful. As success breeds success, the franchisor will be able to sell future franchises for higher fees.

Initially, the franchisor will need to:

- seek legal assistance to draw up and implement appropriate documentation for the franchise structure, such as franchise agreements, patent or trademark protection, disclosure documents, and legal compliance
- write and document training manuals to ensure adequate materials to support staff efforts
- oversee design aspects to ensure that a consistent and appropriate image of the organization will be maintained; this design will ultimately be accountable for a substantial portion of future goodwill
- develop standardized accounting systems to facilitate management and control within each franchise unit.

THE FRANCHISE AGREEMENT

A successful franchise agreement should be as uniform and as standardized as possible. Most agreements will be seen to favour the franchisor, but this is important in order to protect the franchise system as well as provide synergistic benefits for each franchisee.

> **A strong franchise agreement protects all members of the franchise system.**

A franchise agreement will typically require the provision of the following by the franchisor:

- site selection and layout assistance
- the provision of plans and specifications for buildings and improvements
- assistance in purchasing machinery, equipment, and essential products
- franchisee and managerial training
- recruiting assistance
- assistance in advertising and store opening
- provision of operations manuals and accounting systems
- continuing management consultation and site visits

- franchisee seminars, conferences and other ongoing upgrading necessary to effectively operate the franchise.

The obligations of the franchisee as set out in the franchise agreement usually include:

- lease obligations
- construction and opening schedules, if not handled by franchisor
- covenant to construct according to the plans and specifications

> **Consider that all obligations of the franchisee are set out in the franchise agreement.**

- restrictions to territories
- financial reporting and timely payments
- required training
- insurance coverages
- provision of adequate working capital
- full-time commitment to the business
- purchase of products or supplies from the franchisor or designated supplier
- agreement to abide by the terms of the operations manual
- covenant to maintain the franchised premises
- undertaking to ensure proper trademark usage and protection
- use and protection of patents and other proprietary technology, in accordance with a registered user agreement which will typically be part of the total franchise documentation
- participation in franchisor advertising campaigns
- restrictions on transfer of the franchise.

FINANCING ADVANTAGES FOR THE FRANCHISOR

In addition to the general advantages of speedy market penetration, lower overheads, and accelerated profitability, franchising can offer the franchisor a major financing alternative.

Rather than establish its own network of outlets, service facilities or plants, at a significant capital requirement for fixed assets (realty and equipment) and for working capital and marketing costs, the franchisor can subdivide this requirement and transfer the financing burden to the franchisee.

TIP

Carefully plan your step into franchising, considering the financial implications of the different operating structures.

FOR THE FRANCHISEE: IS THIS BUSINESS THE RIGHT FIT?

Franchises can be a complex set of legal and financial structures which need to be carefully reviewed and investigated before committing to purchase a franchise. Of course, the business planning to offer franchises should also look carefully at the following to understand the potential franchisee's concerns. After all, it's rapidly becoming a very competitive business sector.

If you are considering the purchase of a franchise, you need to assess carefully:

- the industry
- the franchisor
- the product or service
- the territory
- the contract.

A list of questions under these categories is provided for your consideration at Quick Check 11.1. Talking to other franchisees can also provide valuable insights. Quick Check 11.2 provides some guidelines.

Quick Check 11.1	Questions to Ask

❑ The Franchisor

To ensure a satisfactory working relationship, it is critically important to know the franchisor and its management. You'll need to assess carefully the following:

✓ Is the company financially stable? How does it make its money? (Money should come from successful franchises and products, not from reselling unprofitable franchises.)

✓ If a subsidiary, who is the parent company?

✓ How long has the company been in business?

✓ Who are the principals?

✓ How long has the present management been with the company?

✓ Does the company franchise other products or services?

✓ Are these products in competition with the franchise under consideration?

✓ On what facts is the profit projection based?

✓ What is the reputation and credit record of the franchisor? Will it help you obtain the necessary financial backing to purchase a franchise?

✓ How many franchises are in operation?

✓ Are there immediate plans for further expansion in your area?

✓ Where will new franchises be located?

✓ Are training programs in place, and are they effective?

✓ Are they paid for by the company?

✓ What continuing assistance in marketing, training and day-to-day operations is provided?

✓ Does the franchisor help recruit and train staff on a continuing basis?

✓ Will there be help in selecting and purchasing/leasing a location? Are there charges for a marketing study?

✓ Does the franchisor offer financial assistance in purchasing the franchise? At what interest rate?

✓ Who pays for initial opening costs, displays and layouts, local and national advertising?

✓ Has the franchisor developed new methods or innovations since it first started?

✓ Does the franchisor provide an operations manual?

✓ Is the price of the franchise variable? How? Why?

Quick Check 11.1   Questions to Ask (cont'd)

❑ The Product or Service

The product or service must be the cornerstone to the franchise operation, bolstered by a strong future competitive position.
- ✓ What is the market demand for the product or service?
- ✓ How long has it been available on the market?
- ✓ Is it seasonal? Is it a luxury? Is it a fad?
- ✓ Can it be successfully marketed in the area under consideration?
- ✓ Are similar products available in this area? At what price?
- ✓ What guarantee is there that the franchisor will be able to continue providing the product at a fair price?
- ✓ What product warranties or guarantees are provided?
- ✓ Who backs them, and carries out and pays for the warranty repairs?
- ✓ Has the franchisor carried out sufficient market research? How many people in the area are potential customers?
- ✓ Is the product protected by a trademark or copyright? Is it patented?

❑ The Territory

The territorial niches, both present and future, will underpin and define the successful opportunity.
- ✓ Is the territory exclusive? What is the size of the territory?
- ✓ Is it clearly defined geographically or only by population?
- ✓ Is the population stable, increasing, or decreasing?
- ✓ Are there proposed changes in traffic patterns or redevelopment which could affect the business in the proposed location? (Check municipal offices about local bylaws.)
- ✓ Is the competition in the area identified? How are these businesses doing?
- ✓ What are the costs for taxes and insurance in the area?

❑ The Contract

Leave nothing to a verbal understanding. Management may subsequently change. Ensure all terms are clearly stated in the written contract.
- ✓ Does the contract clearly define the duration and renewal of the agreement and all costs?

Quick Check 11.1 Questions to Ask (cont'd)

✓ Is there a renewal fee?

✓ Must the franchise purchase a minimum amount of merchandise per year?

✓ Is there a royalty payment? Is it reasonable?

✓ On what basis is it calculated?

✓ What other payments must be made?

✓ Is there a sales quota? Does the company have the right to terminate the contract if the quota isn't met?

✓ Under what other terms can the franchisor terminate the franchise?

✓ Is there provision for repurchasing equipment and inventory? How is price determined?

✓ Does the franchisee have the right to resell, renew, or reassign the franchise? Under what conditions?

✓ Does the family of the franchisee have the right to continue the operation in the event of death? Under what other conditions?

✓ Is there a renewal option for both the franchise contract and the lease of the building? Do they expire concurrently?

✓ Has the franchisor the right to repurchase the franchise? At what price?

✓ Does the franchisee have the right to all innovations and new products offered by the franchisor?

✓ Is there a procedure for settling disputes?

✓ Is the franchisee limited to purchasing all equipment and supplies from the franchisor?

✓ Is the business restricted to only the franchisor's products or services?

Quick Check 11.2 Talk to Other Franchisees

A good initial source for real-world information is to talk to the operators of existing franchises. This can help you determine the reliability of the franchisor and the profitability of the product or service. Some of the things you should explore include:

- ✓ What was the total cost of the franchise?
- ✓ Were there any hidden or unexpected costs?
- ✓ Is there a continuing fee or royalty?
- ✓ Is it reasonable?
- ✓ If there is a minimum sales quota, is it difficult to achieve? How long was the franchisee in operation before the business became profitable?
- ✓ Are products and equipment supplied by the franchisor satis factory and delivered promptly?
- ✓ Is the training program adequate? Were staff members also trained? How is training delivered?
- ✓ Was the profit projection accurate?
- ✓ How are disagreements with the franchisor handled?
- ✓ Is this arrangement workable?
- ✓ What reports are required by the franchisor?
- ✓ Is the marketing, promotional and advertising assistance provided by the company satisfactory to the franchisee?
- ✓ What problems have been encountered?
- ✓ Should any changes be made in the existing contract?
- ✓ Are quality standards enforced?

FRANCHISE OFFERING CIRCULAR

> Carefully review the Franchise Offering Circular.

A Franchise Offering Circular is a statutory legal requirement for the franchisor to sell franchises in some jurisdictions, typically most U.S. states and in Alberta. However, most franchisors will have this document available even in jurisdictions where it is not legally required. The document (analogous to a prospectus for the sale of securities) outlines certain specified financial and legal information about the franchisor and the franchise arrangement. You should request this circular since it will provide considerable informative data.

BE WARY OF SPIN DOCTORS

If the opportunity sounds too good to be true, it probably is. Here are some of the potential negative aspects of a franchise opportunity that others have learned about the hard way:

- Services provided by the franchisor may be expensive or could be purchased more cheaply elsewhere.
- Some of these services may not be of any value to the franchisee.
- The franchisor promises continuing support but fails to live up to that promise.
- If the franchisor operates from another legal jurisdiction and obligations are not fulfilled, it can be difficult, if not impossible, to achieve legal redress.
- Profits are often less than franchisees have been led to believe.
- Some franchises provide no opportunity for flexibility of operation.
- Trade names and symbols may not bring in as much business as projected.
- Misleading promises by franchisors could mean loss of the investment.
- Franchisors could "over-saturate" the market.

TIP

SNAP

Take the time to assess extensively, with professional assistance, all aspects of the proposed franchising opportunity. This investment of time will ensure you avoid a costly mistake.

FINANCING TO PURCHASE A FRANCHISE

When you attempt to arrange your financing, you will discover franchise purchases pose certain unique problems. As many of the costs incurred are "soft," they have little realizable value on liquidation. To counter this risk, obtain the track record and experience of other members of the franchise group. Well-documented track records might provide additional comfort to a lender.

As in most small businesses, financing requirements usually involve funds for working capital (operating loans), long-term assets (term loans), and equity:

- Operating and term loans are traditionally available from institutional sources (often banks).
- Long-term requirements for either realty or equipment may be mitigated by leasing.
- Equity is normally invested into the business by the owner, or by "silent partners."

Operating loans are often supported by assignments of accounts receivable and charges over inventories (Section 427 of the Bank Act or General Security Agreement), if applicable.

Term loans are usually secured by fixed charges on realty, equipment and other long-term assets.

In many cases, a Small Business Loan of up to $250,000 guaranteed by the Federal Government may facilitate the term financing needs.

Some banks offer a complete franchise financing package, covering operating and term requirements, and take as security:

- a General Security Agreement
- limited personal guarantees, plus collateral mortgages on residences
- a mortgage (hypothecation) of lease.

As we approach the millennium, franchising should continue to expand as a business strategy which provides very beneficial and effective means of lessening the financing requirements of both franchisors and franchisees.

RECAP

We have looked at:

- franchising and its growing popularity
- opportunities for growth for the franchisor and franchisee
- evaluating the possibilities for franchising your business
- planning an offering
- the franchise agreement
- evaluating the possibilities from the franchisee's viewpoint
- checking out the proposal, and the possible dangers.

Going Public — Ready, Set, Wait!

Is your company ready to go public? As you start to taste the fruits of business success, the thought of "going public" may evoke feelings of excitement or fear and even confusion. It's one of the most important strategic steps to be taken in the business world, the next move for a company at the top of the heap… but it's not for the faint of heart. If you look at the stats, you will also see that it is a relatively exclusive domain.

GETTING THE PUBLIC TO FINANCE YOU

Whether your company has matured and is in a position to consider a public issue of shares depends on a number of factors. In the preliminary decision-making process, you'll need to assess:

- the size of the company
- its track record of profitability
- its momentum
- depth of management
- use of proceeds
- the business plan and forecasts
- internal systems and procedures
- the board of directors and corporate governance.

Size of Company

Is your company the right size? BIG! REALLY BIG!! While public issues can be structured for as little as $1 million, major underwriters usually focus on issues of $8 to $10 million and up for listing on the Toronto or Montreal stock exchanges. In most circumstances, this would require net after-tax earnings in the range of $1 million or more. However, much smaller underwritings could be considered for listing on the Vancouver or Alberta exchanges in Canada or NAS-DAQ in the U.S.

Track Record of Profitability

What is your company's track record? The ideal candidate has a consistent record of profits and growth over five years or more. Of course, there are always exceptions. A early stage company with a shorter record of profitable history, but with innovative products or services with exceptionally high rates of growth (30 – 50% compounded annually) which can be readily projected into the future may be ready.

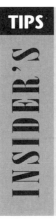

TIPS

- Assess your company and management team carefully.
- Is your company realistically at a stage where it should consider the issue of shares or are there better financing alternatives for the long term?
- Would a better strategy be to bridge the time while you get the business' house in order?

Company Momentum

Investors are always looking for companies with some exceptional and outstanding characteristics that make an interesting "story" (e.g., new products or services that can be rapidly exploited, with highly profitable results). The company must be at the top of its industry and have identifiable competitive advantages or niches. Its past record of growth must be at a rate that exceeds that of its competition so that a strong case can be made for the extension of such growth into the future at equal or greater rates.

Depth of Management

Prospective underwriters pay particular attention to the strength of management. The team must be complete and have the depth, experience and capability to grow with the company. They must be seen as being able to deal effectively with the financial community and shareholders. If key management is unable to assume such a public profile, it is essential to bring that special someone on board well in advance of a public offering.

Use of Proceeds

The company must be able to demonstrate how it will use the funds raised through share issues. A business plan that outlines the application of funds and the expected returns is essential. The

The three big factors are:
• **Management**
• **Management, and**
• **Management**

new funds should be seen to provide enhanced opportunities and profits for the company, rather than pay out shareholders or existing debt.

The Business Plan and Forecasts

You will need to prepare a professional and comprehensive long-term business plan. It's essential for helping underwriters understand the business and appraise its approach, structure and conclusions reached. Additionally, a proven history of accurate budgetary control in recent years will give the underwriters more confidence in the forecast numbers.

Internal Systems and Procedures

A public company must have well structured systems and procedures that will not only support the increased requirements for financial reporting, but will also track the critical aspects of a growing company. A reporting system that covers all facets of operations and is up-to-date and reliable greatly assists management as well as helping underwriters evaluate the company favourably.

The Board of Directors and Corporate Governance

Before going public, you need to look at the composition of your company's Board of Directors. If there are no outside Directors, you will need to find experienced individuals who could offer valuable objective input as board members. In the case of an offering corporation,

TIP

SNAP

If your long-term plan targets going public, your preparations should include appointing some outside directors to your board who can provide a high degree of objectivity and have previously gone through the process of an initial public offering.

the Ontario Business Corporations Act, as an example, requires that at least one-third of the directors shall not be officers or employees of the corporation or its affiliates.

Corporate Structure

A very important part of the preparation to go public is ensuring that the corporate and capitalization structures are in place in a form that will be readily acceptable in the public market. Not only will a clearer and simpler structure emerge, but a significant amount of time and related costs will be saved when preparing a prospectus.

WEIGHING THE PROS AND CONS OF PUBLIC FINANCING

The decision to become a public company is very involved. A company's initial public offering (known as an IPO) is a major undertaking which will have lasting effects and consequences on the company, its shareholders, its officers and directors, and its methods of conducting business.

Why Do Companies "Go Public?"

The rewards of becoming a public company are bottom line and significant. Growth and expansion are enhanced. Personal and corporate prestige evolve.

Corporate Financial Flexibility

Most of the time the public marketplace is substantial and accessible. The availability of funds from a public offering of treasury shares can provide funds for the growth of the company, both by acquisitions and internal expansion.

A stronger equity base will likely result in a lower cost for additional debt financing. There will be increased debt capacity and leverage. In addition, increased exposure to the financial community can result in new sources of capital; for example, institutions whose investment policies restrict or prohibit the purchase of private company debt securities become prospective buyers. The access to a broadly based market for the company's stock may be viewed by lending institutions as a possible debt refinancing source, thereby reducing the perceived lending risk and, therefore, the required yield on incremental debt.

Greater financial flexibility can result from the numerous financing options available to a public company, including a variety of financial instruments (e.g., convertible securities, derivatives, options and warrants).

Liquidity

Marketable securities are generally perceived to have a greater value than privately held securities due to their liquidity. This liquidity is a

> **Liquidity of securities enhance the ability to sell shares and raise capital.**

key factor in making marketable securities more acceptable as collateral to secure loans.

The liquidity afforded to owners of a private company in selling part of their holdings (a "secondary" offering of shares) enables them to diversify their personal risk. Liquidity benefits are extended to residual holdings which also become marketable and are more easily valued.

Tax and Valuation Factors

Estate planning may be simplified by establishing the range of values of the business entity. Principal shareholders can more easily estimate their capital gains tax liability when contemplating the sale of part or all of their holdings.

The payment of debts and other levies attributable to a principal shareholder following death can usually be accomplished more easily through the sale of a portion of the estate's holdings, or with monies borrowed against the security of such holdings, if these holdings are marketable securities.

Unlike a private corporation, a public corporation does not pay taxes on dividends received from other taxable Canadian corporations. Though the Part IV tax paid by a private corporation on dividend income is refundable upon flow-through of the dividends to its shareholders, the tax can still represent a disincentive to the retention of those dividends in the business.

Acquisitions

Unique opportunities become available to public companies in considering acquisition programs as part of their growth strategy, since they have liquid shares which can be used as part of the acquisition consideration.

Because a private company cannot offer shares to the public, in accordance with restrictions in corporate and securities legislation, it is usually restricted to business acquisitions that can be accomplished

A share offering can raise the profile of your company and generate business.

with cash and other tangible assets (or, at a minimum, with debt). Furthermore, the use of shares of a private company to effect transactions can be prohibitively costly, as such shares may be valued at a discount from their worth due to their lack of liquidity. However, publicly traded shares, having a value established by the marketplace as well as ready transferability, may be as acceptable as cash to a prospective vendor. This reduces the dilution of the principal shareholders' interest.

Share ownership in a public company can be an incentive for management of the acquired company to remain with the merged operation. At the same time, public company share ownership or options will provide the incentives to management of the acquired company to improve performance.

The exposure of a public company in the business and financial community may generate unsolicited acquisition or merger opportunities that might not otherwise come to the attention of a private entity.

When a vendor and buyer disagree on the value of a contemplated acquisition, due to a variance in profit-generating projections for the company, a means of reaching an agreement is the setting of a purchase price which varies in relation to future performance (an "earn-out" formula). By using stock instead of cash to settle future earn-out obligations, it is not necessary to set aside cash reserves for contingent payments.

Motivation

Corporate vigour is often enhanced as a result of the incentives implicit in a publicly held company. News of current developments must be communicated over a wider network to the media, public shareholders, investment analysts, and others. The company's share price, a tangible barometer of public reaction, rises and falls accordingly. In the public eye, directors and management may develop greater involvement in and awareness of their broadened responsibilities.

Though stock option plans no longer offer the same attractive tax treatment as they once did, a public company remains in a better relative position if it wishes to implement such a plan to motivate employees toward a profit performance orientation. Marketable securities are favoured by most employees since they are more liquid and easier to use as collateral against borrowed funds applied to the exercise of options. Highly qualified key employees can be attracted to a company via stock options when the company may not otherwise be able to afford to pay the top cash amounts required.

Improved Public Relations and Corporate Image

If properly managed, a public company can enhance its image from the publicity of continuing free and unsolicited media releases, not only with its customers, but also with its employees, suppliers, and creditors.

A successful initial public offering across Canada will see the shares of the company distributed over a wide base. This distribution effectively introduces the company's name and knowledge of its products to new households and businesses in regions where they may not otherwise have had any exposure.

Investment Dealers

A continuing relationship with a major investment dealer can provide a number of benefits such as:

- timely news on economic and industry trends
- information on competitive costs and structuring of various types of capital
- a professional and objective overview of the company's activities as well as a source of specific financial advice
- exposure to business opportunities in the form of acquisition candidates and an ongoing connection with the financial community.

But Wait: There's a Downside

Does the above sound too good to be true? There's always a trade-off. Going public can have significant impact on principals, the company and its management. These are not to be taken lightly.

Factors Affecting Principals

Opportunities for principal shareholders to arrange their financial affairs and those of the company so as to optimize personal tax benefits are curtailed because of full disclosure requirements and regulatory restrictions on non-arm's length transactions.

Some examples of restricted activities:

- Dividend policies cannot be frequently and arbitrarily adjusted in accordance with the tax status of individual shareholders.

- Shareholders' loans and advances are subject to higher scrutiny and, therefore, can be made for defensible business purposes only.
- Expense allowances and other non-taxable benefits often drawn from private companies may have to be sharply reduced, and annual bonuses must be granted as a function of performance rather than the personal financial needs, or tax status, of each owner.
- Transactions among related companies (e.g., holding companies of major shareholders) may be prohibited entirely, or at least severely restricted, with a requirement for independent valuations and/or minority shareholder approval.

Once a corporation becomes a reporting issuer (public company), principal shareholders, directors, and officers are "insiders" and must file public reports revealing the sale or purchase of any of their securities. The untimely selling of shares may be misinterpreted by the market to mean that bad news is imminent. Furthermore, insiders can't sell shares at times when they have knowledge of material facts not yet disclosed to the public.

In the short term (perhaps even on a given day), the personal worth of principal shareholders will fluctuate in accordance with the trends of the market.

The voting rights and inherent power held by the principal shareholder will be diluted to an extent measurable by the number of shares issued. However, dilution does not necessarily mean the loss of control. Maintaining an ownership of the majority of shares outstanding, or retaining "effective" control by continuing, as the principal shareholder with the major block of shares, or even issuing subordinate or non-voting shares to others can retain control in the owner's hands.

The auditors of public companies today are tending to report more *on* management, and less *to* management. Accounting practices may thus impose new constraints which, when combined with minority interests and outside directorships, can become irritants and constraints to the principals.

Factors Affecting the Company

Canadian securities laws require that a public company make "full, true and plain disclosure" of all material facts in its offering prospectus. The corporate information so provided must obviously be detailed and comprehensive. Exemptions may be sought when certain disclosures could be harmful in a competitive sense, but these are sparingly granted by the regulators. This part of the transition to public status is sometimes difficult for private companies to accept for fear that previously proprietary financial information may be of assistance to competitors or customers. Extreme caution is important in

> The disclosure of high profits and high returns on investment might attract new competitors to the industry.

the preparation of all public information releases as sanctions to the company (e.g., cease-trading orders) and its directors and officers can be imposed when news releases are held to be misleading or inadequate.

The disclosure of high profits and high returns on investment might attract new competitors to the industry.

This heightened exposure of success of the company might even attract the attention of takeover companies, where the corporation would become the subsidiary of another major corporation, and become subject to its policies and business practices.

The required periodic reporting of results, especially when coupled with the pressure exerted by institutional investors such as pension funds to demonstrate "performance," may cause a company to seek short-term profit performance to the detriment of longer-term corporate development.

There are ongoing structured costs involved in being a public company, including the costs of quarterly and annual reports (which are becoming more detailed and onerous all the time), stock exchange listing fees, registrar and transfer agency fees, auditing fees, legal fees, and shareholder meetings. Also, there are continuous disclosure requirements by press release and material change reports. In addition, there is substantial encroachment on the time of senior executives. To a larger corporation, these costs are not in themselves onerous; however, inasmuch as these expenses extend beyond the time of the initial public offering, they constitute a continuing and sometimes underestimated cost.

Factors Affecting Management

Management becomes accountable at a higher level to a much greater number of shareholders. The fiduciary responsibility attached to the stewardship of a public company obliges management to devote considerable time to dealing with the bigger issues of corporate governance and with inquiries from shareholders, outside directors, audit committee, financial analysts, and journalists. Of course, this has a significant impact on their time and their managerial effectiveness.

Business must be conducted in a more formal manner and be subject to the many regulations existing for the protection of public shareholders (e.g., proper notice of annual meetings and solicitation of proxies; the need to issue press releases of material changes in the company's affairs, etc.).

TIP

Management and other "insiders" must be very cautious that transactions in the company's securities do not give rise to charges that improper "insider trading" has occurred or that friends or associates have used privileged information to personal advantage.

YOU CAN'T GO IT ALONE

The process of completing a public offering of shares in Canada is affected by extremely complex legislation and regulation. It is absolutely essential that you gather a team of experienced professionals who can provide the appropriate guidance. As much of the work must be done on a timely basis in order to retain flexibility and take advantage of "windows" of opportunity, the team members must be prepared to work long hours to make the offering a successful reality.

The "Going Public" Team

The team will be comprised of management, auditors, legal counsel, board of directors, underwriter, registrar and transfer agent and a financial printer, each of which has a unique role to play in the process. Each team member's responsibility will be discussed further and Figure 12.1 summarizes which member is responsible for which documents and functions.

Management

Certain financial and operational management will play a role in generating and supplying data utilized in the process.

Auditors

A public company may be most appropriately served by one of the large North American public accounting firms which is well recognized by the investing public and which has relevant experience in dealing with public companies.

Legal Counsel

While a company's local counsel will serve it best in operational matters, a public company should also be aligned with a major corporate securities law firm based in a major Canadian city. The complexity of today's securities law suggests that a law firm with ample experience in dealing with securities regulators would be very wise. Where the prospectus is to be filed in more than one province, local counsel opinions are often required in each province as well.

Board of Directors

A public company incorporated in most Canadian jurisdictions is required to have not fewer than three directors, at least two of whom are not officers or employees of the company or its affiliates. In most companies, the board will consist of five to eight directors.

Underwriter

The underwriter will serve as a key advisor to the company on the public issuance of shares, and will also sell these securities to the public. The underwriter must be credible and compatible, and must have an appropriate retail marketing division to ensure a wide national distribution of the share issue.

Registrar and Transfer Agent

A trust company, often with national representation, is necessary to act as registrar and transfer agent in accounting for a public company's share certificates that will be widely distributed. Plan to compare the various services and fees charged by trust companies.

Financial Printer

Once the drafting of a preliminary prospectus has begun, you will need to select a reputable financial printer. The investment dealer can usually recommend a financial printer when requested.

Figure 12.1: The "Going Public" Team — Member's Responsibilities

Document	Responsibility
Preliminary and final prospectus	Working Group
Underwriting agreement	Underwriter
Auditor's comfort letter	Auditors
Certificate to serve as basis for opinion of counsel as to eligibility of the Common Shares for investment	Auditors
Press releases: • Preliminary prospectus • Final prospectus	Company, underwriter and counsel
Tombstone advertisement	Underwriter
Banking and selling group agreements	Underwriter
Various consents	Company counsel, underwriter's counsel and auditors
Resolutions of the board of directors with regard to authorization or approval of: • Issue of shares • Preliminary prospectus • Final prospectus • Underwriting agreement • Application to list shares on stock exchanges	Company and its counsel
Listing applications	Company counsel
Legal opinions: • Company's counsel To transfer agent and registrar To underwriters • Underwriter's counsel • As to translation of the preliminary prospectus into French, if required • Qualifications of Common Shares for sale in various provinces • Eligibility for investment	Company counsel Underwriter's counsel
Other opinions: • As to translation of financial statements, if required	Auditors
Closing Agenda	Company counsel and underwriter's counsel
Closing Documents	Company counsel and underwriter's counsel
Common Share Certificates	Company counsel Registrar

THE PROSPECTUS

When a company makes a public offering of securities (shares or otherwise), it must prepare a prospectus and file this with each provincial securities regulator where the issue will be sold. From planning to offering, it's a long, precise

> **Financial Statements dated not more than 120 days prior to the prospectus must be included.**

and expensive undertaking. It is a complicated, detailed step-by-step process and must be done very carefully with appropriate professional advice.

The prospectus must include a balance sheet as at a date not more than 120 days prior to the date of the issuance of the receipt for the preliminary prospectus as well as at the most recent year end, with a comparable balance sheet for the preceding fiscal year end. As well, statements of surplus and statements of changes in financial position are to be included. In addition, income statements for the previous five fiscal year ends (or less if the company is newer), and for the current fiscal year to the date of the required balance sheet are required.

The underwriter, with the assistance of its lawyers and the company's management, lawyers, and auditors, is responsible for the preparation of the prospectus and the coordination of its component parts.

The legal counsel of the issuing company has a major role in the underwriting process since the prospectus is a legal document which must provide the public with *full, true and plain disclosure* regarding all the company's activities and as such, it must be prepared in accordance with the requirements of the law. The auditors of the company are, of course, responsible for fulfilling the "financials" section of the prospectus.

The preliminary prospectus and the prospectus are disclosure documents which the underwriter will use to market the securities. Of course, the working group wants to put the company in its best light; however, this must be carefully balanced in view of the statutory liability for statements included in the prospectus, or omitted from the prospectus. As the money raised pursuant to the prospectus may be in the several millions of dollars, this potential liability is significant.

> **The prospectus must provide "full, true and plain" disclosure.**

The purpose of this statutory liability is to ensure that the prospectus is as accurate as possible. The parties in question cannot simply rely on the statements of officers and employees of the issuer. All parties concerned must conduct a "reasonable investigation" to ensure that the statements made in the prospectus are true.

All parties concerned must conduct a "reasonable investigation" to ensure that the statements made in the prospectus are true.

Therefore, throughout the procedure of drafting the prospectus, the underwriters and their counsel will ask questions of the officers of the company to ensure that all material information about the company is disclosed and that everything that is disclosed is correct.

Similarly, lawyers for the company will be asking questions on behalf of the directors of the company for the same purpose. Both sets of lawyers will be reviewing material documents including the more important contracts to which the company is a party and the corporate records. Where possible, information contained in the prospectus should be verified through independent means. Shortly before the filing of the preliminary prospectus, there will be a formal "due diligence" session where the key officers of the company will meet with the underwriters and the lawyers for both the company and the underwriters to answer any remaining questions.

Counsel to the company will normally provide the directors with a memorandum describing the nature of the prospectus process and the scope of their potential liability (sometimes called the "scare letter"). Also, a questionnaire is usually sent to the directors and the officers of the company to gather information that must be disclosed in the prospectus or provided to the Securities Commissions, i.e., each director's and officer's full name, date of birth, residential address, current and past employment and remuneration, and indebtedness to, and shareholdings in, the company.

How Long Does It Take?

In an optimal situation with detailed advanced planning and experienced professionals on the team, a public equity offering may be completed in 90 days. However, experience shows that it typically takes 120 to 180 days. Sample 12.1 details a typical schedule.

Sample 12.1:	Timetable for a Public Equity Offering

Deadline	Task
Day 1:	• Organizational meeting
Day 2 to Day 30:	• Prepare preliminary prospectus
	• Due diligence meetings between underwriter and officers of company to verify the material facts contained in the preliminary prospectus
	• Arrange French language translation of preliminary prospectus, if required
	• Begin preparation of the investor presentations for institutional investors and retail account executives in selected cities across Canada
Day 30:	• Company directors' meeting to approve and sign preliminary prospectus
	• File preliminary prospectus with relevant securities commissions across Canada
	• Issue press release announcing the offering
Day 33:	• Receive receipts for preliminary prospectus from all securities commissions
Day 40:	• File listing applications with stock exchanges
Day 47:	• Receive first deficiency letter from securities commissions
Day 54:	• Receive second deficiency letter from securities commissions
Day 58 to Day 60:	• Negotiate resolution of deficiencies
	• Investor presentations to institutional investors and retail account executives in selected cities across Canada
Day 61:	• Pricing meeting between company and underwriters
Day 62:	• Company directors' meeting to approve and sign the final prospectus and underwriting agreement
Day 63:	• Receive receipts for final prospectus
Day 90:	• Closing.

How Much Does It Cost?

Sample 12.2 outlines the typical expenses incurred for an initial public equity offering.

The total cost excluding commissions is generally seen to be in the range of $200,000 – $300,000.

Sample 12.2	Estimated Expenses of an Initial Public Equity Offering	
	To filing of preliminary prospectus	Cumulative to completion of the issue
Company counsel	$ 40,000	$ 75,000
Printing (including share certificates)	40,000	60,000
Auditors	30,000	50,000
Listing fees		15,000
Marketing materials and presentations		15,000
Incidental expenses		15,000
	$110,000	$230,000

The above does not include underwriter's commissions, which could range between 6% and 8% of the amount raised.

Tread Cautiously

This chapter gives only a very brief overview of the going public process — an event which typically occurs only once in a company's lifetime. It is a process that requires extensive study, a high degree of discipline and considerable consultation and liaison with professional advisors.

RECAP

We have reviewed:

- the requirements for "going public"
- the reasons for approaching the public for financing
- the disadvantages of "going public"
- the team you will need if you decide to do so
- preparing the documents and the information you'll need
- some warnings.

Research and Development — Financing the Better Mouse Trap

Got an innovative idea that's bound to make millions but just need a little financing to get it off the ground? Because of the costs, risks, and long-term payback associated with innovation and research, many businesses, particularly small- to medium-sized ones, find financing their sure-fire idea difficult, if not impossible. But with commitment and the right strategies and contacts, it can be done.

Research and development (or colloquially just R & D) has the full attention of today's business and government. Around the globe, research and development has a proven track record of producing substantial rewards and having an overall positive impact on a country's economic growth. Generally occurring in the private sector, expansion through innovation creates jobs and strengthens international trade.

WHAT IS R & D?

R & D, or innovation, includes basic research, applied research or development. In Canada, the federal Income Tax Act defines research and development as:

> ...a systematic investigation or search carried out in a field of science or technology by means of experiment or analysis.

To emphasize the intended broader scope of industrial R & D, the term "Scientific Research" in the Income Tax Act was recently changed to read "Scientific Research and Experimental Development." Certainly, the scope of the definition of

"Development" will be expanded, consistent with the trend in recent years in other government programs.

An Increasingly Important Area of Economic Growth

Research and development is an area that is typically characterized by uncertainty and risk, testing of hypotheses, sound methodology, and qualified staff. Government studies consistently show a clear

> **R&D provides a better return than capital expenditures.**

relationship between expenditures on research and development and economic growth and employment. A recent study entitled *Industrial R & D and Productivity* indicates that R & D investments offer a rate of return that on average is 10 to 15% higher than the rate gained from capital expenditures.

SOURCES OF FINANCING

The major forms and sources of financing for R & D vary significantly, depending on the size of the organization and stage of development of the innovation and include:

- sweat equity
- retained earnings
- new cash equity
- venture capital
- strategic partnering
- turf financing
- government assistance, both tax advantages and funding programs.

As the risk associated with R & D is excessive for small- and medium-sized businesses, partners are usually required to "share the risk." Internal funding, either wholly or partly, may be generated from sweat equity or retained earnings. Assistance then evolves either from the private sector as new cash equity or from the public sector as government funding.

Sweat Equity

In taking an innovation from concept to market, entrepreneurs often complete much of the initial research "in the back garage" with little cash outlay. However, the contribution of energy, emotion and time of the individual engineer/scientist can be very substantial — and too often is not quantified. Certainly at the early stages of development, sweat equity is a cost-effective alternative to employing staff or outside services which must be paid for from cash financing.

It is important to retain and report to financiers the time expended and imputed value along with all out-of-pocket expenses.

Retained Earnings

A few small- to medium-sized companies informally commit large resources to R & D without structured recognition of the risk and of a targeted inherent internal rate of return. The impact on the company's financial well-being can be significant — perhaps even treacherous. On the other hand, the routine expenditure of accumulated earnings, now represented by working capital, usually doesn't incur a debt-servicing cost.

New Cash Equity

As the project moves along, the efforts of the engineer/scientist working on a small scale must now be supplemented with an infusion of cash equity. This cash is needed to contract the supplementary outside services for specialized assistance, testing and prototyping. The entrepreneur usually starts by spending existing savings and then mortgaging his or her house to infuse new funds to continue the efforts; the next step is often personal loans from relatives, friends, employees and business associates. Indeed, even customers or suppliers may be untapped sources of cash, but creative structuring of such a deal will be required.

Once an innovation reaches a certain stage of development, formal seed capital will be needed to further enhance the efforts. Assistance during this "proof of concept" stage can be obtained through nominal equity contributions from provincial venture capital corporations, which have been established to satisfy this need. Organizations such as the federal Business Development Bank of Canada or British Columbia's Discovery Foundation and others offer assistance through early stage financing but take a share of the project in return, often as a royalty on resulting sales.

Venture Capital

At the point of having a developed product with proven market acceptance or clearly defined market research, the project may qualify for conventional institutional venture capital. The major sources of such venture capital are united as members of the Canadian Venture Capital Association. However, most such venture capitalists do not, in practice, make investments of less than $500,000 (although some might go as low as $250,000 if it's an outstanding opportunity). These investors typically prefer a minority equity position, usually in the range of 20 to 40%.

As a result of the recent tax supported program for Labour Sponsored Venture Capital funds, there is currently an abundance of available uninvested venture capital — estimated to be in the order of $7 billion.

Strategic Partnering

Strategic alliances or disposal of certain rights (turf financing) provide the opportunity to raise capital for completing or exploiting R & D. In addition to the cash which may be made available to the R & D enterprise, the business may also gain substantial synergies from its alliance with another entity, such as:

- manufacturing capabilities
- marketing expertise
- distribution networks, or
- complementary product lines.

A strategic association with a large well-known company gives considerable validation and credibility to the technology. Some returns may be in upfront cash, but additional cash flows may also be structured from future royalties.

Turf Financing

The sale of certain rights to a new process/product up front (called turf financing) can often provide early stage capital to reinvest into the development of the new process/product.

REAL LIFE 13.1: Expanding Your Home Market

A company acquired the worldwide patent rights to a new product but needed funds for development and marketing the product.

The company sold the Australian and European rights for $1 million each and used these funds to finalize prototype and product development *and market introduction of the product throughout North America. The $250 million North American market was more than this company could otherwise expect to exploit.*

———

A company was making good progress in developing unique software for a particular Canadian service sector but reached a stage where it needed more capital to continue.

The company pre-sold the rights to the same software for application in another service sector for $500,000 and used these funds as equity to finalize research and development of its primary product.

In return for these benefits, the R & D enterprise may have to give up certain geographical territories or certain product applications. These arrangements generally have the advantage of being long term and inherently leading to the building of a strong and beneficial alliance. In addition, these relationships provide specific expertise perhaps not available to the R & D enterprise, with an inherent acceleration of the enhancement of its R & D efforts.

Government Assistance — Tax-based

Tax legislation includes a number of provisions that are very supportive of research and development. In Canada, the federal Income Tax Act encourages investment in research and development through provisions that allow:

> **R&D tax credits are a simple form of cash assistance.**

- all "current" expenditures to be written off in full in the year incurred, thus reducing income taxes otherwise payable
- an Investment Tax Credit (called an ITC), ranging from 20 – 35% of current and capital expenditures on R & D, is generated which may be utilized in one of two ways:
  - reduction of federal taxes otherwise due (by direct offset against tax instalments), or
  - a refund of the entire ITC upon filing the annual federal tax return.

Provincial tax legislation has similar benefits.

A limited partnership is often used as a vehicle for raising outside capital, and flowing the generous tax benefits for R & D write-offs and investment tax credits to the partners. However, in Canada, this approach is somewhat constrained by the current "at risk" rules which must be met to satisfy Revenue Canada.

In addition to these direct measures, Canadian tax legislation has a number of other provisions which are intended to stimulate the increased availability of capital, some of which may be a means to finance R & D for small- and medium-sized companies:

- the qualification of a portion of RRSP funds for investment in shares of arm's length Canadian-controlled private corporations
- the enticement to pension funds to make a portion of their capital funds available to small- and medium-sized Canadian corporations.

Government Assistance — Cash

Industry Canada, through its Strategic Technologies Programs, focuses certain R & D assistance in the areas of micro-electronics, biotechnology, information technology, and advanced materials.

The National Research Council (NRC) administers the Industrial Research Assistance Program (IRAP) which generates significant forms of assistance in the following areas:

- a network of technology advisors to assist in solving technical problems and provide access at no charge
- a group of technology resource specialists to address specific problems at no charge
- a portion of salary for science or engineering students from universities or colleges on projects representing a new technical initiative for the firms
- a portion of costs for the use of outside technical expertise to solve a specific problem or run tests on a process or product
- a portion of salaries for in-house and/or outside technical support, for R & D on processes or products which show an increment of technical growth from the company's current base.

The Program for Industry/Labour Projects (PILP) provides for technology transfer from NRC laboratories to the private sector, with appropriate supportive funding for enhancement of such transferred technology.

Look for industry specific R&D grant programs.

In addition to these federal cornerstone programs, there are many industry-specific programs for R & D which should also be considered, e.g., energy, pollution control, textiles, oil and gas, agriculture. Many provincial governments also have programs which supplement or fill in gaps in these federal programs.

A number of employment creation programs at the federal level for engineers and scientists provide term subsidies towards new jobs created in the private sector for undergraduates (as co-op students or for summer employment), graduates, post-graduate students, and professors returning to the private sector. As these new employees can be successfully integrated into an R & D project, the government provides yet another source of indirect funding for R & D.

> **Provincial equity corporations also help to share the risk.**

PROVINCIAL VENTURE CAPITAL COMPANIES

To encourage the private sector to commit funds and management expertise for investment as risk capital into small- and medium-sized companies, many provinces have legislated a venture capital program which provides a grant to qualified and registered investing companies in order to help leverage their investments and share the risk. Most programs provide that an investee will be eligible if it is engaged in R & D.

REAL LIFE 13.2: Governments Encourage Enterprise

The Wiz-Kid company was acquiring new technology for Canada which involved a unique process and required specialized equipment, along with concurrent research and development, to bring about successful product application, at a cost of $1 million.

Management sought professional advice and learned that governments often "share the risk" in significant business start-ups or expansions, by providing performance loans or non-repayable contributions (grants) as a tool of economic development. From a financing perspective these funds have the characteristic of equity to the business.

Both the federal and provincial governments supported this program with funding that had the essence of equity, as follows:

Federal
- Grant (DIPP) $400,000

Provincial
- Interest free loan   200,000
- Guarantee of private sector loan   125,000

                                          $725,000

The balance of the funding was arranged through the private sector, generally by leveraging the existing assets of the business.

TIP

Research and development is a high risk business activity (but with a high reward if successful!). It's "good business" to share that risk with other partners or alliances.

RECAP

We have investigated

- the growing importance of R & D
- the various sources for financing R & D, not only with money
- sweat equity, venture funds, and turf financing
- obtaining federal and provincial government assistance and the criteria required
- the value of sharing the risk.

....

CHAPTER 14

And Now... Back to the Bank

Success! Your business has moved beyond survival mode and is once again thriving. It's growing and maybe even reaching out to the global market place. Take a deep breath. It's time to reassess that possibly troubled relationship with the bank that first sparked your search for alternative financing sources.

Back to the bank! You may want to keep your bank as just one of many financing sources. Or you may have outgrown the need for alternative sources of financing altogether and the bank can now meet all of your financing needs.

Or indeed, if you have been fortunate to have had a reasonably good bank relationship throughout your challenging times, there may still be room for improvement.

This chapter will help you understand bank operations and the various financing services they offer and give you some practical guidance for assessing your relationship with your bank.

FIRST... SOME BANKING HISTORY

During the past decade, banking in Canada has undergone many changes. In the next decade, banking will undergo many more, even radical, changes. Understanding where the banks have come from and how their attitudes have evolved are key factors for successful dealings with your bank.

Treading Cautiously

In the first half of the 1990s, banks were "cautious." Most banks adopted very restricted lending practices to specific industries, and many reduced lines of credit and margin ratios to customers.

Logically, caution followed on the heels of the recessionary times of the early 1980s and early 1990s, tumultuous decades for banks.

The recession of 1981-84 caught the entire financial system off guard. It generated:

- substantial business bankruptcies
- annual loan losses of $2.5 billion
- large portfolios of non-performing loans.

Most banks had significant third world non-performing loans while at home they faced economic conditions that varied across the country. The major bank failures in western Canada, with the apparent questionable management practices, further shattered everyone's confidence.

After the Recession: Circle the Wagons!

Still smarting from the troubles of the mid '80s, the banks throughout the late '80s and early '90s began operating in a reactive mode. The guiding principle became *sound* loans rather than *safe* loans. *Sound* loans are made to companies in a stable industry with a specific history of profitable operations and cash flow. A *safe* loan is based primarily on collateral. In seeking *sound* loans, banks:

> Sound loans have become the keynote in banking.

- increased specialization
- became more selective in accounts and weeded out fragile customers and businesses in soft industry sectors
- concentrated efforts on successful businesses
- emphasized cash flow in business plans
- requested back-up security, where possible, from sources outside the business
- took a more proactive role in identifying problem accounts early and in taking corrective action
- ensured that return was commensurate with perceived risk, either by the direct interest rate or by loan administration fees
- enforced closer account supervision with regular financial reports, emphasis on accounts receivable collections, requests that redundant assets be sold, and closer monitoring of financial ratios and covenants.

The downturn and recession of 1989 through to 1995, coupled with a recognition of environmental concerns and collapse of real estate values led to early reactions of banks to reduce outstanding lines of credit, reduce margin covenants, and call for new injections of equity. In the most severe cases, loans were called on businesses in real estate or other targeted industry sectors.

Many bankers may say lending practices and standards have not changed — only circumstances and conditions have changed. From the point of view of small- and medium-sized businesses, however, there is certainly strong evidence of bankers being "gun shy" as a result of their experiences in the 1980s. Basically, the banks have changed the application of their standards!

"I'd Like to Make a Deposit." "R-e-a-d My Screen."

The latter part of the 1990s also marked the burgeoning depersonalization of banking services. The computer is king. Banks strongly encourage their clients to communicate by computer, fax, and voice mail, make your deposits into a machine, and so on. Even the credit process is automated. The account manager simply inputs data into a computer and up pops an appropriate "score" that determines if a loan is granted.

Depersonalization is most readily apparent in the dramatic increase in the number of accounts each account manager now handles; in many instances the account manager's client load has doubled and many predict it will double again.

New information technologies, new international trading blocks, the downfall of domestic trade barriers and the changing face of the capital markets have all contributed to new and innovative approaches in banking in this last decade of the century.

Regardless of a preponderance of automated services, banks are still very much in business and they want *your* business.

Banks want your business.

BANK COMMERCIAL SERVICES

In trying to get your business and your money, all banks promote the broad range of services they offer. You may not necessarily use all of the many services available, but to make the best financial decisions for your particular business, you should be familiar with the most significant products and their benefits. Here's your shopping list; these are discussed as follows:

- Operating Loans
- Non-revolving Loans
- Bankers' Acceptances
- Commercial Term Loans
- Commercial Mortgages
- Eurocurrency Loans
- Letters of Credit
- Other Commercial Services.

Operating Loans

Advances of a short-term nature are provided "at the pleasure of the bank" and are available for day-to-day operating purposes to

> **Operating loans are due on demand — "at the pleasure of the bank."**

supplement working capital requirements of the normal trade cycle. The amount available is established based on anticipated need, which is frequently based on detailed forecasts and cash flow analysis. Typically available in Canadian or U.S. currencies, operating credit lines can be in the form of :

- Direct demand advances
- Overdrafts
- Bankers' Acceptances (BAs), and
- Commercial Letters of Credit.

Rates are on a floating basis for demand advances and overdrafts, usually priced off prime or some other monetary standard such as LIBOR (the London Interbank Offering Rate). Fixed rate terms are available from 30 days to 364 days for BAs.

Operating credits are generally approved for a maximum period of one year and are subject to periodic review, at least annually.

Advances and payments are normally subject to minimum rollover multiples, in thousands of dollars, unless the account is operated as an overdraft.

These loans are typically secured by charges over accounts receivable and inventories. The levels of loans outstanding is usually capped based on specified margin levels, normally:

- Accounts receivable — 65 / 85% of good receivables, under 60 or 90 days
- Inventories — 40 / 50% of cost of finished goods on hand.

When establishing margin ratios, banks will take many factors into account:

- the company's track record of profits and retained cash flow
- the stability of the industry
- the payment terms and collection experience of the business
- the credit rating of the borrower's customers
- the legal jurisdiction of customers
- any prior returns and damaged goods experience
- the availability of contracts to support sales record
- the amounts owing to customers by the business, which could be set-off against an account receivable.

A later section, Understanding Bank Collateral Financing, provides more details on margin determination.

Non-Revolving Loans

Typically these loan agreements provide for repayment to be extended over a longer period of time, usually in excess of 12 months from the date when the initial disbursement of all or any portion of the loan is advanced. However, a non-revolving facility can be for less than one year, similar to bridge financing.

Although a business may use this type of loan for a number of purposes, it is usually used for fixed asset financing with security taken over fixed assets. Loan amounts are established based upon the company's financial position and its needs.

Advances under a non-revolving credit may be by a single drawdown of funds or a series of drawdowns and/or may fluctuate based on fixed asset purchases that are required from time to time.

Funding is usually available in all major currencies.

Utilization of non-revolving loans is in the form of direct advances.

Repayments are generally on a monthly basis, but quarterly, semi-annual, or annual terms are also available by special negotiation and arrangement. Other variations include deferring first or early payments, or having a balloon payment (final lump sum amount) at the end of the agreed repayment period.

Maximum amortization is usually 7 to 8 years; however, this may be extended on an exception basis.

Non-revolving loans are technically on demand and accordingly may be called in "at the pleasure of the bank" should circumstances warrant such action, and regardless of scheduled repayments being up-to-date.

Bankers' Acceptances

A Bankers' Acceptance is a term bill of exchange or draft drawn by an issuer on the bank and accepted by the bank. Upon acceptance, payment of the Bankers' Acceptance becomes a legal obligation not only of the issuer, but also of the accepting bank. Two names on the Acceptance, the accepting bank and issuer, are deemed to enhance its credit quality.

Bankers' Acceptances, (often referred to as BAs or "Acceptances") are one of the world's oldest money market instruments. They have long provided issuers with a convenient, cost-efficient source of short-term funds at fixed interest rates. Equally, Acceptances have provided investors with the advantage of a higher interest short-term investment backed by both the accepting bank and the issuer.

The contemporary use of BAs in Canada, however, dates from 1962 when the Canadian banks collaborated with the Bank of Canada to allow their introduction.

BAs are generally short-term instruments, typically of 30 to 365 days, although they can be written for longer terms as mid-term instruments.

TIP

SNAP

Take advantage of an interest rate window with Mid-Term BAs which are issuable quickly and cost-effectively.

Commercial Term Loans

These loans are available to businesses to finance the acquisition of medium- or long-term assets (specific assets, business expansion or business acquisition), working capital, or debt consolidation.

Terms generally vary from 1 to 5 years, but amortization may be over 8 to 15 years, depending on the nature and condition of the assets and their expected life.

Security is usually based on the fixed assets, rather than on current assets; therefore, there is no margining requirement for this type of loan.

Interest rates may be either floating or fixed. The option may exist to convert from a floating to a fixed rate during the term; however, a fixed rate can usually not be altered (of course, these rates will not be reduced during periods of falling interest rates).

Commercial Mortgages

These are granted against the security of commercial real estate.

Terms vary from 1 to 5 years, but amortization may be from 15 to 25 years.

In most instances, loans will be in the ratio of 60% of property value, although up to 75% may be considered in exceptional circumstances. As a consequence of the decimation of real estate values during the recessions in the 1980s and 1990s, banks have become more conservative in the lending ratio against real estate. As well, they will often only consider a commercial mortgage to an otherwise prosperous company or a property fully leased to prime AAA tenants.

> **Remember that banks are "gun shy" to lend against the security of real estate.**

Eurocurrency Loans

For larger companies, these credits can provide alternative and significant funding. These loans enable borrowers to match assets/liabilities and cash flows by currency.

In certain instances, these loans afford fixed rate funding.

Eurocurrency loans are available in any major currency traded by a bank. However, this market is dominated by U.S. dollar loans.

Borrowings on Eurocurrency markets are simplest when borrowing in round amounts greater than U.S. $250,000 and for round periods (standard "rollover periods" are 1, 2, 3, 6, 9 or 12 months). Borrowings in odd or smaller amounts or for non-standard periods may be available, but at a premium pricing.

Eurocurrency lending is based on the interbank offered rate for equivalent funds — primarily LIBOR (London Interbank Offered Rate), with limited availability in other money centres, such as NYBOR (New York), SIBOR (Singapore) and FIBOR (Frankfurt). Pricing is expressed as a margin over LIBOR and interest is ordinarily payable at maturity of the "rollover period," the market norm. Market practice in Canada is for interest to be collected no less frequently than quarterly.

Eurocurrency lending could be an option in an uncommitted short-term facility and, at the other extreme, in a committed term loan.

Letters of Credit

Letters of credit (LCs) are one of the most commonly used services that a bank offers to its customers. Yet, despite the simplicity and widespread use of LCs, the business community often misunderstands their role in commercial finance.

An LC is the bank's commitment to make a payment on behalf of a customer in connection with a specified transaction. When executed, the LC entitles the bank to reimbursement from the customer.

Canadian companies mostly use LCs when ordering imports. The importer can usually negotiate a better deal by paying with an LC because this eliminates the financial risk to the supplier in regard to the importer's credit worthiness.

To use LCs effectively, a company must understand two fundamental factors:

- the bank's obligations under an LC
- the LC's impact on the company's line of credit.

As soon as the applicant signs the document accepting the terms and conditions, the LC becomes a promissory note. Funds are set aside or reserved by the issuing bank to meet claims against the LC. The bank is committed to paying the LC once it receives certain specified documents, such as bills of lading. The LC must be honoured by the bank if the goods arrive in accordance with their description in the LC, even if they're defective.

That's why the importer should provide a sufficiently explicit description of the product in its application for the LC. The bank will compare the description of the goods in the LC with the description as presented in documents forwarded to it by the customs broker. If there's a notable discrepancy, the bank won't honour the LC.

An LC is a bank loan insofar as its value is the purchaser's liability. Because the bank is obligated to honour the LC, the applicant is required to secure the value of the letter. This security generally reduces its line of credit with the bank. Some banks will automatically reduce the company's working line of credit by the exact value of the LC as soon as the letter is issued. Take, for example, the situation where a manufacturer with a $500,000 credit line applies for an

Letters of credit carve a piece out of your operating line of credit.

LC to pay for $50,000 worth of materials. The bank may immediately reduce the full value of the LC from the working line of credit, leaving only $450,000 remaining.

But in some cases, another bank might only reduce the working line of credit by part of the value of LC; in effect, this bank is increasing the company's line of credit.

Whatever the disposition of goods, a company should pay close attention to the impact of its LCs on commercial finance. An unanticipated shortfall in its working line of credit due to LCs could have significant consequences on its day-to-day cash flow.

Other Commercial Services

Most banks offer some level of venture capital, mezzanine funding and leasing services.

Banks are becoming significantly involved in fee-based services. This may involve merchant banking-type functions (mergers and acquisitions, financial consulting, bridge financing) and money market functions (bankers' acceptances, commercial paper, unrated commercial paper). This is frequently referred to as "intermediation."

TIP

SNAP

Be cautious in arranging a "bridge financing" loan with a bank unless there is a solid take-out loan in place, otherwise a default may occur if repayment is not made when scheduled.

UNDERSTANDING BANK COLLATERAL FINANCING

Collateral or asset-based financing is often used to describe the operating (working capital) financing provided by banks.

The total credit review involves assessment and judgement related to management, cash flows, and business risk. However, the orientation to security or collateral in this lending is critical to a successful financing.

> **Asset-based financing focuses on quality of available security.**

The consequences of the recent recessions have meant more attention is paid to these matters through the close monitoring of margin ratio coverages.

Before reviewing the specific security-related criteria, note that certain businesses and industries are potentially heavily exposed and do not lend themselves to the general principles of collateral financing:

- Service businesses — because of the nebulous nature of the service provided and the propensity for disputes over quality of service.
- Contracting companies — because of the risk associated with unfinished contracts and statutory construction liens.
- Retail stores — consumer receivables are small and may dictate repossession in the event of default of payment.

Accounts Receivable

Receivables are preferred to inventory as a form of collateral because of their relative ease of recovery in the event of liquidation (the conversion of the asset to cash!).

The lender looks for certain favourable considerations:

- customer financial health
- diversified customer base
- warranties
- dilution.

Customer Financial Health

The creditworthiness of a borrower's major customers weighs heavily in a lender's evaluation of the ultimate collectibility of receivables. As credit information is readily available on large companies, these customers will help a lender make an objective and positive credit evaluation of the receivables. Smaller companies with a high credit rating would also provide good collateral to a lender.

In other words, a lender must be able to obtain sufficient credit information to be able to assess the credit worthiness of a borrower's customers.

The industries to which the borrower sells may heavily influence the bank's assessment of the quality of the accounts receivable. Are these industries cyclical? Likely to go out of fashion?

Diversified Customer Base

Lenders are concerned about a borrower's being economically dependent on a limited number of customers. This situation could result in two adverse repercussions:

- The collectibility of a significant percentage of the total accounts receivable could be in doubt as a result of a dispute with just one customer.
- The void created in the sales forecast by the loss of one customer could have a detrimental effect on the company's ability to remain viable.

If you can lessen this risk with mitigating factors, such as a relatively stable demand for the company's products as substantiated by signed contracts with the major customers, bring this to the lender's attention.

Warranties

For lenders, the existence of product guarantees and warranties waves another red flag of potential risk to the collectibility of receivables, especially in distress situations. You should highlight any mitigating factors, such as your company's superior corporate profitability and good product quality control, to reduce the lender's perceived risk.

Dilution

The calculation of the percentage of dilution is one of the most significant criteria lenders use to evaluate the quality of receivables collateral. Dilution is a measure of the erosion in the collectibility of receivables. The most common eroding factors are sales returns, cash and volume discounts, and advertising rebates. A lender's concern in this regard can be lessened if credit notes are processed on a timely basis so that there is assurance that the loan is secured by collectible receivables showing on the borrower's books.

> **Understand the principle of dilution when talking to your banker.**

Collectibility — Building the Bank's Confidence

The bank's major concern is: What is the ultimate collectibility of the receivables? Lenders tend to get nervous when they see red flags from special situations such as:

- overdue receivables
- foreign receivables
- consignment sales
- non-arm's length receivables
- bill and hold
- service receivables
- guaranteed sales
- pre-billing
- interest charges on overdue receivables
- contrary arrangements.

If your company has any of the above, you can still take steps to reassure the lender that you are a good risk.

Overdue Receivables

Generally, lenders will not give an advance against receivables that have been outstanding for more than 90 days where the normal sales terms are 30 to 45 days. Historically, the ultimate collectibility of these past due accounts is significantly impaired. Overdue accounts frequently signal the existence of potential problems — the customer's inability to service the obligation or the presence of a dispute.

In seasonal businesses, however, it is not uncommon to have the specified terms of sale extended beyond 90 days. "Dating," a technique of extending credit beyond normal sales terms, is frequently encountered in the textile and automotive supply industries. Datings allow manufacturers to ship their seasonal product as soon as it is manufactured, and thus avoid paying excessive warehousing costs. By accepting the goods prior to the season in which they are to be sold, retailers are assured the product will be on their shelves at the earliest possible date, without having to pay for it until the selling season actually arrives. If dating is common to the industry in question, lenders will usually advance against such receivables. Lenders, however, do normally finance these receivables beyond their due date.

Foreign Receivables

Foreign accounts receivable are generally not acceptable collateral because of the difficulty involved in registering a charge against them, the problems in establishing and verifying the customer risk and the potential additional costs incurred in their collection. Foreign accounts can be converted into eligible collateral, however, by arranging for insurance from the Export Development Corporation (EDC). Similarly, export insurance may be arranged through provincial development corporations or private insurers.

During the 1980s, the Bank of Montreal enhanced its ability and confidence in lending against U.S. receivables with the acquisition of the U.S.-based Harris Bankcorp. This provided local U.S. knowledge and security expertise. The Canada/U.S. Free Trade Agreement provides further stimulus to other Canadian banks to develop the specific capability to lend confidently against U.S. receivables.

Consignment Sales

In a consignment sale, title does not pass to the receiver of the merchandise. A consignment sale in law represents a bailment and not a valid sale. Therefore, lenders will not advance against such accounts. Because the merchandise is not on the borrower's premises, it will also be excluded by the lender for inventory financing purposes. To improve the borrowing ability, the company should attempt to negotiate a bona fide sale with the customer, rather than a consignment arrangement.

It is important to note that the consignment sale may provide a significant financing advantage to the customer, and so you should carefully evaluate the commercial trade-offs.

Non-arm's Length Receivables

Affiliate and subsidiary accounts are not eligible for financing because ultimate collectibility depends on the financial health of the total entity.

Bill and Hold

Bill and hold exists when the sale has been agreed on by the seller and the purchaser, but the merchandise has not been shipped to the purchaser. Experience has shown that cancellation is significantly higher with this type of sales agreement.

To make this type of receivable more acceptable to a lender, arrange to place the inventory in an independent warehouse at the risk of the customer and acknowledged as a sale by the customer.

Service Receivables

Historically, receivables for services rendered, such as professional services and appliance repairs, have not been acceptable as security for collateral financing, or if acceptable, only at a reduced margin ratio.

Guaranteed Sales

While ownership passes to the buyer in a guaranteed sale, the buyer maintains the absolute right, as distinct from the right of return under warranty or guarantee, to return the goods if he or she fails to resell the merchandise. In exceptional circumstances, lenders may provide financing on guaranteed sales at a reduced advance rate; however, they are normally reluctant to do so because of the uncertainty associated with the sale until such time as the buyer disposes of the goods.

Whenever possible, management should negotiate conventional sales terms with their customers. You don't want to be financing someone else's business!

Pre-Billing

Pre-billing is used as a device to bill a customer for work-in-progress or for merchandise prior to its physical transfer. The uncertainty associated with the collectibility of the related booked receivable contributes to excessive exposure on the collateral. Pre-billings are not usually eligible for collateral financing purposes.

Interest Charges on Overdue Receivables

Banks know from hard experience that the percentage of interest charges collected is small. As a result, these charges are ineligible for financing purposes.

To help the bank readily identify ineligible receivables such as interest charges, make sure your monthly aged trial balance of receivables shows these interest charges separately. This would also communicate to the lender that you are co-operative and forthright.

Contra Arrangements

A contra arrangement is one where the borrower sells to and purchases from the same customer. Contras represent a potential offset against any receivables due from the customer. As a result, lenders will not advance against receivables that have an offset (contra) that can be applied against the receivable.

Where practical, contra arrangements should be kept at a minimum. One of the reasons the banker asks for a list of accounts payable as part of the information monitoring package is to scrutinize for potential contra accounts.

Presenting Receivables in the Most Favourable Light

When presenting receivables as security to lenders, be prepared to make the best impression you can. It is to your benefit to provide:

- an accounts receivable trial balance, aged according to terms of sale
- details of the geographical distribution of customers
- names of major customers
- sales terms
- copies of major sales contracts, if any
- credit information on major customers.

Present details of your accounts receivable to assist your banker.

By going through a detailed analysis of the aged accounts receivable trial balance, the lender will be able to determine the "eligible" receivables. This rate can range anywhere from 50% to 90%, but is usually in the 65% to 85% range.

The lender arrives at the advance rate by looking at the history of the credit notes issued, that is, the number of returns, warranty claims, and all discounts such as volume and cash. These items are the dilution considerations previously discussed.

For example, if the dilution rate were historically 2% to 3%, a lender would not hesitate to advance on eligible receivables in the 75% to 85% range. If the dilution factor is historically 10% to 15%, however, the lender would likely prefer to advance in the range of 65% to 70%.

Inventory

Inventory financing works in a manner similar to accounts receivable financing. Its purpose is to enable borrowers to purchase merchandise when they need it, or to enable them to take advantage of preferential purchase prices or volume discounts.

The advance rate on inventory is usually anywhere up to 60% of eligible inventory, as opposed to 65% to 85% of eligible receivables, because of the following factors:

- A lender cannot monitor changes as easily in inventory as in accounts receivable.
- Experience has shown that complete recovery of the declared inventory value is uncommon since the most marketable inventory is usually disposed of by the borrower prior to liquidation, without being replaced.

Normally, raw materials and finished goods are acceptable for collateral financing purposes, but work-in-progress is usually not. In a distress situation, the cost of completing work-in-progress to a finished state often exceeds the net realizable value. In a liquidation situation, difficulties often arise in completing the product because of a lack of cooperation among the work force, an inadequate mix of components to complete the product, and an unwillingness on the part of customers to pay full value in a distress situation.

When evaluating a loan secured by inventory, the bank and any other lender will consider certain primary factors very carefully:

- liquidity
- seasonality
- perishable goods
- warranties and guarantees
- valuation of inventory.

Liquidity

Liquidity is determined by the inventory's marketability in its present form. The nature of the inventory has a significant effect on a lender's evaluation of its acceptability for financing. Commodities such as grain, lumber, metals and petroleum products, for example, are preferred collateral because their value can be readily monitored.

Other categories of finished goods, such as brand name food products, alcohol, and tobacco are also attractive to lenders because they have an established market. These categories commonly have a high rate of inventory turnover and relatively stable demand. These types of inventory, obviously, also have fewer unfavourable characteristics than products subject to fashion whims and technological obsolescence. High technology products are associated with higher than normal risk in the event of liquidation and, therefore, loan advance rates are often lower.

A lender is keenly aware of the potential shrinkage of inventory value, so you should be prepared to show evidence of your inventory's marketability. A good approach is to provide the lender with a list of firm orders for shipment within the current business cycle, supported by customers' purchase orders, if available.

Seasonality

Inventory of a seasonal nature carries the risk that if it's not sold during that season, it must be carried over for an entire year. For example, Christmas ornaments manufactured in the summer months for fall sales are generally accepted for financing during the summer and fall months. Inventory financing will decrease, however, as the season progresses and, by the end of the Christmas sales season, the inventory loan should be fully paid down or replaced by accounts receivable financing.

Lenders take this position because of the long time before the inventory would become saleable again. In addition, in the event of liquidation, the lenders would be faced with expensive storage, insurance and handling costs before there would be a new market for the inventory. An immediate sale of out-of-season inventory can normally command only "deep discount" distress prices.

You can reduce the lender's concerns by providing a cash flow illustrating the repayment of the inventory loan to coincide with the sale of the majority of the inventory while it is still in season. This cash flow should also be compared to the prior year's positive cash flow pay down.

Perishable Goods

Is your inventory perishable? This is of prime concern to lenders because of the losses that would be incurred in the event of spoilage and the impact this may have on the loan's recovery.

To reassure the lender, demonstrate that your company has taken adequate precautions to safeguard the inventory. You may even wish to invite them to visit your premises to inspect the facilities. You could also highlight the adequacy of the insurance coverage placed on the inventory.

Warranties and Guarantees

Lenders are reluctant to finance inventory that carries with it a warranty or guarantee. The net realizable value of such inventory is reduced significantly if the product is not accompanied by the warranty.

To alleviate this limitation, provide the lender with a performance bond. Or, a third party might be prepared to assume the warranty coverage in the event you, as the borrower, are unable to perform. Obviously, the lender does not want to be put in a position where only the borrower can provide the necessary guarantees and warranties.

Valuation of Inventory

Since the lender's main goal is to establish the reasonableness of the net realizable value of the inventory presented by the borrower, annual audited financial statements will obviously provide some comfort and should be offered in the normal course of events. In fact, detailed reporting of inventory is normally a prerequisite for inventory financing and, therefore, heavy reliance is put on the ability of the borrower to supply this information accurately to the bank.

It is very important to let your lender know that you have good, perpetual inventory records, frequent physical inventory counts and adequate allowance for obsolete or slow-moving inventory. The more comfort you can provide to the lender concerning control, valuation and the ability to report timely and objective inventory information — preferably monthly — the greater the chance for success when it comes time to negotiate or renegotiate a loan.

Other Considerations

Some other considerations that the lender would likely evaluate include:

- age of inventory
- inventory mix
- adequacy of marketing plans
- duty and GST consideration
- physical location of inventory.

TIPS

INSIDER'S

- The bank's willingness to lend against inventory is usually a function of confidence, which is established by understanding.
- A winning proposal will be well prepared and include documented summaries of the business' operating cycle and the inherent cash flow.

IS THE TERM "SERVICE CHARGE" A MISNOMER?

The banking industry's pricing basis for services has shifted dramatically in recent years. Two of the most important factors affecting the cost of financial services are a change in the way business customers use bank services and the general increase in operating expenses. Not to mention profit!

Today's business customers manage their current accounts instead of leaving large sums of money sitting in accounts which do not earn interest. The trend, as a consequence of business efficiency, is to put as much as possible into interest-bearing accounts, term deposits, or other instruments. As a result, the average cost of funds has risen because the banks now have much less low-cost money on deposit to lend out to borrowing customers.

A second factor, higher operating expenses, has affected banks just as it has all businesses. A unique factor of costs to banks is the net cost of capital, which is impacted by the capital adequacy rules set down by the Bank for International Settlements (BIS). Recently increased requirements have affected this major operating cost for the banks.

Each bank's method of dealing with these factors varies, but in general, all banks have moved in two ways:

- to adjust interest rates to a level which covers the actual cost of funds and the credit risk factor
- to introduce fees for other specific financial services.

It All Adds Up!

The banks charge fees to cover their actual expenses and ensure that these costs are paid for, as far as possible, directly by those who are using the services. The latest trend, the "unbundling" of the pricing for identified services, at least makes it possible for you to know the cost and its reason.

> Note how banks have "unbundled" their services to allow them to charge for specific services.

- Application Fee
  The application/evaluation fee is charged for evaluating financing proposals and loan applications and it reflects the time and expertise expended by the bank. Like most professionals, the banker is charging for his or her time. There is an extensive level of review and due diligence to be carried out on every application.

  The application/evaluation fee is, thus, a one-time set-up fee, which may or may not be refundable. It may be expressed as a flat sum or as a percentage of the amount of the loan being requested. Generally, it is paid before the evaluation begins.

- Renewal Fee
  A separate fee may be charged for updating and re-evaluating the financing on each renewal date — often annually.

- Administration Fee
  The administration fee covers the ongoing cost of administering a loan account. The actual amount will be established as part of the agreement between the customer and the bank. As a rule, it is paid at a specified time, either monthly or annually.

- Interest Rate
  The difference between the interest rate paid for deposits (usually called the cost of funds) and the interest rate charged to borrowers

is called the spread. Historically, banks used the spread to cover virtually all of their costs, including administration costs. Customers want more and more information, so the trend for banks to separate or unbundle costs and charge where possible on a user-pay basis is a welcome one.

Interest Rates are More Than Just Interesting

When banks quote on interest rates for a loan, you need to consider several factors, such as term, level of equity and type of account. These factors are a part of the "risk" assessment.

The *length of term* refers to the total time it takes to repay (i.e., to amortize) the loan. Basically, the longer it takes to repay a loan, the more it will cost because the extended term reflects a higher risk factor. There are the possibilities of unforeseen problems developing, such as changes in economic climate or in personal circumstances.

Level of equity refers to how much financing is required from the bank relative to the total amount of financing internally provided or obtained from other investors. If the bank loan is 75% of the total financing requirements, expect to pay a higher rate of interest than if the loan is for 25 or 35% of the total requirements. The greater the amount of equity invested, the smaller the risk to the bank and, therefore, the lower the interest rate.

The *type of account* relates to the industry, the length of time in business, the historical record of earnings and prior experience in borrowing. All of these factors also affect the apparent risk to a banker.

TIP

SNAP

Carefully assess all of the factors when comparing the cost of borrowing — not just the interest rate. Watch out for hidden or separate costs that should be taken into account.

You Got the Loan!

Over the past two to three decades, banks have varied their practices in the use of formal Commitment or Offer of Credit letters/agreements. However, in recent years the banks are standardizing their formats and thereby avoiding client misunderstandings as to the price, terms, and conditions of each credit.

In general terms, the format of a Loan Agreement deals with the following matters:

- definition and amount of credit facilities
- purpose of financing
- repayment terms
- restrictions on availability
- costs
- prepayment conditions
- conditions precedent
- representations and warranties
- covenants
- events of default
- other matters.

TIPS

INSIDER'S

- Read the loan agreement very carefully. If you don't understand a provision, ask questions and expect answers. If you are still unsure, seek outside professional advice before signing on the dotted line.

- Do not agree to understandings or covenants that you cannot possibly meet — they will come back to haunt you. And if the banker suggests otherwise, take in this page!

NICHE BANKS — A NICE ALTERNATIVE FOR SOME

The 1980 revision to the Bank Act divided financial institutions into Schedule A (domestic banks) and B (foreign banks). In 1988, these designations were changed to Schedule 1 and Schedule 2. Schedule 1 banks, with which we are all familiar, attempt to serve the broad needs of all customers. The Schedule 2 banks are generally niche marketers and all but one are foreign-owned.

Schedule 2 Banks

Schedule 2 banks can be controlled or wholly-owned subsidiaries of other institutions. Most are foreign-owned, which is the basis on which major international banks are able to carry on business in

Canada. As a group, they are limited to owning a percentage of the assets of the Canadian banking system. The Canada/U.S. Free Trade Agreement has provided an increased growth opportunity for Schedule 2 banks with a U.S. parent.

Almost all Schedule 2 banks are foreign-owned subsidiaries but there is one bank operating in this category that is indeed Canadian and not an outsider. The Laurentian Bank of Canada is the only domestically owned Schedule 2 bank and is a major force in Quebec retail banking. The bank's focus has been the retail market for the past 143 years.

The Laurentian Bank (until 1987, called the Montreal and City District Savings Bank) and its 130 branches are wholly owned by the Laurentian Group, a financial-services conglomerate. That's the main reason it operates as a Schedule 2 bank. If it were a Schedule 1 bank, ownership by the Laurentian Group or any other shareholder would be limited to 10%. But it certainly has a Schedule 1 mentality! Laurentian is an aggressive competitor in Montreal where it has 114 branches (the other 16 are sprinkled across Canada, as of March 1991). In June of 1991, Laurentian expanded further with the acquisition of the assets and branch network of the insolvent Standard Trust, allowing a quantum leap in growth throughout Ontario and in its status as a truly Canadian bank.

The Schedule 2 Target

> Understand the particular niche of each Schedule 2 bank.

The Schedule 2 banks target narrow market niches and then focus on specializing and capturing a significant portion of that market.

Many of the international banks have extensive worldwide branch networks and they offer strong support in international trade. Others provide significant domestic support in Canada for certain foreign corporations doing export business in Canada. Bank of Boston Canada has been unique in Canada in its specialization in factoring. Citibank Canada, during a period in the 1980s, operated a prominent venture capital division.

In doing business with a Schedule 2 bank, it is important to identify its specific market niche and area of strength to ensure that these services are compatible with your requirements. More recently, certain Schedule 2 banks have introduced branchless banking to Canada. Their low overhead drives a strong competitive force.

Is a Schedule 2 Bank the Right Match for Your Company?

In their marketing efforts, Schedule 2 banks often cite five key factors that set them apart from their Schedule 1 counterparts in servicing the mid-market:

- personal attention
- client uniqueness
- quick response time
- continuity of personnel
- international connections.

Personal Attention

The asset base of Schedule 2 banks is small by Canadian standards and, as such, each account is very important. Unlike the Schedule 1 banks whose lending officers are burdened with existing heavy portfolios, Schedule 2s are generally structured so that each account executive has a significantly smaller portfolio of accounts. In recent years, account managers of Schedule 1 banks have consistently complained of the increasingly large portfolio of accounts assigned to them.

Client Uniqueness

With the smaller portfolios of the Schedule 2s, the executives can take the time to comprehend the unique circumstances surrounding their clients. Unlike larger banks, which lump clients in with other companies of the same industry, they take the time required to know the client's industry and company in greater depth, thereby enabling them to positively respond to often rapidly changing credit requirements.

Quick Response Time

The Schedule 2 banks maintain that they enhance the credit response time in that the clients are dealing with the decision makers, not a branch manager and staff whose every decision seemingly must be approved by "Head Office." Significant credit requests are handled by a credit committee process, presented by the Bank executive, thereby eliminating the multi-layered bureaucratic credit process which often loses the "human" side of the credit.

Turnaround time on new proposals, from receipt of the proposal and prospect contact to the issuance of a discussion letter which outlines the proposed terms and conditions of the credit, is often 24 hours, thereby providing the client with superior service.

Continuity of Personnel

With the Schedule 1 banks, one of the most frustrating experiences that clients face is the continuous turnover of bank personnel. The client is constantly faced with the task of "re-educating" his or her account manager, sometimes annually. Because of the unique operations of Schedule 2 banks, their executives are not faced with the frustrations caused by a large bureaucratic operation. This results in a stable satisfied workforce and less frequent turnover of personnel.

International Connections

The international presence and contacts of a Schedule 2 bank can be a valuable assistance if you are either expanding operations internationally, requiring credit checks on foreign customers or supplying letters of credit to overseas suppliers.

But as Always... Be Wary of the Downside

Negative aspects can surface when dealing with Schedule 2 banks. Key things to be wary of include:

- remote approvals
- ceiling on lending portfolio
- handling of accounts in arrears.

Remote Approvals

Although smaller credits may be approved locally, larger credits will require regional or head office approval at a location outside the country. Also, subsequent alterations or administrative matters may require remote approval. This remoteness may generate an appearance of disinterest in an account or create a reluctance to submit a matter for approval.

Ceiling on Lending Portfolio

Schedule 2 banks in Canada were subjected in total to a limited level of lending in relation to the size of the Schedule 1 banks' marketplace. This limitation has been somewhat relaxed, especially in respect of U.S.-originated Schedule 2 banks.

As well, each Schedule 2 is restricted to a lending portfolio, bearing a specific relationship to its capital base.

These factors can have a bearing on the availability of follow-up funding, if later required.

Handling of Accounts in Arrears

Banks are required to provide for losses on loans with arrears of interest exceeding 90 days. For a bank with a small capital base, a large account in arrears might represent a formidable problem if not corrected in 90 days. As this might require an infusion of outside capital, it would likely put unrealistic pressure on the administration of the arrears circumstance, perhaps leading to a premature call of a loan.

BANK FINANCING FOR SMALL OR STARTING-OUT BUSINESSES

In the early stages of business, when the requirements are less than $500,000, it is hard to interest conventional term lenders — simply because of the fixed cost in administering small loans. Most small businesses turn to their bank for a substantial level of financial support — often more than the bank is able to provide using prudent lending criteria. Also the bank is caught in the same efficiency squeeze. It takes time and money to administer a working capital loan with a modest "interest spread" contribution.

Starting in the 1980s, the approach of some banks to a small business requirement up to $100,000 was to make a personal loan to the entrepreneur, usually secured by outside "hard" security such as a collateral mortgage on a residence. The bank would then allow the entrepreneur the freedom to use these funds at his or her discretion. This trend continues today.

Because of the upsizing of conventional term loans, an increasingly important component of small business financing is the federal guaranteed Small Business Loan (sometimes referred to as a Business Improvement Loan or BIL), which is usually funded and administered by a bank.

The SBLA Solution

Under the federal Small Business Loans Act (SBLA), banks can provide Business Improvement Loans (BILs) to help small business succeed. Since the program was first established in 1961, the SBLA has provided more than 275,000 BILs amounting to over $8 billion.

This is a lot of financial support for small business, yet it has not been a well-known nor well-accepted program.

At first, many banks did not encourage entrepreneurs to use the program because of several factors:

- the limited interest rate spread available because of the statutory capped interest rate mark-up chargeable
- the extra paper work required to register the loan with the government
- the periodic hassles received from the government when a claim has been made
- the limited guarantee, which did not cover 100% of the loan.

However, the program is an important one and it's a good source for finding the first term loan for a small but growing business.

A New and Improved SBL Program

After lengthy lobbying and pressure from the business community, as of April 1993 legislation was passed that significantly enhanced the Small Business Loan program. Many of the changes should serve as a greater incentive to both banks and business people to take advantage of the program.

> Most small businesses should have a BIL to build their operations.

The current criteria include:

- maximum loan amount increased to $250,000
- federal government guarantee is 90%
- allowable interest mark-up is to 13/4%
- financing may be for up to 100% of cost of fixed assets acquired
- fixed assets acquired in the preceding six months may be refinanced, thus restoring working capital
- eligible businesses may have sales of up to $5 million
- restriction on personal guarantees of each individual shareholder to 25% of original loan balance, and prohibition on taking a charge on personal assets to support the guarantee
- broad definition of eligible business.

BILs are ideally suited to small- and medium-sized businesses, particularly start-ups and emerging growth situations. The key advantages of these loans are the high ratio of loan permitted under the program criteria and the ability to restore working capital depleted through fixed asset acquisitions.

SO, HOW GOOD IS YOUR RELATIONSHIP WITH YOUR BANK?

In the coming year, you may deal with one or many banks depending on your business' size, geographic location and complexity of operations. From a strictly objective viewpoint, banks are one of the largest and certainly most critical suppliers to the business.

Banks do not just provide credit. Beyond their lending function, they are also key advisors for:

• cash management
• efficient accounting for incoming and outgoing cash
• international trading
• risk management
• smooth and productive business operations.

Banks now think you are important. They want to nurture their relationship with you. Indeed, the day-to-day interaction between line personnel in the bank and in the client's compa-

Banks think your business is important to them.

ny are just the starting points. Relationships move all the way up the respective organizations. As with any relationship, quality can be a critical factor.

Just as an annual personnel review is fundamental to your business' success, so is an annual review of your bank and your relationship with it.

Your company's financial managers or you as the owner, with input from operating personnel, should evaluate your various bank relationships on an annual basis. Use questions in Quick Check 14.1 as a guide. This evaluation should be the basis for an open, candid, and constructive meeting to discuss the positive and negative aspects of the relationship.

Quick Check 14.1 You and Your Bank: The Annual Check-Up

❑ Account Managers

✓ Is there a clear line of communication, with a designated lead contact person?

✓ Is there knowledgeable back-up to all key people?

✓ Are the account managers proactive in maintaining relationships between the company and senior bank officers?

✓ Do the account managers come forward with new and well thought out ideas?

✓ Do the account managers understand the business?

✓ Are the frequency and format of contacts appropriate?

✓ Is there a feeling of mutual trust and respect?

❑ Attitude

✓ Are bank personnel flexible in reviewing legal documentation, and do they recognize the mutual advantage of having agreements that are fair and balanced?

✓ Do the account persons let you know that your account is important to the bank?

❑ Service

✓ Timeliness of processing transactions?

• Regular?
• Special?

✓ Accuracy in processing transactions?

✓ Responsiveness and timeliness in resolving problems or errors?

✓ Are special requirements handled and processed expediently?

❑ Pricing

✓ Are costs competitive?

✓ Are charges fairly levied?

❑ Staff

✓ Quality of individual line relationships?

✓ Professionalism of bank personnel?

✓ Continuity/turnover of staff?

✓ Availability of knowledgeable back-up to each function?

RECAP

We have reviewed:

- some banking history
- changing attitudes in banks — for the worse
- but they really *do* want your business
- various types of loans:
  - operating and non-revolving
  - bankers' acceptances
  - commercial term and mortgages
  - Eurocurrency
  - letters of credit
- bank collateral financing
- factors affecting the value of your accounts receivable
- building confidence in their collectibility and the factors that can cause concern
- inventory and possible dangers
- service charges and what they mean
- checking out the interest
- and the fine print when you *do* get the loan
- Schedule 2 banks — advantages and drawbacks
- the Small Business Loans Act and the SBL program, and
- use the Quick Check to assess the relationship between you and your bank.

Looking to the Future: Tomorrow's Bank

Banks will continue to undergo many changes throughout this next decade:

- The diennial review of the Bank Act is expected to relax the ownership restrictions on banks, thereby increasing competitive pressures in the industry.
- Foreign entrants into Canada will change the way banking is carried-out, low overhead and minimal service.
- The merger of some of Canada's larger domestic banks will likely move their focus into the large-scale international arena and further from "Main Street" Canada.
- The depersonalizing of bank operations and services and the inherent automation and computerization of many functions will continue.
- Per capita workloads among bank personnel and the focus on customers' use of automated services will continue to increase.
- Alternative accumulations of capital will continue to expand — pension funds, as a result of the ageing population and venture capital resulting from tax driven incentives.
- The need to introduce creative ways to structure deals will continue to increase.

MAKING YOUR BUSINESS THEIR BUSINESS

With these factors and current trends, we can happily anticipate many novel and interesting products, services and marketing approaches in the future. To keep our business, banks will likely:

- demonstrate an improved understanding and determination of business risk, with an inherent higher risk premium recovered in the interest rate or extra charges
- expand industry specialization even further

- increase their focus on environmental concerns in view of the perceived level of risk
- move away from real estate-backed lending
- continue the weakened traditional bank leasing business
- renew their focus on international trade and inherent backing of banking products and services, in support of the emphasis by governments
- with the increasing enhancement of information technologies, expand electronic communication and remote terminal access to bank services and facilities — from funds transfer to balance and transaction verification to issuance of letters of credit and commercial paper
- make networking of EDI (electronic data interchange) and EFT (electronic funds transfer) readily available to all business clients
- enable account managers to improve efficiency and productivity and delegate monitoring of loan covenants by way of compliance certificates
- expand fee-based business through assuming the role of intermediation, where the banker takes an active role in private placements for the benefit of clients and uses the synergy of their investment dealer affiliations
- extend off balance sheet products, such as swaps and long-term standby credits
- package and underwrite the issuance of unrated commercial paper and securitization of bank customer receivables
- move towards a consolidation of banking relationships — syndication of lending deals will be fewer or smaller.

SO, BE NICE TO YOUR BANKER

Here are four basic tenets which will help you develop and maintain a good relationship with your banker.

1. Whenever you must provide information to your banker, make sure the presentation is:
   - clear
   - thorough
   - realistic
   - timely.
2. Make your banker part of your team.
3. Keep your banker informed.
4. Never surprise your banker.

And finally … keep in mind: the bank builds its business by building yours!

GLOSSARY

ABILITY TO PAY (ABILITY TO SERVICE)
Borrower's ability to meet principal and interest payments on long-term obligations out of earnings.

ACCELERATION CLAUSE
Provision, normally present in a debenture agreement, mortgage or other contract, that the unpaid balance is to become due and payable if specified events of default should occur. Such events often include failure to meet interest, principal, or sinking fund payments; insolvency; and non-payment of taxes on mortgaged property.

ACCRUED INTEREST
The amount of interest accumulated since the last interest payment date.

ACID TEST RATIO
Simple ratio of a company's liquid assets to current liabilities. Such assets include cash, marketable securities, and accounts receivable.

AFTER ACQUIRED CLAUSE
Clause in a mortgage or loan agreement providing that any additional mortgageable property acquired by the borrower after the mortgage is signed will be additional security for the obligation.

ANNUAL CLEANUP
A provision normally included in a line of credit agreement. It requires a borrower to "clean-up" its loans (have a zero loan balance) for a specified time during one or more periods a year.

APPRAISED VALUE
An estimate of the current market value used in evaluating the assets pledged as security for a loan.

ASSET COVERAGE
Extent to which a company's net assets cover a particular debt obligation, class of preferred stock, or equity position.

ASSIGNMENT
The sale of a commercial contract or security by one party to another, usually for a lump-sum payment.

BALLOON
An extraordinarily large payment that comes due in some serial or sinking fund bond issues.

BANK ACT
The federal government legislation which governs the way banks operate in Canada.

BANK OF CANADA
Formed in 1934, the Bank of Canada is empowered by statute to regulate credit and currency in the best interests of the country.

BANK FOR INTERNATIONAL SETTLEMENTS (BIS)
Profit-making clearing agency based in Basle for central bank shareholder members in foreign exchange and Eurocurrency markets. The U.S. Federal Reserve Board (FRB) is not a member for technical reasons, and the U.S. sharcholding is through Citibank. The BIS acts as principal forum for routine meetings of central bank governors (always attended by an FRB member). Its financial accounts are denominated in Swiss gold francs. Dividends are paid annually in dollars at the day's Zurich Swiss franc spot rate.

BANK RATE
The minimum rate at which the Bank of Canada makes advances of a short-term nature to the chartered banks, savings banks and investment dealers.

BANKER'S DRAFT
Draft payable on demand and drawn by or on behalf of the bank itself. It is regarded as cash and cannot be returned unpaid. Often used in international trade.

BANKERS' ACCEPTANCES
A bill of exchange, or draft, drawn by the borrower for payment on a specified date, and accepted by a chartered bank. Upon acceptance, the bill becomes, in effect, a postdated certified cheque.

BASE CURRENCY
Currency against which exchange rates are normally quoted in a given centre or country, e.g., the U.S. dollar or U.K. sterling.

BASIS POINT
A measurement unit defined as one hundredth of one percent. Expressed in dollars, for example, a return of 25 basis points means $25 were earned on each $10,000 of assets. Basis points are units in which interest/ discount rates, fees, etc., are quoted: 1% equals 100 basis points.

BEAR MARKET
A market that experiences a period of falling prices, usually brought on by the anticipation of a declining economy. "Bearish" investors are pessimistic about the stock market.

BEARER
Person possessing a bill or note payable to bearer, i.e., ownership is presumed to be with the person bearing or holding the bill or note.

BEARER FORM
A security on which payments are made to the party that has physical possession of the security. There is no registered owner of the security.

BENEFICIAL OWNER
Person who enjoys the benefits of ownership even though title is in another name.

BILL OF EXCHANGE
An unconditional order in writing addressed by one person to another, signed by the person giving it, requiring the person to whom it is addressed to pay at a fixed future date a certain sum in money to the order of a specific person or to bearer.

BOILERPLATE
Standard legal language, often in fine print, used in most contracts, wills, indentures, prospectuses, and other legal documents.

BOND
Usually a fixed interest security under which the issuer contracts to pay the lender a fixed principal amount at a stated date in the future, and a series of interest payments, either semi-annually or annually. Interest payments may vary through the life of the bond. The issuer may be a government, municipal or corporate entity. Bonds maturing in less than 5 years are described as short term, between 6 and 15 years as medium term and more than 15 as long term. In the U.S. a bond is normally for more than 10 years.

BOOK VALUE
Value of a corporation or of a corporate asset according to accounting records. Also known as net asset value. It is determined by dividing the number of issued shares into a company's net assets.

BRIDGING/BRIDGE LOAN
A short-term loan to cover the purchase or construction of an asset until permanent financing, frequently a previously arranged mortgage loan, can be drawn down against the completed asset.

BULL MARKET
A market in which there is a prolonged rise in the price of stocks and bonds. Bull markets usually last a few months and are characterized by a high volume of trading. People who are "bullish" are optimistic about the future of the stock market.

BUSINESS CYCLE
Recurrence of periods of expansion (recovery) and contraction (recession) in economic activity with effects on inflation, growth and employment.

BUSINESS PLAN
A statement in words and numbers of the goals of a business and how and when the owner(s) propose to reach these goals. The business plan should also include a statement of the history of the business and of its owners.

BUSINESS RISK
Sometimes referred to as an economic risk or operating risk, it is reflected in the variability of the firm's earnings (earnings before interest and taxes).

CALL LOAN
Commercial bank loan payable on demand by the lender and repayable at any time by the borrower.

CAPACITY
An assessment of ability and willingness to repay a loan from anticipated future cash flow or other sources.

CAPITAL INVESTMENTS
Money used to purchase permanent fixed assets for a business, such as land, buildings or machinery. Also, money invested in a business on the understanding that it will be used to purchase permanent assets rather than to cover day-to-day operating expenses.

CAPITALIZATION
The total amount of debt and equity issued by a company.

CAPITAL LEASE
Lease that under Financial Accounting Standards must be reflected on a company's balance sheet as an asset and corresponding liability. Generally, this applies to leases where the lessee acquires essentially all of the economic benefits and risks of the leased property.

CAPITAL STRUCTURE
The mix of the various types of debt and equity capital maintained by a firm. The more debt capital a firm has in its capital structure, the more highly levered the firm is considered to be.

CAPITAL TURNOVER
Annual sales divided by average stockholder equity (net worth).

CASH COW
Business that generates a continuing flow of cash. Such a business usually has well-established brand names whose familiarity stimulates repeated buying of the products.

CASH CYCLE
The period of time from the point a firm makes an outlay to purchase raw materials to the point cash is collected from the sale of the associated finished goods. The cash cycle represents the amount of time the firm's cash is tied up.

CASH FLOW FORECAST
An estimate of the timing and amount of money which will be coming in and going out of a business, usually on a month-by-month basis for the period of one or two years.

CASH MANAGEMENT
The management of liquid securities so as to maximize the return, and, at the same time, meet the payment of obligations that come due.

CENTRAL BANK
Major regulatory bank in a nation's monetary system, generally government controlled. Its role normally includes control of the credit system, note-issuance, supervision of commercial banks, management of exchange reserves and the national currency's value as well as acting as the government's banker. In Canada, it is the Bank of Canada; in the United States, the Federal Reserve Board; in the U.K., the Bank of England.

CHARACTER
An assessment of a businessman's dependability as a person.

CHATTEL MORTGAGE
A charge over goods or equipment of a movable nature, as opposed to real estate.

COLLATERAL
An asset/security which is pledged to support/secure a loan, e.g., a collateral mortgage on a house or a pledge of a bond taken as security by a bank to support a term or operating loan.

COLLATERAL MORTGAGE
A loan backed by a promissory note and the security of a mortgage on a property. The money borrowed may be used for the purchase of the property itself or for another purpose.

COMMERCIAL PLEDGE
In Quebec, a form of security whereby machinery and equipment pertaining to a business are given as security for a loan to a business.

COMMITMENT FEE
Fee charged by lenders on the committed loan facility.

COMPENSATION BALANCE
Portion of a commercial loan, usually expressed as a percentage of the loan which the borrower is required to keep on deposit with the bank in lieu of other fees or charges.

CONDITIONS
The limits written into an agreement between a borrower and lender. The limits specify exactly what each party is expected to do in exchange for the benefits each will receive.

CONFORMED COPY
Copy of an original document with the essential legal features, such as the signature and seal, being typed or indicated in the writing.

CONSOLIDATION LOAN
Loan that combines and refinances other loans or debt. It is normally an instalment loan designed to reduce the dollar amount of monthly payments.

CONTINGENCY PLAN
An alternate plan of action to use if circumstances change.

CONVERTIBLE
A bond or other financial instrument which can be exchanged by the holder for a stated number of common shares at a predetermined price.

COST OF CARRY
Out-of-pocket costs incurred while an investor has an investment position, among them interest on long positions in margin accounts, dividends lost on short margin positions, and incidental expenses.

COST OF FUNDS
The interest paid on deposits.

COUNTRY RISK
Risk of lending funds to or making an investment in a particular country.

COUPON
Interest rate payable on bonds, whether bearer or registered. It also refers to the detachable certificate entitling the bearer to payment of the interest.

COVENANT
Promise in a trust indenture or other formal debt agreement that certain acts will be performed and others refrained from.

COVERAGE RATIOS
Ratios, such as times interest earned, total debt coverage, and overall coverage ratio, that measure the ability of a firm to meet its fixed financial obligations.

CREDIT LINES
An uncommitted, unadvised (or a committed, advised) facility opened up by one bank in favour of a customer or another bank.

CREDIT RATING
Overall credit worthiness of a borrower. In the U.S., the two rating agencies are Moody's and Standard & Poor's. In Canada, a top agency is Dominion Bond Rating Service. A top rating is described as "triple A" or "AAA."

CREDIT RISK
Risk that a borrower may default on his obligations; a danger that repayment will not take place.

CREDIT UNIONS
Financial co-operation organizations comprising individuals with a common affiliation, e.g. employer, neighbourhood, nationality. They accept members' deposits in the form of share purchases, pay interest out of earnings while providing consumer instalment credit for their members.

CROSS DEFAULT
Clause in a loan agreement stipulating that default by borrower on any other loans will be regarded as a default on the loan governed by that clause.

CROWN JEWELS
The most desirable entities within a diversified corporation as measured by asset value, earning power and business prospects.

DEBENTURE
A written acknowledgement of a debt; a bond. In the U.S., a debenture, whether straight or convertible, is secured by a general guarantee but not a lien on specific assets, while bonds are unsecured. In the U.K. and Canada, a debenture is usually secured by a charge on corporate assets, while bonds are unsecured.

DEBT/EQUITY RATIO
A comparison of debt and equity used to measure the financial health of a business.

DEBT MANAGEMENT
Manipulation of three aspects of debt: the level of interest rates, the pattern of ownership, and the maturity schedule.

DEBT SERVICE RATIO (REQUIREMENT)
The cash flow available to pay debt principal and interest requirements.

DEFAULT
The failure of a borrower to repay either the interest or the principal according to the conditions governing the loan. In certain cases, the creditors may consent to a rescheduling of the payments to avoid default.

DEMAND FOR PAYMENT
A term which describes an action which may be taken by a lender when a borrower is in default. The demand is usually a formal request for repayment of the outstanding balance in full within a certain period of time.

DEMAND LOAN
A loan which must be repaid in full on demand.

DOCUMENTARY LETTERS OF CREDIT
A letter of credit guaranteeing payment by the issuing or opening bank in favour of an exporter against presentation of shipping and other documents. These instruments are known as commercial letters of credit in the United States.

DUE DILIGENCE
The conducting of reasonable investigative procedures by the underwriter and other persons to provide a defensible basis for believing that there are no misrepresentations contained in a prospectus.

ENTREPRENEUR
A person who starts, organizes, and manages a business, who invests money in it, and who thus accepts the risk of either profit or loss.

EQUITY
The value of a business after all debts and other claims are settled. In addition, the amount of cash a business owner invests in the business. Also, the difference between the price for which a property could be sold and the total debts registered against it.

EVERGREEN CREDIT
Revolving credit with no fixed maturity date, which a bank has the option once annually to convert into a term loan.

FACE VALUE
The nominal value which appears on the face of a document recording an entitlement, generally a certificate or bond. For indebtedness, the amount to be repaid at maturity.

FACTORING
Financial service whereby a firm sells or transfers title to its accounts receivable to a factoring company, which then acts as principal, not as agent. The receivables are usually sold without recourse, meaning that the factor cannot turn to the seller in the event accounts prove uncollectible.

FLOATING CHARGE
Charge or assignment on a company's total assets as collateral for a loan, without specifying a fixed charge on specific assets.

FLOATING RATE
A situation where the interest rate or rate of exchange is determined solely by market forces.

FRONT END FEES
Fees paid when a loan is arranged, such as management fees.

GUARANTEE
An undertaking by a bank or other party (the guarantor) to stand behind the current obligations of a third party and to carry out these obligations should the third party fail to do so, e.g. a loan guarantee under which A makes a loan to B against a guarantee of repayment provided by bank C.

HYPOTHEC
Lien on real estate (Quebec).

HYPOTHECATION
The pledge of property and assets to secure a loan. Hypothecation does not transfer title, but it does provide the right to sell the hypothecated property in the event of default.

INDENTURE
Legal contract spelling out the obligations of a security issuer, and the rights of the holder of the security.

INSOLVENT
Being unable to pay debts as they become due; not strictly the same as BANKRUPTCY.

INTEREST COVER
Ability of borrower to pay the interest payments due on a borrowing from currently available financial resources.

JOINTLY AND SEVERALLY
Legal terminology in relation to a liability. The obligation may be enforced against all obligators jointly or against any one of them separately.

JUNIOR ISSUE
Debt or equity that is subordinate in claim to another issue in terms of dividends, interest, principal or security in the event of liquidation.

JUNIOR SECURITY
Debt with lower priority claim on assets and income than a senior security.

JUNK BOND
A bond with a speculative credit rating. The bonds are called junk because they are issued by companies without long and consistent track records of sales and earnings, or with questionable credit strength. Because junk bonds are risky investments, returns can be high.

LEGAL TENDER
The coin or currency which the supreme monetary authority of a country declares to be universally acceptable therein as medium of exchange.

LETTER OF CREDIT
Financial instrument issued by a bank guaranteeing the payment of a customer's drafts up to a stated amount for a specified period.

LIEN
A charge placed over an asset by such parties as (1) the seller of that asset, or (2) in the case of construction or repairs, by the person (contractor) who carries out the work. The lien holder may take possession until the asset/work is paid for in full. Liens must be registered under the various provincial laws in order to be protected and enforceable.

LINE OF CREDIT
An agreement negotiated between a borrower and a lender which establishes the maximum amount against which a borrower may draw. The agreement also sets out other conditions, such as how and when money borrowed against the line of credit is to be repaid.

LIQUID ASSETS
Also quick assets. Cash and readily disposable current assets.

LIQUIDATION
Dissolution or winding up of a company, either voluntary or compulsory. Disposal of assets for cash.

LOAN AGREEMENT
Contract between the bank and the borrower in which the terms and conditions of a credit commitment are recorded.

LONDON INTERBANK OFFERED RATE (LIBOR)
Rate that the most creditworthy international banks dealing in eurodollars charge each other for large loans.

MARKETING PLAN
A statement in words and numbers of how a business proposes to sell its product and/or services and to whom. It is an integral part of the business plan.

MERCHANT BANK
Originally a bank which specialized in financing international trade and as such developed specialist knowledge of the countries with which it dealt. Now it plays a much broader role by acting as an issuing house for stocks, bonds, by raising loans, equity, capital, dealing in bills and foreign exchange. Merchant banks also act for and advise companies, e.g., in merger situations, and some deal in bullion.

MEZZANINE LEVEL
Stage of a company's development just prior to its going public.

MORATORIUM
A situation where a borrower makes a formal statement that he is unable to meet all or part of his debts. It is usually a holding action designed to lead to re-negotiation of outstanding debt repayments. Not to be confused with default.

MORTGAGE
Debt instrument by which the borrower (mortgagor) gives the lender (mortgagee) a lien on property as security for the repayment of a loan.

MOVEABLE PROPERTY
In Quebec, assets that can be moved, for example, machinery and equipment.

NEGATIVE COVENANT
An undertaking not to do certain things. It is frequently argued that negative covenants are preferable to positive covenants because it is easier to establish if something which was not to have been done has in fact been done, rather than vice versa. The breaking of a covenant, say in a debenture, usually constitutes a default which, in turn, gives rise to certain specified remedies that can be taken by the debenture or other security holder.

NICHE
Particular specialty or market segment in which a firm has garnered a large share.

OVERTRADING
Practice of a firm that expands sales beyond levels that can be financed with normal working capital.

PARI PASSU
To rank equally or in a stated ratio with another portion of the company's capital structure or debts.

PERSONAL GUARANTEE
A personal promise made by an individual on behalf of the borrower to repay the debt if the borrower fails to repay as agreed.

POWER OF ATTORNEY
A legal document authorizing one person to act for another, either for a specific time and/or purpose in general.

PRIME RATE
The interest rate that is charged by the banks to their most creditworthy customers.

PRIOR CHARGES
Charges on debentures, loan stock, or notes, which rank ahead of share capital. The service of interest on such charges is a cost of running the company which must be met before any dividend is paid, and in the event of default on the conditions of the issue, the repayment of such indebtedness is a charge ranking before share capital.

PRIVATE PLACEMENT
The sale of stock or debt to a limited group of investors which therefore, doesn't have to comply with all the rules and regulations of disclosure that restrict the normal placement procedure.

RECOURSE
In the event of default, recourse gives the right to take possession of the asset.

RESTRICTIVE LOAN PROVISIONS
Provisions that place constraints on the operations of term borrowers, such as restrictions on working capital, fixed asset, future borrowing, combinations, salaries, security investments, the use of loan proceeds, and the payment of dividends. Sometimes called "restrictive covenants."

REVOLVING CREDIT
Line of credit against which funds may be borrowed at any time, with regular scheduled repayments of a predetermined minimum amount.

RISK

Used interchangeably with the term "uncertainty" to refer to the variability of returns associated with a project or forecast values of the firm. In a statistical sense, risk exists when a decision maker can estimate the probabilities associated with various outcomes.

SALE AND LEASEBACK

A transaction in which a lessor purchases assets and then leases them back to the party from whom they were purchased.

SAVE HARMLESS

A contract clause whereby one party to a transaction tries to protect himself from a past or subsequent liability caused, usually unwittingly, by the other party.

SEED CAPITAL

The proceeds raised by a one-time sale of securities to a restricted number of purchasers, usually to finance the initial development of the company's business. This initial sale is exempt from prospectus requirements.

SENIOR DEBT

Debt securities whose claim is prior to junior obligations and equity on a corporation's assets in the event of liquidation.

SENSITIVITY ANALYSIS

Study using modelling techniques for measuring the effect of a change in a variable on the risk, or profitability of an investment, often referred to as "what if" analysis.

STANDBY CREDIT

Arrangement with a lender (either a bank or banks, or the IMF in the case of a member country) that a fixed amount of credit will be available for drawing during a given period, if required.

STANDBY FEE

A fee charged on the unused portion of the credit under a revolving credit or line-of-credit arrangement.

STANDSTILL AGREEMENT

Agreement between a company and its lenders, whereby the lenders agree to hold their current position without any unilateral action for a given period of time, in order to allow the company to develop a restructuring proposal.

SUBORDINATED DEBT

Where one lender has agreed in writing to rank behind another in claiming against an asset, he/she will only receive capital back after the other has been fully paid out. A bank will often insist that shareholder loans be subordinated to the obligations of the bank. This is also known as "subrogation."

SUBROGATION

See Subordinated Debt.

TERM

The length of time which a loan agreement covers. The maximum time during which a loan is to be repaid.

TERM LOAN

Loan for a fixed period, usually more than a year.

TRANSACTION RISK

The risk that results from the effect of changes in currency rates on balance sheet assets.

ULTRA VIRES ACTIVITIES

Actions of a corporation that are not authorized by its charter and that may therefore lead to shareholder or third-party suits.

UNBUNDLING

Trend in banking toward costing and pricing separately for services provided.

UNDERCAPITALIZATION

Situation in which a business does not have enough capital to carry out its normal business functions.

UNENCUMBERED

Property free and clear of all liens (creditors' secured claims).

VARIABLE RATE (FLOATING RATE)

Financial instrument or security bearing a variable interest rate. Can be applied to Certificates of Deposit issued for a normal minimum period of 360 days with the interest rate set at a specified spread over the current rate of 90-day CDs. Such CDs are adjusted every 90 days.

VENTURE CAPITAL

An individual or institution that provides "high risk" debt or equity capital unavailable from traditional sources, for the growth (or in some instances, seed funding) of small businesses at any stage before they go public.

WAREHOUSE RECEIPT
Negotiable instrument listing goods or commodities kept for safe-keeping in a warehouse.

WORKOUT
In the case of a bad loan or troubled firm, remedial measures being taken.

INDEX

THE WRITING TEAM

PRINCIPAL AUTHOR — GARY A. FITCHETT, CA

Gary Fitchett is sometimes called the guru of business financing in Canada. A chartered accountant for over 30 years, Gary has practised with specialization in Financial Consulting, 11 years as a partner of a National Accounting Firm and most recently as managing partner of Management Synergistics. He has helped hundreds of small- and medium-sized businesses solve their financing problems — from as low as $10,000 to as high as $65,000,000 — and from bank issues to factoring to venture capital – and from the east coast to the west coast.

Gary's particular areas of focus are entrepreneurship, new business formation and expansion, technology development, financing, mergers and acquisitions, and strategic planning.

Gary is well-known across Canada for his lively, anecdotal seminar presentations on a broad range of finance topics in which he translates theory into practical application. He has been Chairman of the Business Financing Congress presented in Montreal, Vancouver and Toronto and co-sponsored by The Canadian Institute of Chartered Accountants and the Society of Management Accountants of Canada.

Gary is the principal author of *The Canadian Business Financing Handbook,* a 3-volume, 2,200 page loose-leaf service published by The Canadian Institute of Chartered Accountants. Leading a team of financial professionals, Gary produced this highly valued professional reference publication to meet the needs of financial professionals.

In the world of business, Gary is the President and CEO of NuPro Innovations Inc., a start-up company with facilities in Georgia, Arizona and Mexico, involved in the development and introduction of a unique composite manufacturing material. NuPro is a public company on NAS-DAQ. He was formerly the founding President and CEO of Gresham Resources Inc., a U.S. based junior oil and gas company listed on the Vancouver Stock Exchange. Also, Gary was a Director of Cansib Energy Inc., a VSE listed company active in oil and gas projects in Russia.

When Gary's not travelling and tending to his many business interests, he resides lakeside in Port Perry, Ontario with his wife, Marilyn, and their four children.

JOHN D. ALTON, MBA, CA

Also a chartered accountant, John Alton began his career with a national accounting firm where he specialized in Management Consulting. In 1974, he attained his MBA at the University of Western Ontario. John is Gary's partner in Management Synergistics and an experienced financial consultant. As co-author of the mammoth project, *The Canadian Business Financing Handbook,* John continues to contribute to the annual updates. John also recently joined The Osborne Group, a Toronto-based contract executive management firm as a Principal.

A member of the Institute of Internal Auditors and a frequent lecturer for Durham College and private sector organizations, John has a unique blend of training and experience. He has consulted in areas of financing, business valuations, investigations and the growing financial technologies in micro-computing.

John has also presented talks and seminars to the Canadian Hospital Association, Bank of Montreal, Canadian Institute of Chartered Accountants, Association of Colleges of Applied Arts & Technology of Ontario, Chambers of Commerce and the Federal Business Development Bank of Canada on a wide variety of business topics.

John resides in Woodville, Ontario with his wife, Cynthia, and their daughter.

KATHLEEN ALDRIDGE, B.A., B.ED.

Kathleen Aldridge (nee Biggs) is a writer/editor of business/technical marketing communications, newsletters, and publications. She attained her B.A. at York and then her B.Ed. at Althouse College of Education at the University of Western Ontario. Kathleen spent the first part of her career teaching English and Theatre and Film Arts at York Mills Collegiate. From there, she moved to the Canadian Institute of Chartered Accountants (CICA) as a Manager of Professional Development. She now works out of her home office providing communications services to corporations and professional associations.

Kathleen worked with Gary and John as editor throughout the development of *The Canadian Business Financing Handbook* and is editor of the annual updates.

Kathleen resides in Markham, Ontario with her son.

other books in the

SMALL
OFFICE
HOME
OFFICE

S O L U T I O N
S E R I E S

FROM McGRAW-HILL RYERSON

THE SMALL BUSINESS REFERENCE SERIES

 FROM McGraw-Hill Ryerson

0-07-552899-1 / $24.99 PAPERBACK (P)

0-07-551558-x / $22.95 PAPERBACK (P)

0-07-552815-0 / $24.99 PAPERBACK (P)

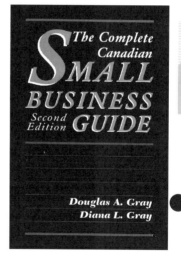

0-07-551661-6 / $39.99 HARDCOVER (T)